Why the Russian Constitution Matters

The Constitutional Dark Arts

William Partlett

·HART·
OXFORD · LONDON · NEW YORK · NEW DELHI · SYDNEY

HART PUBLISHING

Bloomsbury Publishing Plc

Kemp House, Chawley Park, Cumnor Hill, Oxford, OX2 9PH, UK

1385 Broadway, New York, NY 10018, USA

29 Earlsfort Terrace, Dublin 2, Ireland

HART PUBLISHING, the Hart/Stag logo, BLOOMSBURY and the Diana logo are trademarks of Bloomsbury Publishing Plc

First published in Great Britain 2024

Copyright © William Partlett, 2024

William Partlett has asserted his right under the Copyright, Designs and Patents Act 1988 to be identified as Author of this work.

All rights reserved. No part of this publication may be reproduced or transmitted in any form or by any means, electronic or mechanical, including photocopying, recording, or any information storage or retrieval system, without prior permission in writing from the publishers.

While every care has been taken to ensure the accuracy of this work, no responsibility for loss or damage occasioned to any person acting or refraining from action as a result of any statement in it can be accepted by the authors, editors or publishers.

All UK Government legislation and other public sector information used in the work is Crown Copyright ©. All House of Lords and House of Commons information used in the work is Parliamentary Copyright ©. This information is reused under the terms of the Open Government Licence v3.0 (http://www.nationalarchives.gov.uk/doc/open-government-licence/version/3) except where otherwise stated.

All Eur-lex material used in the work is © European Union, http://eur-lex.europa.eu/, 1998–2024.

A catalogue record for this book is available from the British Library.

A catalogue record for this book is available from the Library of Congress.

Library of Congress Control Number: 2024940187

ISBN:	PB:	978-1-50997-219-7
	ePDF:	978-1-50997-222-7
	ePub:	978-1-50997-221-0

Typeset by Compuscript Ltd, Shannon
Printed and bound in Great Britain by CPI Group (UK) Ltd, Croydon CR0 4YY

To find out more about our authors and books visit www.hartpublishing.co.uk. Here you will find extracts, author information, details of forthcoming events and the option to sign up for our newsletters.

To Anastasiya, for your inspiration and patience
To Roma, for your enthusiasm and criticism
To Philip, for the time to think about this book on those sleepless nights
May this book help good triumph over anti-politics

Preface

AUTHORITARIANISM IS ON the rise. This growing threat involves more than just the challenge posed to democracies by a powerful China or aggressive Russia. It also includes the erosion of key democratic norms and practices within well-established democracies. Moreover, this authoritarian threat relies on something we often associate with democracy: constitutional law.

Constitutional law is an unlikely tool for an authoritarian resurgence. We normally think of authoritarian leaders deploying non-legal mechanisms such as ideology, intimidation, or violence to build authoritarianism. Russia has long played a central role in this story. During the Cold War, the Soviet Constitution of 1936 became the classic example of a 'sham' Constitution.[1] And, more recently, a 2010 study described the current Russian Constitution as one of the 'Ten Worst Sham Constitutions'.[2]

But, in recent decades, authoritarian leaders have increasingly used constitutional law to entrench their power. This legalistic turn in authoritarianism raises important questions. Why do established authoritarian leaders and aspiring dictators spend so much time amending and reforming Constitutions? What purpose does this constitutional reform serve? The answers to these questions will help to better understand the relationship between Constitutions and different types of political ordering.

Scholars have begun to address these questions. They have described how Constitutions can be powerful tools for authoritarian leaders to coordinate power or signal their programmatic goals or ideology.[3] This book will expand this understanding by examining a neglected practice

---

[1] Richard Sakwa, 'The Struggle for the Constitution in Russia and the Triumph of Ethical Individualism' (1996) 48 *Studies in East European Thought* 115.
[2] Mila Versteeg and David Law, 'Sham Constitutions' (2013) 101(4) *California Law Review* 863, 899. See also R Sakwa, *The Crisis of Russian Democracy The Dual State, Factionalism and the Medvedev Succession* (Cambridge, Cambridge University Press, 2012) 42 ('Post-communist Russia has been in a permanent state of exception, exercised not through constitutional provisions of some sort defining a state of emergency but through an informal and undeclared derogation from constitutional principles').
[3] Tom Ginsburg and A Simpers (eds), *Constitutions in Authoritarian Regimes* (Cambridge, Cambridge University Press, 2014).

that I call the 'constitutional dark arts'. This practice falsely claims that constitutional democracy and rights are best secured in a system that concentrates constitutional power in one elected leader. It has helped to fuel the recent surge in authoritarianism.

This book will study this deceptive practice by looking at Russia's post-Soviet constitutional experience. This experience shows that the Russian Constitution is not a sham. Instead, it is an example of the 'constitutional dark arts'. Since 1993, the Russian Constitution has claimed to guarantee democracy and rights protection in a constitutional order that also centralises broad authority in the President.

This book will show the corrosive effects of this constitutional order on Russian governance over time. It has constituted a form of top-down, presidentially dominated politics that has not just undermined democratic and rights guarantees. It also has generated a dysfunctional form of governance that has damaged the quality of governance.

This experience teaches us important lessons about Russia. Russian political ordering is more than the personal project of Vladimir Putin. It is also the product of a constitutional system that gives vast rational-legal authority to the *office* of the Russian President. This constitutional order will shape politics in a post-Putin Russia. After Putin leaves the presidency, we could see a destabilising struggle between different factions to capture the office of the presidency. Even if we do not, whoever succeeds Putin will attempt to use this centralised constitutional system to maintain authoritarianism. Moreover, long-term democratic reform will require more than just Putin leaving office. It will also require a new Russian constitutional foundation that reduces the power of the office of the President and instead creates a balanced constitutional system that values political competition, deliberation, and compromise. This will not only help to build a more democratic Russia; it will also help to create better quality Russian governance.

Russia's constitutional experience also helps to understand the growing relevance of Constitutions in authoritarianism more generally. Authoritarian Constitutions are not just the tool of one leader. They also help to anchor a normative system that values the centralisation of power and allows authoritarian leaders to justify their domination of politics.

Russia's experience also shows how these authoritarian Constitutions and their justifications can be countered. In fact, Russian experience shows that, over time, these systems are open not only to criticism that they undermine democracy and rights protection. They also are prone to arguments that they are dysfunctional and provide poor quality governance. The constitutional dark arts are therefore far better at projecting the image of strong and stable governance than actually delivering it.

Finally, the concept of the constitutional dark arts sheds important light on current threats to established democracy. In these settings, elected leaders argue that concentrated authority is best able to ensure democracy and rights by allowing them to overcome a corrupt elite or decisively respond to pressing problems. Defending and renewing democratic constitutionalism requires returning our focus to the detailed structural provisions that apportion power between different institutions. These kinds of provisions do more than just limit state power. A long tradition of anti-centralist political philosophy has argued that this kind of balanced Constitution constitutes a pluralistic form of politics that ensures better quality governance over time.

The Russian Constitution therefore matters. In addition to anchoring its own system of authoritarianism, Russia's constitutional order presents a challenge to the West. This challenge is no longer based on class and economics as it was during the Cold War. Instead, it involves the supposed democratic benefits of a centralised form of politics dominated by one elected leader. This claim is central to the arguments of many populist politicians in established democracies such as Donald Trump. Countering it requires remembering the reasons why we should value a balanced constitutional order that disperses power between public institutions and fosters a pluralistic form of political ordering.

Contents

Preface vii

Introduction 1
    I. The Conventional Answer 1
   II. My Answer 2
  III. The Constitutional Dark Arts 3
  IV. The Constitutional Dark Arts in Russia 4
   V. A New Constitutional History of Post-Soviet Russia 6
  VI. Methodology 8
 VII. Lessons 9
VIII. Plan of the Book 12

1. The Constitutional Dark Arts: Concept and Consequences 14
    I. Constitutional Centralisation 17
   II. The Centralised State Tradition 19
  III. The Constitutional Dark Arts 22
  IV. Identifying the Constitutional Dark Arts 24
   V. The Constitutional Dark Arts in Action 26
  VI. Conclusion 32

2. The Russian Democratic Constitutional Movement 34
    I. Russia's Centralised State History 35
   II. The Intellectual Roots of Russian Democratic
        Constitution-Making 37
  III. Sakharov's Constitutional Draft 39
  IV. Early Russian Democratic Development: 1988–91 40
   V. Rumiantsev's Constitutional Commission 42
  VI. The Rise of Boris Yeltsin, 1992–93 44
 VII. Yeltsin's Constitutional Draft 50
VIII. Conclusion 52

3. The Foundation of the Constitutional Dark Arts in Russia 54
    I. Russian Crown-Presidentialism 60
   II. President as Monarch 63

	III.	President as Chief Executive Officer 67
	IV.	Justifying Russia's 1993 Constitution 70
	V.	Conclusion 73
4.		The Personal President (1994–99) 75
	I.	Centre-Periphery Relations 76
	II.	Economic Reform 81
	III.	Effectiveness 83
	IV.	Popular Accountability 84
	V.	Domestic Legal Accountability 86
	VI.	International Legal Accountability 92
	VII.	Conclusion 94
5.		The Managerial President (2000–08) 95
	I.	Presidential Institution-Building 97
	II.	Dictatorship of the Law 100
	III.	Recentralising Power in Moscow 102
	IV.	Controlling the Oligarchs 104
	V.	Effectiveness 106
	VI.	Popular Accountability 109
	VII.	Domestic Legal Accountability 110
	VIII.	International Legal Accountability 114
	IX.	Conclusion 115
6.		The Constrained President (2008–12) 117
	I.	The Compliance Pull of the Presidential Term Limit 118
	II.	Constraining the New President 119
	III.	Impact on Domestic Policy 122
	IV.	Impact on Foreign Policy 125
	V.	Popular Accountability 128
	VI.	Domestic Legal Accountability 129
	VII.	International Legal Accountability 134
	VIII.	Conclusion 136
7.		The Imperial President (2012–the Present) 138
	I.	The Closing of Russian Politics 139
	II.	Confrontation with the West 141
	III.	2020 Constitutional Reforms 142
	IV.	Full-Scale Invasion of Ukraine 148
	V.	Effectiveness 150

	VI.	Popular Accountability 152
	VII.	Domestic Legal Accountability 153
	VIII.	International Legal Accountability 157
	IX.	Conclusion 157

8. Constitutional Law in a Post-Putin Russia 160
    I. Status Quo Successor: Continuing the
       Constitutional Dark Arts 161
    II. Real Democratic Reform: The Need for
        a New Constitutional Foundation 164
    III. A New Constitutional Structure 170
    IV. Building a More Effective and Accountable
        Russian State 174
    V. Conclusion 178

9. Countering Constitutional Authoritarianism 180
    I. Authoritarian Populism 181
    II. The Populist Threat to Democracy 187
    III. Strengths of the Constitutional Dark Arts 190
    IV. Weaknesses of the Constitutional Dark Arts 194
    V. Conclusion 200

10. Renewing Democratic Constitutionalism 201
    I. The Dangers of Legal Constitutionalism 202
    II. The Political and Normative Foundations
        of Democratic Constitutionalism 211
    III. A Balanced and Energetic Constitutional Democracy ... 213
    IV. Engaging with Anti-Centralist Political Philosophy 215
    V. Conclusion 221

Conclusion: Constitutions at the End of History 223
    I. Better Understanding Russia 224
    II. An Old Ideological Debate Continues 224
    III. Democratic Constitutionalism in the
         Twenty-First Century 226

Bibliography 228
Index 239

Introduction

ON 24 FEBRUARY 2022, the world changed. At 03:40 am Kyiv time, Russia launched a volley of missiles against major Ukrainian cities while Russian troops and armoured vehicles thundered across the border. Russia's full-scale invasion of Ukraine took many by surprise, including those at the highest levels of Russian government.[1] The decision had been made by one public official: Russian President Vladimir Putin. The secrecy and concentration of power in the office of the President was so great that Russia's Prime Minister – constitutionally the second most important official in the Russian system – was only informed of the decision to invade the day before it began.[2] How is it possible that one man could single-handedly start the largest war in Europe since World War II?

I. THE CONVENTIONAL ANSWER

The conventional answer is that Vladimir Putin's dominance over the Russian political system is the product of his personal, non-legal authority. This account – reproduced in a procession of Putin biographies – focuses on Putin's control over the murky world of Russian elite politics.[3] And there is little question that Putin has used the techniques he learned as a KGB agent to impose himself on Russian politics. Numerous commentators have documented Putin's role as the 'godfather' of Russia's informal politics of patronage.[4]

---

[1] A Pertsev, 'The Death of the Collective Putin' (in Russian) (*Meduza*, 30 December 2022) https://meduza.io/feature/2022/12/30/smert-kollektivnogo-putina (discussing how Russian elites went from being advisers to servants).

[2] A Pertsev, 'He Does Not Speak Out Even behind Closed Doors' (in Russian) (*Meduza*, 21 July 2022) https://meduza.io/feature/2022/07/21/ne-vyskazyvaetsya-dazhe-pri-zakrytyh-dveryah.

[3] See, eg C Belton, *Putin's People: How the KGB Took Back Russia and Then Took on the West* (New York, Farrar, Straus and Giroux, 2020); M Gessen, *The Man Without a Face: The Unlikely Rise of Vladimir Putin* (New York, Riverhead Books, 2012).

[4] M Kimmage, 'The Godfather in the Kremlin' *The Wall Street Journal* (26 August 2023) www.wsj.com/world/russia/the-godfather-in-the-kremlin-e39be66a.

2 *Introduction*

Using Max Weber's famous typology, Putin undoubtedly draws on non-legal, personalised 'traditional' and 'charismatic' forms of authority to dominate Russia.[5] His charismatic authority relies heavily on official state messaging (particularly on television) which shows him to be an energetic leader who can restore Russian power in the world. In this strongman image, Putin himself plays an exceptional role in protecting Russia and ensuring its safety. At the same time, Putin also appeals to traditional authority by associating himself with Russia's historical legacy and the Russian Orthodox Church. In fact, the Kremlin's messaging machine frequently describes how Putin has stepped into a historical role that Russia has long needed for ensuring its unity and wellbeing.[6]

This personalised authority, the conventional view goes, makes the 'rational-legal' authority of Russia's 1993 Constitution irrelevant. A recent comparative study of constitutional authoritarianism describes Vladimir Putin as a 'master of deformalisation'.[7] Another influential study classifies Russia's constitutional order as one of the 'Ten Worst Sham Constitutions' in 2010.[8] A recent book argues that the Russian Constitution's initial embrace of the 'European/Western liberal tradition' has failed in the face of Russia's 'idiosyncratic' history.[9]

II. MY ANSWER

This book challenges this conventional answer. It shows how rational-legal, constitutional authority has been the forgotten foundation of

---

[5] C Matheson, 'Weber and the Classification of Forms of Legitimacy' (1987) 38 *The British Journal of Sociology* 199.
[6] SL Myers, *The New Tsar: The Rise and Reign of Vladimir Putin* (New York, Alfred A Knopf, 2015).
[7] G Frankenberg, *Authoritarianism: Constitutional Perspectives* (Cheltenham, Edward Elgar, 2020) 114.
[8] DS Law and M Versteeg, 'Sham Constitutions' (2013) 101 *California Law Review* 863, 899. See also R Sakwa, *The Crisis of Russian Democracy: The Dual State, Factionalism and the Medvedev Succession* (Cambridge, Cambridge University Press, 2011) 42 ('Post-communist Russia has been in a permanent state of exception, exercised not through constitutional provisions of some sort defining a state of emergency but through an informal and undeclared derogation from constitutional principles').
[9] J Henderson, *The Constitution of the Russian Federation: A Contextual Analysis* 2nd edn (Oxford, Hart Publishing, 2022) 9. See also R Sakwa, *The Crisis of Russian Democracy The Dual State, Factionalism and the Medvedev Succession* (Cambridge, Cambridge University Press, 2012) 42 ('Post-communist Russia has been in a permanent state of exception, exercised not through constitutional provisions of some sort defining a state of emergency but through an informal and undeclared derogation from constitutional principles').

Russian authoritarianism since 1993. This authority can be found by looking beyond the early chapters of the Russian Constitution to the detailed structural constitutional rules in its later chapters. These structural rules centralise authority in the office of the Russian President, giving the occupant of this office vast *sovereign authority* to build a presidentially dominated constitutional system. It has allowed the Russian President to occupy the same dominant position that the General Secretary of the Communist Party or the Tsar once occupied.

In a perfect world, this centralised presidential authority would be exercised in accordance with the democratic principles and rights guarantees in the early chapters of the Constitution. But, in reality, this broad presidential authority has reinforced Russia's deep tradition of centralised, authoritarian governance and has effectively nullified the individual rights and democracy guarantees in the early chapters of the Constitution. This is particularly noticeable since 2000, when the constitutional rules centralising power in the Russian President became a key foundation for the reconstruction of Russian authoritarianism around President Vladimir Putin.

III. THE CONSTITUTIONAL DARK ARTS

In centralising constitutional power in the President in a constitutional order guaranteeing democracy and rights protection, Russia's constitutional drafters (and their supporters in the West) in the early 1990s relied on a neglected constitutional practice that I call the 'constitutional dark arts'. This practice – which has grown in influence globally since the 1980s – guarantees democratic principles and individual rights within a highly centralised constitutional structure. This book will show how this constitutionally centralised system creates the illusion of democracy while in reality undermining both democracy and rights-protecting governance.

The practice is a form of the constitutional 'dark arts' because it *falsely* argues that a centralised state is necessary for securing democratic institutions, principles and rights. Its proponents make two misleading claims. First, they assert that the all-powerful sovereign is elected and therefore answerable to the people. This *popular* accountability rests on the assumption that there is a unified people able to hold the sovereign leader to account. Second, they argue that centralised power ensures stable governance and a unified system of legality. This allows courts to hold the state *legally* accountable for any democratic or rights violations.

Russia's post-Soviet constitutional experience shows why both forms of accountability are likely to fail over time. Constitutional centralisation forms the foundations of a political system in which one sovereign office can use its concentrated authority not just to dominate politics but also to justify this centralisation of power. In this political system, the sovereign institution can deploy its sovereign authority to manipulate both popular and legal accountability. In some cases, it can transform elections and courts from tools of accountability to tools of central legitimation.

The Russian experience also shows the best ways of countering the constitutional dark arts. This constitutional practice does more than just undermine democracy and rights protection. It also undermines the overall quality of governance by degrading the ability of public institutions to deliver basic goods to its citizens.[10] These systemic governance problems show that centralisation is better at projecting the image of strong and effective government than actually delivering it. Shattering this image can be a potent defence against the constitutional dark arts.

IV. THE CONSTITUTIONAL DARK ARTS IN RUSSIA

The use of the constitutional dark arts in Russia has its roots in the Soviet period and its democratic movement seeking a reason-based form of constitutional democracy grounded on universal human rights. The central objective of this movement was not to break with Russia's deep tradition of centralisation by adopting a balanced Constitution that dispersed power between public institutions and placed *political* checks on the concentration of power. Instead, its goal was the adoption of a Constitution that would open the Russian legal system to international human rights law and empower courts to place *legal* checks on centralised power.[11]

This rights discourse and its focus on legal accountability shaped the struggle for power between President Boris Yeltsin and the Russian legislature between January 1992 and October 1993. To break this deadlock and cement what he and his team thought to be the rightful place of the elected Russian President in the Russian political system,

---

[10] V Gel'man, *The Politics of Bad Governance in Contemporary Russia* (Ann Arbor, University of Michigan Press, 2022).

[11] R Horvath, *The Legacy of Soviet Dissent: Dissidents, Democratisation and Radical Nationalism in Russia* (New York, Routledge Curzon, 2005).

President Yeltsin – with the backing of the West – dissolved the legislature and successfully pushed through a new Constitution in a December 1993 referendum. This exercise of the constitutional dark arts created a hybrid Russian Constitution that guaranteed democratic principles and individual rights while creating a 'crown-presidential' constitutional system that concentrates broad rational-legal authority in the office of the President.[12]

President Yeltsin and his team justified this order on three bases. First, they argued that broad presidential powers were necessary to avoid the dangers of state disintegration and economic crisis that faced Russia. In particular, President Yeltsin described the Constitution as a way to avoid the problem of 'dual power' which would threaten the existence of the Russian state.[13] Many of his supporters also argued that a powerful President was necessary to push through the 'correct' policy of rapid marketisation.[14] This system was underpinned by a kind of anti-politics that dismissed the validity of any opposition to Yeltsin's reformist programme.

Second, Yeltsin and his supporters described this sovereign President as consistent with democracy. They argued that centralised presidential power was appropriate because the President was elected and therefore the representative of and accountable to the people.[15] Third, and finally, they argued that this centralisation was necessary for the implementation of democracy and rights. Without strong state power, they argued, there would be no stable legal system.[16] This legal system – open to the precedents of international human rights law – would then empower courts to limit any attempts by the state to abuse individual rights.

Western supporters of this Constitution made similar claims. One stressed how rapid market reform spearheaded by a powerful Russian President (who could circumvent checks from opposition parties in the

---

[12] W Partlett, 'Crown-Presidentialism' (2022) 20 *International Journal of Constitutional Law* 204.
[13] For more on these justifications, see ch 3.
[14] B Sautman, 'The Devil to Pay: The 1989 Debate and the Intellectual Origins of Yeltsin's "Soft Authoritarianism"' (1995) 28 *Communist and Post-Communist Studies* 131; D Kurnosov, 'Beware of the Bulldozer: What We Can Learn from Russia's 1993 Extra-Constitutional Constitution-Making' (*Verfassungsblog*, 7 January 2022) https://verfassungsblog.de/beware-of-the-bulldozer/ (describing how Russian President Boris Yeltsin was described as a bulldozer by a colleague).
[15] For more on these justifications, see ch 3.
[16] Tatyana Boiko, Interview with Mikhail Krasnov, Professor of Constitutional Law, Higher School of Economics (*Daily Journal*, 4 October 2018) https://svop.ru/main/27667/.

legislative branch) would eventually bring democratic politics to Russia.[17] Others saw periodic elections as a critical way to hold the President accountable. Finally, individual rights were seen as an important check on the otherwise broad powers of the President. For instance, the Venice Commission report on the 1993 Constitution repeatedly stressed the importance of judicial checks on power as part of its overall assessment that the Constitution 'does not give rise to any serious question' as to whether it is democratic.[18] In sum, many Western supporters saw the Constitution as a necessary 'framework for reform'.[19]

V. A NEW CONSTITUTIONAL HISTORY OF POST-SOVIET RUSSIA

This centralised constitutional system has shaped Russian politics ever since 1993. From 1993 until 2000, President Boris Yeltsin drew heavily on the decree powers of the President to avoid compromise with the legislature in his pursuit of economic and political reform. His personalised style of presidential dictatorship created a class of powerful (but often corrupt) business oligarchs and regional leaders that limited the power of the President. Although these checks and balances allowed pluralism to flourish, this personalised system created a dysfunctional economy and a democratically unaccountable political system. This was most clear in the poorly managed and brutal invasion of Chechnya and the 1996 presidential election. Finally, neither courts nor international human rights law were able to limit the abuses of this personalised presidency.

From 2000 to 2008, newly elected Russian President Vladimir Putin and his team deployed the constitutional authority of the President to create a new form of anti-politics. Turning away from Yeltsin's attempt to build a free market system by decree, they instead drew on both the guardian and management powers of the presidency to rebuild the power of the central state around the office of the President. This managerial presidency created a streamlined presidential bureaucracy and

---

[17] See, eg HJ Ellison, *Boris Yeltsin and Russia's Democratic Transformation* (Seattle, University of Washington Press, 2006).

[18] Venice Commission, Council of Europe, 'Opinion on the Constitution of the Russian Federation as Adopted by Popular Vote on 12 December 1993' (24 March 1994) www.venice.coe.int/webforms/documents/default.aspx?pdffile=CDL(1994)011-e (arguing, for instance, that the provision creating a strong Constitutional Court is important because it will play a 'decisive role' in ensuring that 'political conflicts' are solved by reason).

[19] W Pomeranz, *Law and the Russian State: Russia's Legal Evolution from Peter the Great to Vladimir Putin* (London, Bloomsbury, 2018) 123.

established a 'dictatorship' of the law.[20] The new system allowed Putin to entrench his own power but did not solve the systemic problems of poor quality governance in Russia. Meanwhile, the courts and international human rights tribunals remained unable to constrain this new centralised presidential dictatorship.

The foundational rational-legal powers of the managerial President also helped Vladimir Putin to accumulate non-legal forms of authority. First, the constitutional powers declaring the Russian President to be head of state and guarantor of the Constitution allowed Putin to compare himself to a Tsar who embodies the people and ensures the unity of the Russian state. He has since justified this traditional authority on a narrative about Russia's historical identity and safety requiring a single leader to ensure the unity and direction of the state. Second, the broad executive management powers have enabled the President to personally intervene in solving problems and bolster a media image that demonstrates his charismatic authority.

This system was tested from 2008 to 2012 when Putin stepped down as President and became Russian Prime Minister. During this period, Prime Minister Putin primarily relied on his non-legal, charismatic authority to constrain newly elected President Medvedev's presidential powers. These constraints were successful in domestic policy-making but President Medvedev was able to use the guardian powers of the presidency to make independent decisions in foreign policy. Despite these two power centres, both domestic and international courts grew less able to constrain the centralisation of power in the president.

Since returning to the presidency in 2012, Putin has used this rational-legal, constitutional authority to build a far more closed form of authoritarianism centred around a strengthened President who would protect Russia's imperial identity from enemies internal and external. This imperial presidency was cemented in the highly choreographed, top-down constitutional reform of 2020. The full-scale invasion of Ukraine on 24 February 2022 shows this system in action – one increasingly reliant on the decisions of one individual and ineffective. Furthermore, courts have become legitimators of this new system as Russia has decisively turned away from international human rights law.

This constitutional history raises an important question: Could Vladimir Putin have built his power without the vast constitutional authority of the President? It is unlikely. As chapters two and three will

---

[20] R Sharlet, 'Putin and the Politics of Law in Russia' (2001) 17 *Post-Soviet Affairs* 195.

show, Boris Yeltsin – a far more talented charismatic politician than Vladimir Putin – ultimately needed more than non-legal, personal authority to dominate Russian politics. Putin needed this authority as well. In fact, the broad legal powers given to the President in the Constitution and the centralised state justifications underpinning them were critical in allowing Putin to consolidate control over the Russian political system in the early years of his presidency. As chapter five will describe, these legal tools did not just allow Putin – a trained lawyer himself – to bring the powerful oligarchs and regional governors to heel. They also allowed Putin to justify his growing authority as a better form of political ordering.

This constitutional history of post-Soviet Russia therefore reveals that we have misjudged the role of the Russian Constitution in Russian politics. The Russian Constitution is not a sham. Instead, since 1993, its detailed structural rules have reinforced a long-standing normative commitment to the benefits of a centralised state. These rules have given the President – and particularly Vladimir Putin – a powerful set of tools and justifications to dominate Russian politics. This presidentially dominated system has done more than undermine popular and legal accountability. It has also weakened the authority and competence of other public institutions and contributed to poor quality governance. This constitutional history therefore reveals the role that President Boris Yeltsin and his supporters in the West played in creating a centralised constitutional system that continues to underpin Russian authoritarianism today.

VI. METHODOLOGY

In telling this story, this book focuses on the political and normative consequences of constitutional law. It therefore looks beyond judicially enforceable rights provisions and democratic guarantees to the detailed constitutional rules that organise power politics. It views these structural constitutional rules as more than just a reflection of existing power relations but as the foundation of a broader normative system for how politics should be organised. This 'structural-normative' approach seeks to understand how the Constitution structures a form of politics grounded not just on the basis of power but on the basis of reason-giving and justification.

Intellectual history reveals two competing normative traditions about how politics should be organised. Both traditions come with a set of justifications and reasons for the best form of politics. On one side is the 'balanced state tradition', which argues that the dispersion of constitutional authority is better because it stops tyrannical or despotic governance and encourages pluralistic politics. On the other side is the 'centralised state tradition' which argues that the centralisation of constitutional authority is preferable because it avoids civil war and fosters a politics of unity and harmony. This book then seeks to understand how Constitutions influence the debate between these competing traditions.

This approach requires identifying the detailed structural constitutional provisions and determining how they interact with one another to create a normative blueprint for arguing about political power.[21]

Structural constitutional rules then influence the broader normative understanding of the best organisation of the state. In some cases, these structural rules reinforce pre-existing commitments. For instance, in a constitutional setting where the centralised state tradition has historically been dominant, centralising constitutional provisions will bolster this dominance by stressing how one sovereign institution can ensure political unity and internal peace. In other cases, the structural constitutional text can work to transform existing constitutional culture. For example, in places where the centralised state tradition has been dominant, constitutional provisions that disperse public power will work to amplify competing arguments about the value of dispersing constitutional authority. These effects remind us that structural constitutional rules are not technical and value-free. On the contrary, they play a critical and often decisive role in shaping the normative debate about the best organisation of the state.

VII. LESSONS

This book applies this structural-normative approach to Russia's post-Soviet constitutional experience. This constitutional history does more than yield new lessons about the nature of Russian politics and its possible future. More broadly, it provides important insights into populist authoritarian systems such as Turkey, Hungary, Zimbabwe and Kazakhstan. It also helps to better understand democratic

---

[21] KL Scheppele, 'The Rule of Law and the Frankenstate: Why Governance Checklists Do Not Work' (2013) 26 *Governance: An International Journal of Policy, Administration, and Institutions* 559.

constitutionalism and how to defend it against the deceptive claims of the constitutional dark arts.

First, and most specifically, Russia's constitutional development sheds important light on the foundations of Russian authoritarianism. The centralising provisions in the later chapters of the Russian Constitution have reinforced the dominance of the centralised state tradition in Russia and have been critical in supporting authoritarian governance since 1993. Most notably, in the early 2000s, these provisions helped Vladimir Putin to use the authority of the Presidency to eliminate checks on his power and dominate politics. Today, this constitutional system enables Putin to use the power of the Presidency to withstand external shocks (such economic sanctions) and reinforces an internal Russian normative system that is committed to centralised presidential rule. In the long term, it shows that Russian authoritarianism is more than just a product of Vladimir Putin's personal, non-legal authority; it is also rooted in Russia's constitutional structure and its ability to (falsely) justify centralisation as producing democracy and good governance.

These findings challenge the dominant historical account that Putin broke with the Constitution in rebuilding Russian authoritarianism.[22] They also contribute to recent work by scholars seeking to understand authoritarianism in Russia and its impacts.[23] It suggests that the departure of Putin from power could generate a destabilising struggle to capture the sovereign office in Russian politics: the presidency. Even if it does not, a successor will likely attempt to use the centralised constitutional system to rebuild authoritarian governance.

Real democratic change will require amending the Constitution to reduce the power of this presidential office and creating a balanced state with checks on the concentration of power. This balanced constitutional system will seek to break with Russia's long commitment to centralisation by establishing a new kind of competitive and pluralistic politics. In justifying this break with the past, democratic reformers can and should argue that a balanced constitutional system is not only more accountable and rights-protecting – it is also more likely to provide effective

---

[22] See, eg Pomeranz (n 17).
[23] See, eg T Frye, *Weak Strongman: The Limits of Power in Putin's Russia* (Princeton, Princeton University Press, 2021); V Gel'man, *Authoritarian Russia: Analyzing Post-Soviet Regime Changes* (Pittsburgh, University of Pittsburgh Press, 2015); Taylor, B, *State Building in Putin's Russia: Policing and Coercion After Communism* (Cambridge, Cambridge University Press, 2011); M Krasnov, *A Personalist Regime in Russia: The Experience of Constitutional Analysis* (in Russian) (Moscow, Liberal Mission, 2006).

governance. In making this argument, they can draw on the example of late Tsarist liberal tradition which argued that a balanced Constitution does more than limit state power; it also ensures a more effective and stable system of Russian governance.

Second, the Russian experience teaches us more broadly about the relationship between written Constitutions and populist authoritarianism. Centralised Constitutions have traditionally complemented non-legal forms of authority in monarchies or one-party (communist) states. Now, in authoritarian populism, centralised Constitutions make an all-powerful, elected leader the guarantor of democracy and individual rights. These Constitutions provide the populist leader with more than just tools to dominate politics; they also allow centralised authority to justify their actions as democratic and rights-promoting. This deceptive practice underpins constitutional politics from Turkey to Hungary to Kazakhstan.

This finding contributes to the recent literature on the role of written Constitutions in authoritarian state-building globally.[24] It shows how dictators can use Constitutions to rebuild their centralised authority even after the collapse of legitimacy of a monarchical or one-party state. It also shows how Constitutions can be a tool for aspiring dictators looking to dismantle checking institutions and entrench their personal power in established democracies. The Russian experience also shows how these populist threats to democracy can be countered. In particular, opponents of centralisation must show that the claims underlying this practice are illusory. Centralised power does not lead to stable, democratic governance. Instead, it undermines not just democracy but also effective, good governance.

Third, the fact that Russia's constitutional system remains so poorly understood carries an important lesson about the foundation of democratic Constitutions. Most importantly, it demonstrates that democratic Constitutions are more than just *legal* documents that empower courts to *limit* state power on the basis of rights and democratic principles. Instead, they are more fundamentally documents that contain *structural* legal rules which disperse power between the institutions of state and support a normative system committed to a pluralistic form of politics.

---

[24] T Ginsburg and A Simpser (eds), *Constitutions in Authoritarian Regimes* (New York, Cambridge University Press, 2014); Frankenberg (n 7); D Landau, 'Abusive Constitutionalism' (2013) 47 *University of California Davis Law Review* 189; KL Scheppele, 'Autocratic Legalism' (2018) 85 *University of Chicago Law Review* 545.

12 Introduction

This finding contributes to a turn in constitutional theory that seeks to understand the role of Constitutions in enabling more effective and democratically accountable forms of state power.[25] It also contributes to recent work that seeks to connect detailed work on constitutional design with normative democratic theory.[26] Finally, it turns our attention to a long tradition of anti-centralist political philosophy that focuses on the benefits of balanced systems of constitutional governance. This tradition contains important lessons for contemporary democratic constitutional theory. In particular, this philosophical tradition shows that a properly balanced Constitution does more than limit the concentration of state power; it also arranges power so that the state can effectively advance the well-being of its citizens.

VIII. PLAN OF THE BOOK

The rest of this book will be organised as follows. Chapter one will describe the concept of the constitutional dark arts and its consequences. The following six chapters will examine how the constitutional dark arts developed in Russia. Chapter two will describe the centrality of an anti-political form of legal rights constitutionalism to Russia's post-Soviet democratic Constitution-making movement. Chapter three will detail how President Boris Yeltsin drew on this anti-political legacy and the constitutional dark arts to successfully advance a presidentially dominated Russian Constitution in December 1993. Chapter four will examine how President Yeltsin used this Constitution to build a system of personalised rule focused on radical market reform and decentralised power. Chapter five will describe how newly elected President Vladimir Putin drew more broadly on the powers of the Russian presidency to entrench his own power as part of his call for a 'strong state' in Russia. Chapter six will explain how this presidentially dominated system operated from 2008 to 2012 when Putin stepped down from the presidency.

---

[25] NW Barber, *The Principles of Constitutionalism* (Oxford, Oxford University Press, 2018); M Khosla and M Tushnet, 'Courts, Constitutionalism, and State Capacity: A Preliminary Inquiry' (2022) 70 *The American Journal of Comparative Law* 9; J King, 'The Rule of Law' in R Bellamy and J King (eds), *The Cambridge Handbook of Constitutional Theory* (Cambridge, Cambridge University Press, forthcoming 2024) (describing the importance of a social dimension of the rule of law). This will be discussed in more detail in ch 10.
[26] S Ganghof, *Beyond Presidentialism and Parliamentarism: Democratic Design and the Separation of Powers* (Oxford, Oxford University Press, 2021).

Chapter seven will describe how Putin's return to the presidency in 2012 has led to the creation of an imperial President that has taken a far more hostile approach to the opposition and the outside world. Chapter eight will examine the role of constitutional law in a post-Putin Russia and why a democratic Russia will need a new constitutional foundation. Chapter nine will explain how Russia's post-Soviet experience helps to better understand the increasing relevance of Constitutions in authoritarianism globally and how to counter this trend. Chapter ten will explore what our failure to understand the Russian Constitution teaches us about the political and normative foundations of democratic constitutionalism.

1

The Constitutional Dark Arts: Concept and Consequences

WRITTEN CONSTITUTIONS BURST on to the world stage and into the popular imagination during the American revolution.[1] Democratic revolutionaries in the American colonies seized power and sought to build new forms of governance that drew their authority from the people rather than divinely empowered monarchs. To do this, they drafted written Constitutions that dispersed power between public institutions to ensure individual rights and a better form of pluralistic politics. In creating these written Constitutions, they were influenced by a normative tradition that argues that a Constitution which balances power between different public institutions is the best way to ensure individual liberty and good governance.[2]

This 'balanced state tradition' and its normative understanding of 'good' political ordering has shaped the understanding and implementation of written democratic Constitutions ever since. Courts frequently rely on its justifications in questions of interpretation. For instance, the United States Supreme Court has repeatedly blocked the over-concentration of power in one institution on the basis of protecting individual rights.[3] This protection of dispersed *institutional authority* not only protects individual liberty but also 'good government'.[4] It does so by preserving the authority of a diverse range of institutions to participate in the exercise of public power. This tradition is so influential that

---

[1] GS Wood, *Power and Liberty: Constitutionalism in the American Revolution* (New York, Oxford University Press, 2021).
[2] JGA Pocock, *The Machiavellian Moment: Florentine Political Thought and the Atlantic Republican Tradition* (Princeton, Princeton University Press, 2016); see ch 10 for more on this 'balanced state tradition'.
[3] *United States v Lopez* 514 US 549, 552 (1995) ('constitutionally mandated division of authority was adopted by the Framers to ensure protection of our fundamental liberties').
[4] MJC Vile, *Constitutionalism and the Separation of Powers* 2nd edn (Indianapolis, Liberty Fund, 1998) 3.

the use of written constitutional rules to centralise power is viewed as an aberration from the norm and an example of 'abusive constitutionalism'.[5]

Written Constitutions, however, have not always dispersed institutional authority between institutions. Soon after the American founding, written Constitutions provided concentrated *sovereign authority* to monarchs in continental Europe and Asia. These top-down written constitutional texts were used to complement and strengthen the monarch's traditional, divine authority to direct the political system.[6] Later, centralised Constitutions have become the tool of one-party communist parties. These Constitutions build a centralised state that complements the non-legal authority of the Communist Party.[7]

These centralised constitutional systems are grounded on more than just self-interest. They are underpinned by the 'centralised state tradition' which explicitly rejects the dispersed institutional authority of the balanced state tradition. This normative tradition criticises the constitutional dispersion of power for allowing civil war, anarchy, and division. Instead, it argues that a good Constitution must be centred around a sovereign office that represents the 'indivisible nation or people, unitary royal or popular sovereignty, a general will that cannot err'.[8]

This tradition values a kind of 'anti-politics' that condemns political pluralism and compromise. It holds that good political ordering requires a Constitution that encourages unity by 'subsuming or eliminating internal rivals in favour of a central power'.[9] This harmony is guaranteed by the sovereign office's will which should be wielded to avoid anarchy and ensure peace and order. In this politics of unity, some measures of top-down coercion are justified so that individuals will accept the authority of the sovereign. For instance, Rousseau argued that this unity can often require education, where the public is 'taught to recognize what it desires. Such public enlightenment would produce a union of understanding and will in the social body'.[10]

These two traditions and their competing visions of good political ordering vie for influence in every national constitutional discourse. This

---

[5] D Landau, 'Abusive Constitutionalism' (2013) 47 *UC Davis Law Review* 189.
[6] L Colley, *The Gun, the Ship and the Pen: Warfare, Constitutions and the Making of the Modern World* (London, Profile Books, 2021).
[7] R Tucker, 'The Theory of Charismatic Leadership' (1968) 97(3) *Daedalus* 731, 738.
[8] NL Rosenblum, *On the Side of Angels: An Appreciation of Politics and Partisanship* (Princeton, Princeton University Press, 2008) 26.
[9] J Harrison, 'Sovereignty: Dual, Plural, and One' in N Aroney and I Leigh (eds), *Christianity and Constitutionalism* (New York, Oxford University Press, 2022) 174.
[10] Quoted from Rosenblum (n 8) 28.

competition is dynamic and ongoing; the dominance of one over the other can change over time. For instance, the centralised state discourse was influential in Germany for much of the nineteenth century and in the 1930s. Post-war Germany has embraced the balanced state tradition. The terms of this debate are set out in Table 1 below.

Table 1 Competing traditions of proper state ordering

	Balanced state tradition	Centralised state tradition
Nature of politics	Compromise and negotiation between plural institutions and interests	Top-down managerial anti-politics
Type of representation	Claims to represent the 'part'	Claims to represent the 'whole'
Constitutional system	Dispersed authority	Centralised power
Key institution	Multi-party legislature	Sovereign leader
Form of authority	Institutional authority	Sovereign authority
Main justification	Stops tyranny and protects individual liberty and democratic accountability	Avoids civil war and ensures unity and harmony

For many years, centralised constitutional systems largely supported monarchical and one-party governance. Since the 1980s, however, constitutional centralisation has been increasingly justified as a better way to achieve democracy and individual rights. This deceptive claim envisions an anti-political constitutional system where an elected sovereign leader oversees a state limited by judicially enforced rights and democracy guarantees. This kind of Constitution is then justified as the best of both worlds: Able to create a strong, unified state that is also democratic and rights protecting.

I call this practice the 'constitutional dark arts.' The 'dark arts' refers to the sinister or duplicitous use of technique.[11] The use of constitutional centralisation to achieve democracy and rights protection is a form of the constitutional dark arts because it falsely claims that a centralised state under one leader can secure democracy and individual rights.

---

[11] *Oxford English Dictionary* 3rd edn (Oxford, Oxford University Press, 2021) (most recently modified version published online in December 2023).

Over time, a centralised constitutional system is likely to constitute a form of top-down politics that undermines the institutional and judicial independence necessary for popular accountability and robust rights protection. In some contexts, elections and courts can develop into mechanisms for further *enabling* central power. Moreover, it is likely to contribute to bad governance that is often highly inefficient and unable to deliver basic goods to its citizens.[12]

This chapter will examine the concept of the 'constitutional dark arts' in more detail. It will first describe the history of constitutional centralisation. It will then describe the growing popularity of the 'constitutional dark arts' since the 1980s as leaders have claimed that centralisation can better secure democracy and rights protection. Finally, it will examine why centralising constitutional authority is likely to foster a form of politics that undermines democratic and rights guarantees.

I. CONSTITUTIONAL CENTRALISATION

Not long after the rise of democratic written Constitutions underpinned by the balanced state tradition in late eighteenth-century America, written Constitutions also became tools for centralising authority in the hands of the monarch. These constitutional texts reinforced the centralised state tradition in these monarchical systems by intentionally centralising 'rational-legal' *sovereign authority* in the monarch to complement the monarch's charismatic and traditional authority. This allows the *office* of the monarch to wield the tools of modern bureaucratic governance through power to make 'Administrative acts, decisions, and rules'.[13] These monarchies were then described as better able to secure the common good because of their basis in law.

A key early example was France's Constitutional Charter of 1814.[14] Describing itself as a 'monarchical constitution' that the King 'grant[s] and concede[s]' to his subjects, it gave the King vast power, including to

---

[12] V Gel'man, *The Politics of Bad Governance in Contemporary Russia* (Ann Arbor, University of Michigan Press, 2022).

[13] M Weber, *Theory of Social and Economic Organization* (T Parsons (ed), AM Henderson and T Parsons (trans)) (New York, Free Press, 1947) 338.

[14] 'Constitutional Charter of 1814' (*The Napoleon Series*) www.napoleon-series.org/research/government/legislation/c_charter.html; see also MJ Prutsch, '"Monarchical Constitutionalism" in Post-Napoleonic Europe Concept and Practice' in KL Grotke and MJ Prutsch (eds), *Constitutionalism, Legitimacy, and Power: Nineteenth-Century Experiences* (Oxford, Oxford University Press, 2014).

appoint the upper house of the legislature (Chamber of Peers), the judiciary, and to suggest and promulgate the laws.[15] This document ensured the King could control the growing French bureaucracy. Furthermore, underlying this French Charter was the argument that centralisation was needed to avoid anarchy and to advance the general good (including rights protection) after the 'chaos' of the French Revolution. For instance, the preamble of the document states that the restoration of the authority and prerogatives of the King are necessary to banish 'all the evils which have afflicted the fatherland during our absence'.[16] This includes the right to 'peace' which is 'the first need of all of our subjects'.[17]

Prussia's 1850 Constitution also followed this model, concentrating significant power in the hands of the King.[18] The King possessed the rational-legal power to not only serve as the head of state but also to engage in the 'active exercise of the unified power of the State'.[19] Alongside a list of rights guarantees, the King had the power to appoint the upper house of the legislature as well as the judiciary.

The use of written Constitutions to centralise power to complement monarchical power was also influential outside of Europe. Mid-nineteenth-century Japan drew heavily on this practice to systematise power and compete with the European powers. After the Meiji restoration, the Japanese Emperor drafted a new Constitution that concentrated significant rational-legal authority in the Office of the Emperor.[20] This practice of using written Constitutions in monarchies remains a common practice today. For instance, the Constitution of the Kingdom of Saudi Arabia creates a monarchical system that complements the traditional, divine power of the King by concentrating vast rational-legal power in the office of the King.[21]

Constitutional centralisation has not just emerged as a technique of centralised monarchical governance. Since the early twentieth century, constitutional centralisation has also played a key role in one-party states. Constitutions in communist states such as China, Vietnam, and

---

[15] 'Constitutional Charter', ibid.
[16] ibid.
[17] ibid.
[18] JH Robinson (trans), *Constitution of the Kingdom of Prussia* (Philadelphia, American Academy of Political and Social Science, 1894).
[19] Vile (n 4) 270.
[20] I Miyoji (trans), 'Constitution of the Empire of Japan' (*National Diet Library*) www.ndl.go.jp/constitution/e/etc/c02.html#s2.
[21] 'Saudi Arabia 1992 (rev 2013)' (*Constitute*) www.constituteproject.org/constitution/Saudi_Arabia_2013 ('Constitution of Saudi Arabia').

Cuba create a centralised state that is meant to serve as a battering ram to build a communist future.[22] This centralised system of sovereign authority is then deliberately placed under the leadership of the Communist Party.[23]

This use of a Constitution to centralise the state under Party leadership is underpinned by two concepts in socialist ideology. First is the Leninist concept of 'vanguardism', in which Party members play the leading role in formulating policy and directing the state.[24] Second is the Leninist principle of 'democratic centralism' that fundamentally rejects the separation of powers as a barrier to realising the will of the people.[25] The written constitutional system thus centralises power in a hierarchy of legislative bodies which are to serve as 'transmission belts' of Party policy. This legislative system therefore bears little resemblance to western-style parliamentarism and instead concentrates vast power in the legislative chairman.[26] This centralised state system is then an instrument of Party leadership.

II. THE CENTRALISED STATE TRADITION

Underpinning these Constitutions is the centralised state tradition, which dates back to the seventeenth century and includes a set of justifications for why centralisation is better able to ensure stability and advance the common good. These justifications have varied over time but they fundamentally reject pluralistic politics because 'no political recognition and arrangement of parts, no dynamic of cooperation, and certainly no dialectic of conflict can illuminate the common good and move from fragmentation to unity'.[27] Instead, they all value a form of anti-politics in which the sovereign officeholder ensures harmony and unity.

---

[22] BN Son, *Constitutional Change in the Contemporary Socialist World* (Oxford, Oxford University Press, 2020).
[23] See, eg Article 1 of the Chinese Constitution ('Leadership by the Communist Party of China is the defining feature of socialism with Chinese characteristics') (*Constitute*) www.constituteproject.org/constitution/China_2018 ('Constitution of the People's Republic of China').
[24] W Partlett and EC Ip, 'Is Socialist Law Really Dead?' (2016) 48 *New York University Journal of International Law and Politics* 463, 470–71.
[25] R Ludwikowski, 'Judicial Review in the Socialist Legal System: Current Developments' (1988) 37 ICLQ 89.
[26] Partlett and Ip (n 24) 482–83.
[27] Rosenblum (n 8) 28.

A key early thinker in the centralised state tradition was Thomas Hobbes. Nancy Rosenblum describes how Hobbes – writing amidst civil war in seventeenth-century Europe – rejected the idea of a mixed or balanced Constitution as 'not government at all' but instead the 'fragmentation of the commonwealth into factions'.[28] In a chapter describing the factors that the tend to 'weaken' or lead to the 'dissolution' of the state, Hobbes likened a system of balanced institutional authority to a 'disease in the natural body' and the distribution of power as 'worms in the entrails of the natural man'.[29] Hobbes's anti-politics therefore delegates political decision-making exclusively to the sovereign. Any criticism of this sovereign or attempts to 'dispute his power', Hobbes argued, are dangerous because they would 'slacken' the obedience of the people and therefore threaten 'the safety of the Commonwealth'.[30] For Hobbes, politics is a technical science, involving the knowledge and application of 'certain Rules, as doth Arithmetique and Geometry'.[31]

This anti-political tradition has had a powerful influence on absolutist monarchical systems. For instance, a key Prussian thinker argued that centralisation was necessary to avoid division and ensure that the 'force and authority of the government [is] not be diminished, but rather enhanced, through [the Constitution]'.[32] In addition, German thinkers like Von Mohl attacked the traditional democratic separation of powers doctrine for being 'logically false, and leading in practice to the destruction of the State and to anarchy'.[33] In this understanding, the separation of powers was only a luxury that could be afforded by wealthy and powerful countries that already had established nation-states. Germany, by contrast, was still in the process of building a modern nation state from a set of independent localities. As will be discussed in more detail in the following chapter, Russian constitutional thinkers like Nikolai Karamzin made similar arguments about the necessity of centralised power for maintaining Russia's imperial position, unity and identity.

---

[28] ibid 30.
[29] T Hobbes, Chapter XXIX (2007) The University of Adelaide Library https://resources.saylor.org/wwwresources/archived/site/wp-content/uploads/2012/09/chapter29.html.
[30] T Hobbes, *Leviathan*, vol 2, N Malcolm ed (Oxford, Oxford University Press, 2012) 526.
[31] ibid 322.
[32] W von Humboldt, 'Denkschrift über ständische Verfassung (October 1819)' in B Gebhardt (ed), *Wilhelm von Humboldts Gesammelte Schriften*, vol 12 (Berlin, De Gruyter, 1904) 389, 391, quoted from M Levinger, 'Kant and the Origins of Prussian Constitutionalism' (1998) 19 *History of Political Thought* 241, 260.
[33] R von Mohl, *Die Geschichte und Literatur der Staatswissenschaften*, vol 1 (Erlangen, 1855) 273, quoted from Vile (n 4) 270–71.

This anti-political tradition also shaped twentieth-century communist Constitution-making. A key foundational text was Vladimir Lenin's *The State and Revolution*, which made the case that the communist party must use a highly centralised state to build communism.[34] A centralised state would therefore be a key catalyst in allowing the Party to accelerate the inevitable transition from capitalism to communism. The adherence to centralisation in communism also draws on 'high modernist ideology' and its view of politics as a technical practice grounded on 'the rational design of social order commensurate with the scientific understanding of natural laws'.[35] The carriers of high modernism are 'optimistic about the possibilities for the comprehensive planning of human settlement and production'.[36] It therefore requires a form of politics that prefers 'certain forms of planning and social organization (such as huge dams, centralized communication and transportation hubs, large factories and farms, and grid cities)'.[37]

These justifications can be rational and persuasive in the short term when unity is needed to avoid anarchy or overcome an emergency. But, over time, these justifications are less persuasive as the centralised state fosters state weakness and instability. In the long term, therefore, its justifications are more emotional, exploiting fears of state breakdown and anarchy. This book will show how a fear of chaos and disorder frequently appears in Russian justifications for strong presidential power, from the speeches of Boris Yeltsin in the 1990s to the more recent extra-curial writings of the Chairman of the Russian Constitutional Court, Valery Zorkin.

Moreover, when it shapes constitutional text, this centralised state discourse often links centralisation with national identity. This identarian link can then serve as an additional justification for a centralised state by making this form of politics look natural and inevitable. As will be described in more detail later, Russia's adherence to a centralised state draws heavily on the idea that it is natural to Russia's constitutional identity and position in the world. As we will see in chapter seven, the 2020 amendments were a particularly good example of this identarian association between a centralised state and Russia's historical identity. Another example of this identarian argument is the 'Asian values' discourse,

---

[34] VI Lenin, *The State and Revolution*, R Service trans (London, Penguin, 1992).
[35] JC Scott, *Seeing Like a State: How Certain Schemes to Improve the Human Condition Have Failed* (New Haven, Yale University Press, 1998) 4.
[36] ibid.
[37] ibid 5.

which holds that a centralised and strong state is part of a specific set of values that are held closely in a number of Asian countries (and that are frequently set against Western values).[38]

III. THE CONSTITUTIONAL DARK ARTS

Proponents of monarchical and communist forms of constitutional centralisation have normally rejected elected institutions, the separation of powers or judicial review. In these systems, the ultimate source of authority for the sovereign leader lies outside the Constitution; the Constitution itself only reinforces this non-legal authority. For instance, Saudi Arabia's monarchy explicitly states that the authority of the King stems from 'the Holy Qur'an and the Prophet's Sunnah which rule over this and all other State Laws'.[39] Moreover, the Chinese Constitution delegates a 'leadership role' to the Communist Party, an institution that is regulated by its own Party Constitution and which draws heavily on the charismatic authority of its leader.[40]

Since the 1980s, however, centralised Constitutions have become the foundation of a new form of populist authoritarianism. These Constitutions concentrate vast sovereign authority in one elected office in a system that also guarantees rights and democracy.[41] In contrast with the centralising Constitutions of the past, the foundational (popular) authority of the sovereign is located in the Constitution itself.

This centralised version of democratic rights constitutionalism has been the product of at least two factors. First, with the end of the Cold War, written Constitutions that create elected institutions and guarantee rights have become important generators of state legitimacy.[42] Second, despite the growing influence of democratic ideas and institutions, centralisation and its anti-political justifications have remained attractive, particularly when Constitution-making takes place in conditions of state breakdown or emergency.

---

[38] MD Barr, 'Lee Kuan Yew and the "Asian Values" Debate' (2000) 24 *Asian Studies Review* 309. See also T Li-Ann, 'Varieties of Constitutionalism in Asia' (2021) 16 *Asian Journal of Comparative Law* 285.
[39] Constitution of Saudi Arabia (n 21) Art 7.
[40] Constitution of the People's Republic of China (n 23) Art 1.
[41] Roberto Gargarella, *Latin American Constitutionalism, 1810–2010: The Engine Room of the Constitution* (Oxford, Oxford University Press, 2013).
[42] F Fukuyama, *The End of History and the Last Man* (New York, The Free Press, 1992).

These factors combine to form a constitutional practice that I call the 'constitutional dark arts'. This practice is grounded on the claim that democracy and rights can better be realised through a highly centralised constitutional system of anti-politics. This book will examine one of its most common forms: a hybrid written Constitution which guarantees democracy and rights in its early foundational chapters while centralising vast legal power in an elected sovereign officeholder in its later chapters.

Proponents of the constitutional dark arts justify this centralised democracy on two misleading bases. These arguments draw from the anti-politics of the centralised state tradition. First, they claim that the sovereign office is elected and therefore is directly accountable to the people.[43] This *popular accountability* relies on the anti-political assumption that there is a unified and identifiable will of the people and that it can actively hold their representative to account. In constitutional text, this is frequently found in a foundational provision declaring 'the people' to be the sole source of authority and later claiming the President represents the people. Eric Posner and Adrien Vermeule recently have argued that centralisation is 'inevitable' in today's world and nothing to worry about because there are robust 'political constraints' that have emerged to control the abuse of power by these powerful officials.[44]

Second, they claim that the centralised sovereign office guarantees a stable system of legality that allows courts to limit the state through judicially enforced democratic and rights guarantees. This claim is often linked with the international human rights movement. It views democratic and rights disagreement as resolvable through adjudication and reason. This anti-political *legal accountability* asserts the primacy of law over politics where powerful courts can credibly serve as a kind of 'insurance' against the excesses of state power.[45]

This judicially centred understanding of Constitutions grew in influence in the post-World War II order. As democratic Constitutions increasingly came to be seen through this *legal* lens, constitutional law became the realm of lawyers and judges. This legal paradigm saw reason-based interpretation rather than political mobilisation as the basis of

---

[43] Rosenblum (n 8). Chapter 1 describes the deep roots of holistic claims in political philosophers such as Hobbes and Rousseau.
[44] EA Posner and A Vermeule, *The Executive Unbound: After the Madisonian Republic* (New York, Oxford University Press, 2010) 5.
[45] T Ginsburg, *Judicial Review in New Democracies: Constitutional Courts in Asian Cases* (Cambridge, Cambridge University Press, 2003) (arguing that judicial review facilitates democracy by putting constraints on government and is sought as a solution to the problem of uncertainty in constitutional design).

constitutional democracy. In this vision, therefore, a constitutional order was democratic when it included democratic and rights guarantees in its early foundational chapters. The technical structural rules in the later chapters of the Constitution that create a normative blueprint for the state were less important.[46]

IV. IDENTIFYING THE CONSTITUTIONAL DARK ARTS

The constitutional dark arts therefore generate a constitutional system that combines broad rights and democratic guarantees with detailed structural rules that concentrate vast sovereign authority in one elected office. This system therefore contains two different types of constitutional rules.

The first type of constitutional rule draws from the tradition of balanced Constitutions. These rules guarantee a vast array of abstract principles such as republican governance, the separation of powers and the rule of law. They also include guarantees of individual rights as well as a commitment to independent and impartial courts. They are often found in the 'foundational' parts of the Constitution and are often harder to amend than later provisions. They are easy to identify.

The second type of rule concentrates authority in one elected office and is underpinned by a set of justifications drawn from the centralised state tradition.[47] These detailed *structural* rules serve as the 'engine room' of the Constitution by creating a normative system of anti-politics in which one elected sovereign office can justify its domination on the basis of harmony and unity.[48] In many contexts, this concentrated authority is contained in the later sections of the Constitution that describe the way in which the elected offices of state relate to one another. Legally, these provisions are often considered to be less fundamental to the order and are easier to amend. These provisions and their consequences can be harder to identify.

---

[46] S Levinson, *Framed: America's 51 Constitutions and the Crisis of Governance* (New York, Oxford University Press, 2012) 19–28.
[47] In some constitutional systems, critical structural rules are not in the actual text of the Constitution but are instead contained in conventions or settled practices. See, eg G Appleby, 'Unwritten Rules' in C Saunders and A Stone (eds), *The Oxford Handbook of the Australian Constitution* (Oxford, Oxford University Press, 2018) 209.
[48] Gargarella (n 41).

In identifying the structural provisions of the constitutional dark arts, we must avoid a checklist approach that considers these provisions in isolation. A checklist approach asks questions like 'Does the Constitution require the legislature to approve the presidential appointment of the Prime Minister?' or 'Can the legislature vote no confidence in the government?' Kim Lane Scheppele describes why this checklist approach to structural provisions can be misleading.[49] She describes how many centralising Constitutions combine otherwise normal, democratic structural mechanisms in a way that leads to centralisation. This, she argues, fosters a 'Frankenstate' in which 'perfectly reasonable pieces' interact with one another in a way that creates a 'monster'.[50]

To spot this kind of Frankenstate, one must take a *structural-normative* approach that seeks to understand how particular structural rules combine with one another to create an overall *system* of public power. This reading requires understanding the 'interaction effects' of provisions that describe the authority of key institutions such as the President, legislature and Prime Minister. Scheppele argues that this kind of approach requires the reader to ask a series of targeted 'what if?' questions about the overall functioning of the constitutional system.[51] These questions might include the following: What if the lower house rejects the President's candidate for Prime Minister or votes no confidence vote in the government? What if the Prime Minister disobeys the President? What if the legislature wants to remove the President from office?

Take, for instance, the power of the Russian President to appoint the Prime Minister. The Russian Constitution requires the lower house of the legislature to 'consent' to the President's nomination.[52] Taken in isolation and using a checklist approach, this provision suggests that the legislature shares power with the President over the selection of the Prime Minister, a key executive branch officer. This would demonstrate that Russia has a French-style semi-presidential system. But later provisions show that this power to consent is not binding. If the legislature rejects the presidential candidate three times, the President has the authority to dissolve the legislature and unilaterally appoint the same candidate.[53]

---

[49] KL Scheppele, 'The Rule of Law and the Frankenstate: Why Governance Checklists Do Not Work' (2013) 26 *Governance: An International Journal of Policy, Administration, and Institutions* 559.
[50] ibid 560.
[51] ibid 562.
[52] Art 83(a), Constitution of the Russian Federation (*Council of Europe*) https://rm.coe.int/constitution-of-the-russian-federation-en/1680a1a237.
[53] ibid Art 111.4.

Taken together, these provisions make it clear that legislative consent is not necessary to a determined President intent on appointing a particular Prime Minister. Instead, the President has unilateral rational-legal authority to appoint the Prime Minister.

This systemic reading of particular rules can be painstaking. In fact, it is often the case that small constitutional details are critical in the creation of a centralised state. The old phrase is therefore correct: The devil is in the details. One way to help to identify the normative intent of these rules is to look at their historical context. In particular, what were the drafters saying at the time of drafting about these structural provisions? Were they stressing the centralised state tradition's focus on a politics of unity and harmony? Or were they discussing the balanced state tradition's value for dispersed institutional authority and pluralistic politics?

Understood this way, structural constitutional rules are more than just a technical rule book or the simple product of individual self-interest. These centralising provisions draw on the justifications of the centralised state tradition. They therefore *value* a particular kind of politics for solving collective political problems and therefore shape the broader ongoing debate about the best form of politics.[54] Because they are placed in the Constitution, this system of politics is then associated with national identity. Structural constitutional rules are not, therefore, value-free; on the contrary, they signal the best form of political ordering.

V. THE CONSTITUTIONAL DARK ARTS IN ACTION

Once we have identified this kind of hybrid constitutional system, a key question emerges: How do these two types of rules interact with one another? Roberto Gargarella describes three common theories for understanding how these two different types of rules relate to one another. First is that the two types of rules are essentially 'autonomous' and the constitutional guarantees will allow courts to protect rights and democratic values even despite the centralisation of power in the hands of one sovereign office.[55] A second approach is that democratic and rights provisions will 'compensate' for any democratic or rights abuses stemming from the centralisation of power.[56] This argument is often

---

[54] LH Tribe, *The Invisible Constitution* (Oxford, Oxford University Press, 2008) 10.
[55] Gargarella (n 41) 157–58.
[56] ibid 158–59.

supported by constitutional provisions allowing domestic courts to apply international human rights law. A third approach is that 'a system of concentrated authority is a necessary condition for making a politics of rights possible'.[57] We often see this kind of argument in the context of social or economic rights.

These explanations might hold in the short term. Centralisation can be an important temporary mechanism to counter emergencies or crises and therefore to secure democracy or rights protection. For example, temporary centralisation can restore legitimate authority and therefore create the foundations for courts to protect rights. We see examples of this kind of temporary centralised governance in democracies through history. For instance, the Roman republic famously had the position of 'dictator' that would rule for six months at a time to overcome serious emergencies.[58] The archetypal example was Cincinnatus, who assumed dictatorial powers to save the Roman republic and then immediately gave up this power to return to his farm.

But, placed in a permanent constitutional text, centralised sovereign authority has political consequences that are very likely to undermine democracy, rights protection, and good governance over time. Legal theory helps us understand why. It demonstrates that detailed structural rules are more likely to be self-enforcing and shape the political system than abstract constitutional provisions guaranteeing democracy or rights.

A. The Weakness of Rights and Democratic Guarantees

Legal rules are frequently implemented outside of court. This is particularly true for constitutional rules, which are often implemented and shaped by political actors acting in the political process.[59] The self-enforcing nature of constitutional law is particularly relevant in places with weak courts. In this extra-judicial process of constitutional implementation, all rules are not created the same. A decisive factor in the self-enforcing nature or 'compliance pull' of any legal rule is its 'textual determinacy' and the 'ability of the text to convey a clear message'[60] in

---

[57] ibid 160–61.
[58] Marc de Wilde, 'The Dictator's Trust: Regulating and Constraining Emergency Powers in the Roman Republic (2012) 33(4) *History of Political Thought* 555.
[59] J Goldsmith and D Levinson, 'Law for States: International Law, Constitutional Law, Public Law' (2009) 122 *Harvard Law Review* 1791.
[60] ibid 1713.

a way that helps to 'promote compliance'.[61] In other words, it must be clear on what 'is permitted' and what is 'out of bounds'.[62] The clearer and more determinate the rule, the more likely it is to be self-enforcing.

Rights and democratic guarantees are generally indeterminate rules that do not convey a clear message. Take, for instance, provisions guaranteeing judicial independence, the separation of powers, or democracy. These are highly abstract concepts that are open to a number of different interpretations. For instance, you could have the separation of powers but few checks and balances on the concentration of power.[63] Article 10 of the Russian Constitution is a good example. Moreover, individual rights provisions themselves are always subject to reasonable limitation through law. Rights enforcement therefore requires the application of a balancing test between the interests of the individual and the state. Finding this balance cannot be reduced to 'simple binary categories' and instead invites more complex questions which 'suffer the costs of elasticity'.[64]

This elasticity and indeterminacy allows powerful players to claim that they are complying with these guarantees even while following their preferred course of action. In fact, their preferred approach can be justified on a number of different grounds. For instance, an individual speech right can be rejected on the basis that speech is being limited to pursue a compelling state interest. These kinds of provisions therefore are unlikely to constrain powerful players in the exercise of power. In the hybrid orders of the constitutional dark arts, these provisions are likely to be underenforced, particularly when it involves the interests of the sovereign office.

Detailed structural constitutional rules, by contrast, assign specific powers to institutions (such as appointment powers) and determine how institutions relate to one another. They are more likely to be binary and therefore are 'capable of being resolved by an objective test of compliance involving a choice between only two options'.[65] This is not to say that all structural rules are binary or clear. It is instead to say that these structural rules are more likely to be clear and determinate than democracy or

---

[61] ibid 1721.
[62] ibid 1716.
[63] W Partlett, 'Separation of Powers without Checks and Balances: The Failure of Semi-Presidentialism and the Making of the Russian Constitutional System' in T Borisova and WB Simons (eds), *The Legal Dimension in Cold War Interactions* (Leiden, Martinus Nijhoff Publishers, 2012).
[64] Goldsmith and Levinson (n 59) 1724.
[65] ibid 1722.

rights guarantees. This is so because structural rules must allow political actors to coordinate their behaviour in the exercise of public power. Sanford Levinson explains that:

> These rules encompass such factors as establishing the institutional contexts for the making and enforcement of laws, including setting out the basic ground rules for the election (or appointment) of officials and the length of the terms of their offices.[66]

These detailed structural provisions exercise a powerful compliance pull, even in the absence of external enforcement. They do so by encouraging gratification deferral because one can expect that it will be enforced in the same way in the future. From a self-interested perspective, structural rules become important focal points that are in the long-term interests of these actors to comply.[67] Powerful actors will choose to be bound by those rules in order to gain benefits in the future.

Moreover, even in centralised systems, these clear structural rules place limits on the sovereign. In order to benefit from the coordination benefits of constitutional centralisation, the sovereign leader must also accept limitations on its power. This includes the constitutional structures through which the state operates. A good example is the constitutional process of lawmaking in Russia.[68] Despite the broad constitutional authority of the Russian President, the President's ability to determine the content of legislation is constrained by the constitutional requirement that legislation be passed by both the lower and upper houses of the legislature. This procedural constitutional requirement allows opponents of a presidentially sponsored law to mobilise against it and force the President to compromise.

For instance, in 2013, a coalition of powerful executive officials were able to stall the adoption of a law endorsed by President Vladimir Putin. This delay ultimately forced the office of the President to compromise on the law's details. Ben Noble argues that this is a broader phenomenon in which 'non-democratic parliaments' can matter as a 'mechanism for the resolution of intra-executive factionalism'.[69] This case shows how structural rules in the constitutional system constrain the power of the sovereign office. The sovereign dictator cannot simply ignore clear rules

---

[66] S Levinson, 'Do Constitutions Have a Point? Reflections on "Parchment Barriers" and Preambles' (2011) 28(1) *Social Philosophy and Policy* 150, 151.
[67] See, eg T Ginsburg and A Simpser, 'Introduction' in T Ginsburg and A Simpser (eds), *Constitutions in Authoritarian Regimes* (New York, Cambridge University Press, 2014) 2.
[68] B Noble, 'Authoritarian Amendments: Legislative Institutions as Intraexecutive Constraints in Post-Soviet Russia' (2020) 53 *Comparative Political Studies* 1417.
[69] ibid 1445.

like the constitutional requirement that legislation requires the ratification of the text of the law by both the upper and lower house. To get the coordination benefits of centralising constitutional provisions, the President must accept these limitations on his power.

Another example of the constraints of Constitutions in this context is the surprising compliance pull of presidential term limit provisions. Even in well-established authoritarian systems, powerful officeholders have often been unable to simply ignore these clear constitutional limitations. As will be discussed later in chapter six of this book, President Vladimir Putin stepped down from the office of the presidency in 2008 due to a constitutional term limit. He did so despite strong popular support for his leadership and calls by the elite to ignore the constitutional term limit. In giving up the Presidency, Putin is one of the few healthy Russian leaders to voluntarily give up power in Russian history.

Finally, the compliance pull of structural constitutional rules is shown by efforts to amend structural provisions in authoritarian systems. Turkmenistan is a good example. There is little question that Turkmenistan is a well-established authoritarian regime. In 2020, however, the office of the President amended the Constitution to create a formal upper house of the legislature.[70] This new upper house is now partially appointed by the President and has wide powers to confirm presidential appointments.[71] The constitutionalisation of this upper house now provides the President with additional legal tools to control legislative power that the President did not enjoy before. This suggests the importance of expanding rational-legal authority even in well-established authoritarian regimes.[72]

In sum, centralising structural rules simply matter more. They create a self-enforcing political order dominated by one institution. In this kind of system, constitutionally guaranteed elections are unlikely to hold the powerful sovereign to account. Examining almost two centuries of Latin American constitutional experience, Roberto Gargarella argues that voting is an 'extremely limited tool' in shaping the actual exercise of power because 'the citizenry may want to give multiple and different orders or messages through the vote, but they only have one chance to

---

[70] T Saeedi, 'Turkmenistan Switches to Bicameral System of Parliament – Why?' *News Central Asia* (27 September 2019) www.newscentralasia.net/2019/09/27/turkmenistan-switches-to-bicameral-system-of-parliament-why/.

[71] Turkmenistan Constitution 1992 (with amendments until January 2023) arts 78, 80². *Zakon* https://online.zakon.kz/Document/?doc_id=31337929.

[72] 'Turkmenistan Tinkers with Constitution in Apparent Transition Strategy' (*Eurasianet*, 25 September 2020) https://eurasianet.org/turkmenistan-tinkers-with-constitution-in-apparent-transition-strategy.

express all those different meanings'.⁷³ Moreover, the sovereign can use its vast authority to ensure that it wins elections by, for instance, excluding opponents from the ballot. This exercise of authority turns elections into rituals that build legitimacy for the sovereign office-holder rather than actually providing any real choice to the people.

Moreover, in this centralised system, judicially enforceable rights guarantees are also unlikely to limit the power of the sovereign leader over time. Courts are weak actors. As Alexander Hamilton wrote, courts have 'no influence over either the sword or the purse'.⁷⁴ In addition, they are appointed by the executive and must rely on the actions of political branches (particularly the executive) to implement their judgments. This is true even in balanced Constitutions with dispersed institutional authority.⁷⁵ For instance, Barry Friedman argues that the United States Supreme Court has carefully ensured that its decisions do not stray too far from public opinion.⁷⁶

The weakness of courts is particularly evident in contexts with little tradition of the rule of law and concentrated constitutional authority. In these places, even if courts were initially impartial and attempted to check the power of the sovereign, it is likely that they will eventually be forced to bend to the will of the sovereign officeholder. This sovereign possesses numerous tools to intimidate and control courts; these include broad appointment and removal powers as well as the authority to abolish this institution. Roberto Gargarella has described in the Latin American context 'how a system of concentrated power begins to conflict with the social demands generated in the name of constitutional rights'.⁷⁷

B. Authoritarian Legitimacy

In creating a self-enforcing system of centrally dominated politics, these structural rules also have important normative consequences.⁷⁸ These detailed structural rules are part of a normative blueprint for how the

---

[73] Gargarella (n 41) 163–64.
[74] Federalist 78 (Alexander Hamilton, 28 May 1788) *National Constitution Center* https://constitutioncenter.org/the-constitution/historic-document-library/detail/alexander-hamilton-federalist-no-78-1788.
[75] ibid (describing courts as the 'weakest branch' of government).
[76] B Friedman, *The Will of the People: How Public Opinion Has Shaped the Meaning of the Constitution* (New York, Farrar, Strauss, and Giroux, 2010).
[77] Gargarella (n 41) viii.
[78] This understanding is akin to the constructivist theory of how international legal rules work. See, eg HG Cohen, 'Can International Law Work? A Constructivist Expansion'

state *should* operate in solving collective political problems. They reinforce and bolster the central argument of the centralised state tradition that the concentration of power is the best way to foster a unified, secure and harmonious politics.[79] These justifications in turn seek to describe the centralisation of power as inevitable, necessary or natural.

The later chapters of this book will show how the Russian Constitutional Court has relied on these justifications to under-enforce rights provisions. It has also upheld broad interpretations of presidential power on similar bases. This activity helps explain why courts in a constitutionally centralised system are not just politically weak and unable to check the abuses of power by the centralised sovereign. They actually become institutions that actively *strengthen* the centralised authority of the sovereign.

The normative consequence of this constitutional centralisation does more than just impact judicial decision-making; it also shapes the values of the broader political system. The upcoming chapters of this book will demonstrate how these justifications for centralised power have increasingly influenced broader political discourse in Russia. In so doing, they have helped to create a kind of authoritarian legitimacy that allows the sovereign office to justify its growing power on reasons rather than threats of force or intimidation. This is a reminder of the ideological potential of constitutional law overall and how Constitutions can establish a system for ensuring obedience and normalising the commands of one sovereign office.

VI. CONCLUSION

This chapter has introduced the concept of the dark arts of constitutional law and the constitutional order it produces. It has then examined why constitutional centralisation is likely to overwhelm constitutional guarantees of rights and democracy. The following chapters will closely examine the development of this practice in the Russian context to better understand both the causes and consequences of the constitutional dark arts. These chapters will show how the presidential centralisation of Russia's 1993 Constitution had its roots in the anti-politics of the Soviet democracy movement. It will then describe how President Boris Yeltsin – with

---

(2009) 27 *Berkeley Journal of International Law* 636. See also A Wendt, *Social Theory of International Politics* (Cambridge, Cambridge University Press, 1999).
[79] Rosenblum (n 8) 27.

the support of the West – deployed the constitutional dark arts by pushing through a centralised Constitution on the basis that it would help to secure stability as well as democracy and rights guarantees.

The following chapters then examine how this hybrid constitutional order has shaped Russian governance since 1993. They will show how constitutional centralisation has taken different forms, depending on the time and personal commitments of the individual occupying the presidency. One constant, however, has been the increasing concentration of power in the President. This trend has intensified problems of democratic accountability and weak rights protection over time. It has also generally weakened the ability of Russian public institutions to provide good quality governance.

2
The Russian Democratic Constitutional Movement

IN 1975, SOVIET scientist and democratic dissident Andrei Sakharov was awarded the Nobel Peace Prize 'for his struggle for human rights in the Soviet Union, for disarmament and cooperation between all nations'. Although he was unable to attend, his wife – Elena Bonner – read his speech at the ceremony. Sakharov's speech tied democracy and human rights to a broader, universal moral struggle for cooperation and peace. Sakharov linked his political struggle with a desire to improve 'the future of mankind'.[1]

Sakharov's words reflected the understanding of constitutional democracy amongst key Soviet-era dissidents and reformers. Their approach to democracy was part of a broader, cosmopolitan movement in the 1970s. Samuel Moyn describes how the international human rights movement represented a shift in reformist thinking. Visions of a better and more just form of domestic politics were replaced by 'claims to make a difference not through political vision but by transcending politics. Morality, global in its potential scope, could become the aspiration of humankind'.[2] Rights offered a way to build a better world and 'make a difference not through political vision but by transcending politics'.[3]

This anti-political form of rights constitutionalism struck a chord in the late Soviet Union amidst the exhaustion of the state-based revolutionary tradition and doubts about the possibilities of political mobilisation. Furthermore, democratic dissidents were often members of the intelligentsia and were attracted to a reason-based form of governance. Rights guarantees offered a way to transcend political disagreement and violence

---

[1] A Sakharov, 'Acceptance Speech' (*The Nobel Prize*, Oslo, Norway, 10 December 1975) www.nobelprize.org/prizes/peace/1975/sakharov/acceptance-speech/.
[2] S Moyn, *The Last Utopia: Human Rights in History* (Cambridge MA, Harvard University Press, 2012) 213.
[3] ibid.

by appealing to morality and the universal common good. Soviet dissidents therefore consistently described themselves as operating outside of normal politics, defenders of a universal form of rights-based politics.

This movement's moral call for a rights-based democracy became an inspiration for many reformers seeking to break with the Soviet past and build a democratic Russia in the late 1980s and early 1990s. It drove the constitutional drafts that envisioned a newly democratic Russia. In these drafts, Constitutions were no longer primarily focused on distributing power between the public offices of the state. They were instead unifying texts that empowered courts to limit the power of the state. They did this by opening the domestic legal system to international human rights law and empowering courts to protect the individual against the state. This approach focused constitutional attention squarely on rights and democracy guarantees. Structurally, it envisioned a unifying elected President that represented the whole people and would guarantee a stable system of legally enforced democracy and rights. This vision would help Boris Yeltsin become the leader of Russia's post-Soviet democratic movement.

I. RUSSIA'S CENTRALISED STATE HISTORY

Sakharov and his fellow democratic dissidents operated in a highly centralised constitutional system. For centuries, Russia's dominant constitutional tradition had stressed the necessity and benefits of a centralised state. As William Pomeranz writes, in Russia the dominant 'theory of "state and law"' is underpinned by 'the essential idea of unity'.[4]

The roots of this Russian centralised state tradition can be traced back at least to the time of Peter the Great. At that time, Theofan Prokopovich, the leading ideologist of Peter the Great's imperial project, argued that Russian imperial development required the concentration of power in the hands of the Tsar.[5] This argument was not drawn from Russian thought. Instead, Prokopovich imported these ideas from the centralised state thinkers in Western Europe such as Thomas Hobbes and Jean Bodin, who argued that legal sovereignty, political unity and internal peace required the centralisation of power.

---

[4] WE Pomeranz, *Law and the Russian State: Russia's Legal Evolution from Peter the Great to Vladimir Putin* (London, Bloomsbury, 2018) 165.
[5] GM Hamburg, *Russia's Path toward Enlightenment: Faith, Politics, and Reason, 1500–1801* (New Haven, Yale University Press, 2016) 245.

Despite these broader European roots, Tsarist Russian writers soon begin to describe state centralisation as uniquely necessary to Russian political identity in the nineteenth century. This line of justification can be most clearly found in the work of Nikolai Karamzin, who argued that the study of national history yields specific laws that govern the present. He argued for the 'historical necessity' of centralised autocracy for Russia which, he claimed, had been established for 'the good of the people and not for the special use of the autocrat'.[6] For Karamzin, ideas of a balanced Constitution coming from England and the United States were not compatible with Russia's historical needs and identity.

Karamzin developed this identarian argument in his now-famous, 12-volume work called *The History of the Russian State (Istoriia Gosudarstva)*. This book romanticises the centralisation of power. For instance, Karamzin described Ivan the Terrible's subjugation of the republic of Novgorod to be an important moment in Russian history. He wrote that although it is 'characteristic of the human heart to wish well to Republics. The dangers of it ... captivate the young and inexperienced'.[7] Karamzin then described how the arguments of the 'friends of liberty' in Novgorod promised only 'a glorious death among the horrors of starvation and bloodletting'. The better approach, he argued, was that of 'peaceful citizenship' under the Tsar and its yield of 'life, security, calmness, and intact estates'.[8]

Karamzin advanced similar arguments in other work, stressing the importance for Russia of a powerful sovereign leading an autocratic form of government (*samoderzhavie*) and writing that 'Autocracy is the Palladium of Russia'.[9] Contrasting Russia's needs with those of more decentralised states, he argued that history shows that 'Russia is not England ... Not to fear the sovereign is not to fear the law'.[10] Constructing a historical narrative about the necessity of centralisation, he argued that Russia's 'ancient' form of authoritarian governance has 'magical strength'.[11] Karamzin therefore supported Tsars who exercised 'undivided personal authority'.[12]

---

[6] JL Black, *Nicholas Karamzin and Russian Society in the Nineteenth Century* (Toronto, University of Toronto Press, 1975) 188.
[7] Quoted from ibid 106.
[8] ibid.
[9] Quoted from ibid 76.
[10] R Pipes (ed), *Karamzin's Memoir on Ancient and Modern Russia* (New York, Atheneum, 1969) 197.
[11] Black (n 6) 188.
[12] Hamburg (n 5) 722.

Echoing Hobbes, Karamzin argued that nations that allow competition between individuals and factions will find themselves plunged into 'endless disputes, and the people will become the unfortunate instruments of a few powerful men intent on sacrificing the good of the commonwealth for the sake of their own selfish advantage'.[13] Karamzin made this position particularly clear in his opposition to the nineteenth-century constitutional movement led by a group of nobleman would come to be known as the Decembrists. He supported their repression, declaring their ideas to be 'alien' to the Russian people.[14] He argued that 'love for monarchs' and 'devotion to the throne' were 'native characteristics' of the Russian people.[15]

The Soviet Union continued this centralised state tradition, repackaging it in the language of socialist ideology. Vladimir Lenin advanced this argument in *State and Revolution*, calling for a centralised state that would become a battering ram to destroy the bourgeoisie and build a communist state.[16] By the 1930s, this had become the Soviet constitutional model.[17] The written constitutional system – contained in the succession of Soviet and republic Constitutions – created a centralised hierarchy of legislative bodies that largely served as 'transmission belts' of Party policy. This legislative arrangement was underpinned by the Leninist principle of 'democratic centralism' that fundamentally rejected the separation of powers as hindering the will of the people.[18] Finally, much as its Tsarist predecessor had, socialist constitutional thought viewed any arguments for a balanced Constitution as 'bourgeois' and counter-revolutionary. Centralised Constitutions were now to be a way of ensuring a powerful state that could ensure a transition to communism.

II. THE INTELLECTUAL ROOTS OF RUSSIAN DEMOCRATIC CONSTITUTION-MAKING

The late Soviet-era democratic reform movement did not seek to confront this long tradition of state centralisation by proposing a new democratic

---

[13] Quoted from ibid 712.
[14] R Wortman, *Russian Monarchy: Representation and Rule* (Boston, Academic Studies Press, 2013) 238.
[15] ibid.
[16] VI Lenin, *The State and Revolution*, R Service trans (London, Penguin, 1992) 88–89 (writing that 'the first stage' of communism cannot 'be fully free from traditions or vestiges of capitalism' and that 'it follows that under communism there exists not only bourgeois law but also the bourgeois state').
[17] W Partlett, 'The Historical Roots of Socialist Law' in F Hualing et al (eds), *Socialist Law in Socialist East Asia* (Cambridge, Cambridge University Press, 2018).
[18] R Ludwikowski, 'Judicial Review in the Socialist Legal System: Current Developments' (1988) 37 *ICLQ* 89.

Constitution that balanced power between the institutions of state or recognised plural sites of authority. Instead, this movement viewed a democratic Constitution as placing judicially enforced *legal* checks on the abuse of power by the state. The struggle for rights and democracy thus was a court-centred struggle for legal accountability based on 'morality' and reason.[19] This movement would play a critical role in helping to 'lay the foundations of Russian democracy' by shaping the drafting of a new democratic Russian Constitution after the collapse of the Soviet Union.[20]

The emphasis on legal accountability led this movement to initially focus heavily on the rights provisions in the Soviet Constitution.[21] Valdimir Bukovsky's 1972 trial is a good example. In his defence, he argued that the application of the Soviet Criminal Code to his activity violated Article 125 of the 1936 Soviet Constitution, which guaranteed freedom of speech and assembly.[22] This legal strategy reflected the movement's conscious renunciation of traditional politics and desire to avoid 'any sort of constructive solutions in this area [political struggle]'.[23] This approach led members of this movement to became known as 'rights protectors' (*pravozashitniki*) who viewed democracy as a commitment to a rights-centred system of rule of law.

The legal approach to democracy gained further momentum in the mid-1970s as the international human rights movement grew in influence.[24] When the Soviet Union signed the Helsinki Accords of 1975, Soviet democratic dissidents could expand their legalist strategy. In addition to Soviet rights guarantees, dissidents could now appeal to international human rights law to reform the Soviet system. Andrei Sakharov – who received the Nobel Peace Prize in 1975 – emerged as a key leader of this movement. Sakharov viewed 'traditional politics' to be a 'dangerous anachronism'.[25] Instead, the struggle for human rights was a universal one that involved the 'future of humankind'.[26]

This vision was grounded on the idea that 'democracy is the only attempt in history to try to construct a society on a rational foundation'.[27]

---

[19] R Horvath, *The Legacy of Soviet Dissent: Dissidents, Democratisation and Radical Nationalism in Russia* (New York, RoutledgeCurzon, 2005) 205.
[20] ibid 206.
[21] ibid 73–74.
[22] ibid 74.
[23] ibid 76.
[24] ibid 80–88.
[25] S Kovalev, 'Andrei Dmitrievich Sakharov: Meeting the Demands of Reason' in *Andrei Sakharov and Human Rights* (Strasbourg, Council of Europe Publishing, 2010) 134.
[26] ibid.
[27] ibid 138.

In the mid-1970s, an important debate demonstrated Sakharov's commitments. For Sakharov, the struggle for democracy and human rights transcended domestic politics and was an international project. Sakharov argued that real reform would need to come from outside, from international human rights pressure from the international community.[28] He and his supporters therefore deliberately refused a political program that sought to fundamentally change the institutional position of the communist party or introduce political pluralism. On the contrary, they appealed to the universal, moral and international principles of individual rights.

III. SAKHAROV'S CONSTITUTIONAL DRAFT

The anti-politics of this Soviet democratic movement shaped visions of democratic Constitution-making amidst a collapsing Soviet Union. A key model was Andrei Sakharov's proposed Constitution for a reformed Soviet state to be named the 'Union of Soviet Republics of Europe and Asia'.[29] Released in 1989 just before his death, this draft would exert a significant influence on the later drafts produced at the Russian level as well as Russia's post-Soviet constitutional order. The anti-politics of the democratic, rights movement influenced the entire text.

First, individual rights are foundational in Sakharov's constitutional order and ultimately transcend the organisation of the state and its corresponding politics. Rights are universal, apply to all of humanity, and are derived from the international legal order. For instance, Article 5 states that the 'UN Covenants on Human Rights … have direct effect on the territory of the Union and take precedence over the laws of the Union and the republics'.[30] It also draws on the experience of the 'rights protectors' when it guarantees that 'no one can be subject to criminal or administrative punishment for their beliefs'.[31] The Constitution therefore opens the domestic legal system to the rights that apply across the world.

---

[28] B Martin, 'The Sakharov-Medvedev Debate on Détente and Human Rights: From the Jackson-Vanik Amendment to the Helsinki Accords' (2021) 23 *Journal of Cold War Studies* 138.
[29] AD Sakharov, 'The Constitutional Project of the Soviet Union of Europe and Asia' https://constitution.garant.ru/history/active/1024/.
[30] ibid Art 5.
[31] ibid Art 6.

Second, the system of state power created by the Constitution reflects the anti-politics of this movement. The proposed Constitution calls for a common political future and 'a reciprocal pluralistic rapprochement (convergence) of the socialist and capitalist systems as the only cardinal solution to global and domestic problems'.[32] In addition, this state is led and unified by an elected head-of-state President who is forbidden from leading a political party.[33] The precise powers of this President, however, are left unenumerated. In a reflection of the Soviet tradition, the legislature (Congress of People's Deputies) is more powerful than the President: the legislature chooses the executive branch Council of Ministers and judge.[34] But, other than this, the precise details of state organisation are only included in eight provisions.[35] Sakharov's understanding of democracy thus placed little emphasis on the domestic organisation of the state.

IV. EARLY RUSSIAN DEMOCRATIC DEVELOPMENT: 1988–91

This Soviet-era legacy had a powerful impact on liberal democratic and constitutional reform during the late Soviet era of openness (*glasnost*') and restructuring (*perestroika*). One example was the creation of the Soviet Committee of Constitutional Supervision, which had limited advisory powers except for a broad power to invalidate republic laws on the basis of the Soviet Constitution or international human rights law.[36] When it acted on this power, the Committee invalidated republic-level laws on the basis of international human rights provisions, such as the International Covenant on Civil and Political Rights.[37] This reliance on the implementation of international human rights reflected the centrality of rights discourse to understandings of Soviet reform and demonstrated the remarkable legitimacy of international rights claims at the time.[38]

Rights constitutionalism also pervaded the Russian independence movement. The Declaration on the State Sovereignty of the Russian Federation adopted by the Russian legislature in 1990 drew heavily on

---
[32] ibid Art 4.
[33] ibid Arts 28, 35.
[34] ibid Arts 31, 34.
[35] ibid Arts 28–36.
[36] H Hausminger, 'From the Soviet Committee of Constitutional Supervision to the Russian Constitutional Court' (1992) 25(2) *Cornell International Law Journal* 305, 309.
[37] ibid 311.
[38] ibid.

international law.[39] The Declaration itself was proclaimed in the name of the 'highest aims' drawn from international law including the 'inalienable right to a life of dignity, to free development and use of his native tongue, and to each people, self-determination in the national-State and national-cultural forms which they choose'.[40] This document also guaranteed individual rights to Russians on the basis of international law. For instance, Article 10 states that 'the rights and freedoms provided for by the RSFSR Constitution, USSR Constitution, and generally-recognized norms of international law shall be guaranteed to citizens and stateless persons residing on the territory of the RSFSR'.[41] Finally, it clearly owed a debt to Sakharov and his movement with its proclamation that Russia

> declares its adherence to generally-recognized principles of international law and readiness to live in peace and harmony with all countries and peoples, to take all measures not to permit confrontations in international, inter-republic, and inter-nationality relations, upholding in so doing the interests of the peoples of Russia.[42]

The *perestroika* period itself also involved the democratisation of the Russian constitutional system. Russia amended its republic Constitution to create a fully elected Congress of People's Deputies with broad power to amend the Constitution, pass laws, elect a chairman and approve the head of government as well as other state officials. These broad powers reflected the continuing importance of parliamentary sovereignty to the Soviet tradition. When the first elected Congress convened on 16 May 1990, it chose Boris Yeltsin as chairman, drawing his support from a coalition of democratic activists and conservative Russian nationalists.

This elected Congress made a number of amendments to Russia's republic Constitution that further implemented aspects of the Sakharov model. Most notably, in April 1991, the Congress enacted legislation to amend the Constitution and create the first Russian Presidency.[43] This change was made after a referendum in which 70 per cent of Russians supported the creation of the presidency.[44] This change placed the

---

[39] 'Declaration on the State Sovereignty of the RSFSR', adopted by the First Congress of the People's Deputies (12 June 1990), https://soviethistory.msu.edu/1991-2/eltsin-and-russian-sovereignty/eltsin-and-russian-sovereignty-texts/russian-state-sovereignty.
[40] ibid Art 4.
[41] ibid Art 10.
[42] ibid Art 14.
[43] Law 'On the President of the RSFR' (*Presidential Library of the Russian Federation*, 24 April 1991) www.prlib.ru/en/history/619190.
[44] ME Urban, 'Boris El'tsin, Democratic Russia and the Campaign for the Russian Presidency' (1992) 44 *Soviet Studies* 187.

President at the head of the executive branch and gave the President the authority to veto laws, the power to name the head of the government with the agreement of the Supreme Soviet, and broad ability to issue decrees 'to stabilise the Russian economy'.[45] Finally, the drafters sought to maximise Russia's democratic legitimacy and specified that the President was to be directly elected. This would prove to be an important choice as it placed an elected presidency within an existing constitutional system of parliamentary sovereignty. The tension between the popular authority of the new Russian President and the constitutional authority of the Congress would prove explosive in the coming years.

V. RUMIANTSEV'S CONSTITUTIONAL COMMISSION

In 1990, the newly elected Congress of People's Deputies created a special commission to draft a new Constitution for the Russian Republic (then still part of the Soviet Union). The leader of the Commission was a young lawyer named Oleg Rumiantsev. Rumiantsev – who was dubbed the 'James Madison' of Russia by David Remnick at the Washington Post – travelled widely in the United States in developing the early drafts of the Constitution and was widely influenced by American rights constitutionalism.[46] The Commission published a journal that included articles on American constitutionalism, including on the separation of powers and Alexander Hamilton.[47] Furthermore, in early 1993, senior staff of the Commission met with experts on the US Constitution for a week-long conference in Washington, DC. This was the culmination of a long-standing collaboration between the commission and western experts.[48]

The anti-politics of the rights movement inevitably shaped this draft. Rumiantsev described a new democratic Constitution as 'a legal document' that will 'enable the courts to decide the constitutionality of any action'.[49] Rights were therefore placed in the initial chapters of the constitutional draft. The first 11 chapters – including the foundational

---

[45] ibid 189.
[46] D Remnick, 'Meet Oleg Rumyantsyev, The James Madison of Russia' *The Washington Post* (Moscow, 30 September 1991) www.washingtonpost.com/archive/politics/1990/09/03/meet-oleg-rumyantsyev-the-james-madison-of-russia/73cc7091-3ed8-43d8-97ce-18acf6347734/.
[47] V Schwartz, 'The Influences of the West on the 1993 Russian Constitution' (2009) 32 *Hastings International and Comparative Law Review* 101, 111.
[48] ibid 146–48.
[49] O Rumiantsev, 'Russia's New Constitution' (1991) 2 *Journal of Democracy* 37, 39.

ones – guarantee democratic principles and rights. These chapters included one on 'civil society' that guaranteed a free media.[50] Much as in the Sakharov draft, these constitutional rights were themselves linked to international human rights norms. For instance, Article 2 'ensures the rights and freedoms of man and citizen in accordance with the provisions of the Constitution of the Russian Federation and the generally recognized principles and norms of international law'.[51] Article 3 made it clear that the 'rule of law' included the direct application of international law.[52]

Following the Sakharov model, the draft Constitution detailed the organisation of the state in the later chapters. It also created an elected President. But, unlike the Sakharov model, the later structural chapters did attempt to break with Russia's centralising past. In fact, the draft created a balanced constitutional system that placed checks on the centralisation of power. The legislature (still called the Supreme Soviet) was described first, and had important powers, including to remove members of the government.[53] These provisions meant that the President and legislature shared 'management' power over the executive-branch ministers. The President was given significant guardian powers, but not enough to dominate the political system.[54] As Rumiantsev himself explained, 'a new Constitution must contain institutional and organizational guarantees forbidding a return to a monolithic structure of power, making social pluralism irreversible'.[55] Rumiantsev's constitutional system, therefore, broke with Russia's long anti-political, centralised state tradition.

This vision of a balanced Russian state, however, was increasingly unpopular as the stakes of Russian Constitution-making rose amidst the collapse of the Soviet Union. The leadership of the elected Russian legislature had little interest in adopting a new constitutional order that placed constitutional checks on its vast constitutional power under the amended Soviet-era Constitution. On the other side, President Yeltsin and his supporters were also not interested in constitutional checks on presidential power. As the next section will demonstrate, they favoured a President with broad powers to continue Russia's reforms.

---

[50] 'Draft Constitution of the Russian Federation', prepared by the Constitutional Commission of the Congress of People's Deputies of the Russian Federation (16 July 1993) https://constitution.garant.ru/history/active/101201/. Art 51.
[51] ibid Art 2.
[52] ibid Art 3.
[53] ibid Art 99.
[54] ibid Arts 93–96.
[55] OG Rumiantsev, 'From Confrontation to Social Contract' (1991) 5 *East European Politics and Societies* 113, 126.

VI. THE RISE OF BORIS YELTSIN, 1992–93

The anti-politics of the Soviet-era rights movement played an important role in the ability of a young former communist apparatchik and populist named Boris Yeltsin to become the leader of the Russian liberal democratic reform movement. In particular, the rights movement's disdain for ordinary politics and belief in legal accountability allowed Yeltsin to persuade them that a strongman President was compatible with democracy and rights protection. In fact, as we will see, Yeltsin was able to persuade many that a powerful President would actually further those democratic goals.

Yeltsin was not initially well liked by Russian human rights advocates because of his background as a communist apparatchik. But, over time, many increasingly supported him. This was partly a product of Yeltsin's vocal support for rights. In the late 1980s, Yeltsin actively embraced the rights movement, claiming to continue the 'path that Sakharov began'.[56] Bill Keller of the *New York Times* described Yeltsin's increasing appeal to key members of the Soviet democratic rights movement. For instance, he reported how a key Sakharov ally and rights campaigner, Sergey Kovalev, stated that 'The impression of Yeltsin among people like me and in intellectual circles started to change gradually and slowly'.[57]

The Russian democratic movement's alliance with Yeltsin stemmed not just from his embrace of rights discourse. It was also pragmatic. Yeltsin was popular. He handily won the first ever Russian presidential election in June 1991 with 57.3 per cent of the vote. President Yeltsin described this popularity as empowering him as the representative of the Russian people to overthrow a corrupt and sclerotic Soviet system. He described how the President's embodiment of popular sovereignty would ensure that state interests were no longer 'put above those of the individual'.[58] Now, he argued, the President would represent the entire people and ensure their 'well-being'.[59]

Yeltsin's understanding of democratic politics was therefore deeply populist, viewing the elected President as the unmediated representative

---

[56] Horvath (n 19) 102.
[57] B Keller, 'Boris Yeltsin Taking Power' *The New York Times Magazine* (Moscow, 23 September 1990) www.nytimes.com/1990/09/23/magazine/boris-yeltsin-taking-power.html.
[58] D Remnick, 'Yeltsin Sworn in as Russian President' *The Washington Post* (Moscow, 10 July 1991) www.washingtonpost.com/archive/politics/1991/07/11/yeltsin-sworn-in-as-russian-president/533c96df-a858-44a7-8827-eab25130a551/.
[59] ibid.

of the Russian people. Luke March describes how Yeltsin's populism was based on this idea of a popular leader 'separate from the Communist Party' who 'focus[ed] on the corruption of the communist bureaucracy'.[60] This populist strongman understanding of the President was shared by other significant public figures at the time. At Yeltsin's inauguration as President, the head of the Russian Orthodox Church stated that 'by the will of God and the choice of the people, you are bestowed with the highest political office in Russia'.[61] It was also shared by many leading liberals, who supported a transitional form of authoritarian liberalism headed by a powerful President who would reform by decree.[62]

A key moment in Yeltsin's appeal to this kind of unmediated popular representation was when he stood on top of the tank in August 1991, opposing a coup meant to preserve the old Soviet system. When the coup failed, power quickly shifted from the General Secretary of the Communist Party, Mikhail Gorbachev, to President Boris Yeltsin at the Russian republic level. With the Soviet Union collapsing, the stakes of Russian politics were now far higher than before. Yeltsin was no longer just the elected leader of a national republic. He was now the President of an entity that would soon become the successor state to the Soviet Union.

Initially, President Yeltsin was not focused on constitutional change. In the days after the failed coup, Yeltsin began to work on building a personalised 'vertical of power' that would help him carry out his presidentially led radical reform.[63] To do this, he constructed a hierarchy that would extend from himself, the President, to leaders at the provincial and local level. First, he established a system of presidential representatives to ensure the extension of his personal power into Russia's region. Second, he created a new institution in the region – the head of administration (*glava administratsii*) – each of which would replace the power of the Communist Party in each respective region:

> The executive and administrative functions of state government in territories, provinces and autonomous provinces and regions are henceforth to be exercised by heads of administration appointed by the RSFSR President and

---

[60] L March, 'Populism in the Post-Soviet States' in CR Kaltwasser et al (eds), *The Oxford Handbook of Populism* (Oxford, Oxford University Press, 2017).
[61] Remnick (n 58).
[62] B Sautman, 'The Devil to Pay: The 1989 Debate and the Intellectual Origins of Yeltsin's "Soft Authoritarianism"' (1995) 28 *Communist and Post-Communist Studies* 131, 137–41.
[63] ibid 140.

accountable only to him. The head selects a 'team' at his own discretion, and he has broad powers – for example, he can veto the decisions of local soviets.[64]

This top-down hierarchy closely approximated the centralised form of power exercised by the Communist Party of the Soviet Union.[65]

Yeltsin did not just build a top-down vertical of power. He also unilaterally pursued radical economic reforms by decree. This broad decree power was not a formal constitutional power of the President. Instead, the legislature continued to delegate to Yeltsin wide but time-limited decree powers to implement his vision of radical economic reform. This support was the product of a rapidly changing political landscape. In particular, the legislature had supported Yeltsin because the 'deputies [in the legislature] could not ignore the new political situation after the [August 1992] coup [when the Communist Party of the Soviet Union was disbanded]'.[66]

These broad and unilateral decree powers suited Yeltsin, who was suspicious of the bargaining and compromises of normal politics. He and his supporters were aware that radical market reform would be painful for the Russian people and was likely to be unpopular over time. Democratic deliberation and compromise would undermine the necessary pace of these reforms. They therefore viewed a presidentially led form of anti-politics as the only way to carry out the necessary reforms required to overcome the Soviet legacy. Underpinning this approach was the common belief at the time that market reform would inevitably bring democratic reform as well. Timothy Snyder has described this 'politics of inevitability' as reflecting the idea that there is only one correct path in politics.[67] For this reason, they saw no basis for disagreement with their views.

This increasingly centralised form of presidential rule brought Yeltsin increasingly into conflict with the newly created Constitutional Court. From its first judgment, this Court – led by a very active Chairman named Valery Zorkin – refused to recognise any broad implied

---

[64] A Dergachov, 'The First Days of the Russian President's Local Representatives' (*Izvestiia*, 28 August 1991) 2, in 43(35) *Current Digest of the Post-Soviet Press* (2 October 1991) 21–22.

[65] Sautman (n 62) 138–40 (describing how a KGB report at the time called for 'a strong authoritarian regime in our country in a moderate national democratic wrapping').

[66] Quoted from W Partlett and M Krasnov, 'Russia's Non-Transformative Constitutional Founding' (2019) 15 *European Constitutional Law Review* 644, 661.

[67] T Snyder, *The Road to Unfreedom: Russia, Europe, America* (New York, Tim Duggan Books, 2018).

presidential powers.[68] To do this, Zorkin took a very active role in personally 'controll[ing] the agenda of the Court and select[ing] politically salient cases for consideration'.[69] For instance, in its first case, the Russian Constitutional Court struck down a presidential decree seeking to merge the internal state security ministry with the police.[70] The Court argued that the President did not have this power; this power was exercised by the legislature. It further reasoned that the decree undermined the system of 'checks and balances' found in the separation of powers in the amended Russian Constitution that was critical for ensuring human rights.[71]

The Zorkin Court grew worried that President Yeltsin's personalised style of governance and calls for Russia's regions to assume more powers were dangerous to Russia's legal development and unity. In particular, Zorkin frequently 'expressed his fear of Russia disintegrating into a multitude of microstates as the USSR had broken up earlier'.[72] In its third major decision, the Court struck down language in a regional republic's Declaration of Sovereignty that limited the applicability of Russian law on its territory.[73]

President Yeltsin's personalised style of anti-politics did not just lead him into conflict with the Constitutional Court. It also eventually led to a confrontation with the Congress of People's Deputies. This elected body was very large but did not operate as a deliberative legislative body. Instead, reflecting the centralised Soviet state tradition, it was a 'tool' in the hands of a small leadership. During much of the Soviet period, this centralised system simply carried out the commands of the Party. In 1992 and 1993, the Congress was controlled by Ruslan Khasbulatov and

---

[68] A Trochev, *Judging Russia: The Role of the Constitutional Court in Russian Politics, 1990–2006* (Cambridge, Cambridge University Press, 2008) 108.
[69] ibid 103.
[70] Decision of the Russian Constitutional Court N 1-P of 14 January 1992 'On the case of Verifying the Constitutionality of the Decree of the President of the RSFSR of December 19, 1991'; 'On the Formation of the Ministry of Security and Internal Affairs of the RSFSR' (in Russian) (*Garant*) www.garant.ru/products/ipo/prime/doc/12011601.
[71] ibid.
[72] ibid 141.
[73] Decision of the Russian Constitutional Court No 3-P of 13 March 1992 'On the case of verifying the constitutionality of the Declaration of State Sovereignty of the Tatar SSR of August 30, 1990, the Law of the Tatar SSR of April 18, 1991 'On Amendments and Additions to the Constitution (Basic Law) Tatar SSR', Law of the Tatar SSR of November 29, 1991 'On the referendum of the Tatar SSR', resolution of the Supreme Council of the Republic of Tatarstan of February 21, 1992 'On holding a referendum of the Republic of Tatarstan on the issue of the state status of the Republic of Tatarstan" (in Russian) (*Garant*) www.garant.ru/products/ipo/prime/doc/1675704/.

his associates. This leadership had originally sought to cooperate with Yeltsin by delegating wide decree powers to reform the economy. But, as these reforms grew increasingly controversial and the Russian economy worsened, the leadership of the Congress moved to exploit its broad rational-legal authority to limit the powers of President Yeltsin and curb his decree-based economic reform.

Legally, there was little that Yeltsin and his team could do as broad rational-legal, constitutional authority was lodged in the Congress.[74] Reflecting its foundational principle of parliamentary sovereignty, Article 104 of the 1978 Russian Constitution stated that 'The Congress of People's Deputies of the Russian Federation is entitled to accept for its consideration and resolve any issue within the jurisdiction of the Russian Federation'.[75] In addition, the Congress was the complete 'master' of the Constitution-making process, possessing a monopoly over adopting a new Constitution as well as making changes and additions to the existing one. At the same time, the Congress could repeal decrees and orders of the President of the Russian Federation, as well as the decisions adopted by the Supreme Court and laws signed by the President.

When the Congress refused to renew Yeltsin's decree powers in December 1992, Yeltsin appealed to his unmediated relationship with the Russian people as the basis for his power:

> [I]n this situation, I consider it necessary to appeal directly to the citizens of Russia, to all the voters. My proposal is based on the constitutional principle of people's rule, on the President's constitutional right to appeal to the people, and on the President's constitutional right of legislative initiative. ... The Congress and the President have but one judge – the people.[76]

President Yeltsin's appeal had no grounding in rational-legal, constitutional authority at the time. As the struggle with the Congress continued, Yeltsin and his team realised they would need rational-legal, constitutional authority. This required adopting a new constitutional order that envisioned the newly created President much as Yeltsin did: as an elected leader who could become a new guiding force in Russian politics.

---

[74] See generally W Partlett and M Krasnov, 'Russia's Non-Transformative Constitutional Founding' (2019) 15 *European Constitutional Law Review* 644.

[75] *Constitution of the Russian Soviet Federative Socialist Republic* (in Russian) (1978, as amended 15 December 1990) Art 367, http://constitution.garant.ru/history/ussr-rsfsr/1978/red_1978/5478725/.

[76] 'The President of Russia Sees Holding a Nationwide Referendum as the Only Way Out of the Crisis', *Izvestiia* (10 December 1992), 1, in 44(50) CDPSP (13 January 1993) 1.

Yeltsin increasingly argued that a centralised constitutional document was now necessary for continuing Russia's reforms. In making this argument, Yeltsin's supporters drew heavily on the arguments of the centralised state tradition:

> Russia has always needed strong executive authority at major turning points in its history. [I]f we want Russia to be preserved and not to break up into appanage principalities, it needs that kind of authority – both because of its geopolitical position and large dimensions and because of its ethnic makeup, which has always been a special problem for us.[77]

This crisis eventually boiled over in March 1993 when Yeltsin attempted to declare martial law and rule by decree. To defuse the crisis, the Congress scheduled a referendum for 25 April 1993 which asked Russians who they trusted more: the President or the Congress. In response to a petition from a group of parliamentarians, the Russian Constitutional Court ruled that the question asking the Russian people whether they 'trust' the Russian President or 'approve' of the President's socio-economic policy were of moral significance and not binding legal significance.[78]

After receiving more than 50 per cent support on these questions, however, Yeltsin and his supporters proclaimed that 'The Russian Soviet Federation Socialist Republic has been peacefully replaced by the Russian Federation. The state has changed its legal identity'.[79] This position was popular amongst other liberal democratic reformers leaders. For instance, Gavril Popov – a leading liberal and former Mayor of Moscow – openly called for a temporary presidential dictatorship.[80] Yeltsin and his team embraced this moment as a critical one in reshaping the constitutional system of power relationships. Rather than once again trying to declare presidential dictatorship, Yeltsin and his team focused their attention on the creation of a new Russian constitutional order that

---

[77] Interview by Aleksandr Sidiachko, Megapolis-Express (19 May 1993), 23, in 45(19) Current Digest of the Post-Soviet Press (9 June 1993), 4.

[78] Decision of the Russian Constitutional Court N 8-P of 21 April 1993 'On the Case of Verifying the Constitutionality of Part Two of Paragraph 2 of the Resolution of the Congress of People's Deputies of the Russian Federation dated March 29, 1993'; 'On the All-Russian Referendum on April 25, 1993, the Procedure for Summing Up its Results and the Mechanism Implementation of the Referendum Results' (in Russian) (*Garant*) www.garant.ru/products/ipo/prime/doc/12011596/.

[79] V Kononenko, 'President of Russia begins Promised Changes by Presenting Draft of New Constitution', Izvestiia (30 April 1993), 1–2, in 45(17) Current Digest of the Post-Soviet Press (26 May 1993) 7.

[80] 'The Russian Democratic Reform Movement is for Presidential Rule', Nezavisimaia Gazeta (5 November 1992), 2, in 44(45) Current Digest of the Post-Soviet Press (9 December 1992) 1.

would give the Russian President the rational-legal authority it needed to safeguard Russian reform.

VII. YELTSIN'S CONSTITUTIONAL DRAFT

As Yeltsin turned to Constitution-making, he and his team already had a draft in mind. In 1992, a leading pro-Yeltsin party, the Russian Democratic Reform Movement, produced a draft Constitution that would empower a strongman President to reform the country without parliamentary interference.[81] A key drafter of this Constitution was Anatoly Sobchak. A law lecturer and influential liberal, Sobchak spoke of using 'semi-dictatorial methods' to create 'a strata of owners on which the new political authorities can lean'.[82] Sobchak would go on to become Mayor of St Petersburg and mentor to a young Vladimir Putin. Sobchak's vision of a strongman Constitution to enable Russia's transition reflected broader views among other liberals about the need for authoritarian presidential leadership to reform Russia. They broadly saw centralised presidential power as necessary for dismantling the Soviet system and building a rights-protecting Russian democracy.

The April 1993 referendum result brought this draft Constitution to the forefront of Russian politics. Citing his strong backing in the April 1993 referendum, Yeltsin published a decree creating a constitutional convention (*soveshchanie*) that would produce a draft Constitution for Russia.[83] Working from Sobchak's 1992 presidential draft, this conference was fully appointed by President Yeltsin. Its working process was also heavily controlled by key members of Yeltsin's inner circle who strongly believed that a presidentially dominated Constitution was the only way to reform Russia.

When this convention finally met, Yeltsin made it clear that it must produce a Constitution that would give the President adequate authority to both oversee and drive Russia's reforms. In an early speech to the entire delegation, Yeltsin described the ongoing struggle for power between the President and the parliament in binary terms. He explained

---

[81] 'Draft Constitution of the Russian Federation, Political Council of the Russian Movement of Democratic Reforms' (in Russian) (*Garant*) https://constitution.garant.ru/history/active/101203/.
[82] Sautman (n 62) 138.
[83] Presidential Decree No 718 of 20 May 1993 'On Convening the Constitutional Conference and Completing the Preparation of the Draft Constitution of the Russian Federation' (in Russian) (*Yeltsin Presidential Archive*) https://yeltsin.ru/archive/act/35993/.

that 'In opposition are not two branches of government, but instead two independent political systems'.[84] Yeltsin associated parliamentary government with the Soviet Union, arguing that assembly-based power (*sovetskaia vlast'*) was unable to achieve reform. He also drew from the centralised state tradition by declaring assembly-based governance as 'dangerous [and] chaotic'.[85] This led him to conclude that 'assemblies [*sovety*] and democracy are not compatible'[86] and that only a presidentially dominated system could effectively build democracy.

The convention's final constitutional draft was released in July 1993.[87] It included a long list of rights provisions as well as commitments to a constitutional court and international human rights law norms. Reflecting its populist roots, it made popular sovereignty a key foundational principle of the democratic system.[88] The constitutional draft left the arrangement of public power to the end of the Constitution. Much as the Sakharov Constitution, it made a unifying elected President the head of state and the 'guarantor of the Constitution'. But it went into far more detail, deliberately placing the President above the system of separated legislative, executive, and judicial power and giving it broad decree power. It also gave the President broad powers to dissolve the legislature if there was a dispute about the Prime Minister[89] or a vote of no confidence.[90] It also created a diminished legislative assembly divided into an elected upper and lower house.[91]

In order to keep the support of Yeltsin's allies in the Russian regions, the draft did provide one key check on the centralisation of power in the office of the President. Most notably, it included the full text of the 1992 Federation Treaty, which granted significant autonomy to Russia's regional subunits. This treaty created the basis for a real form of asymmetrical federalism. The republics that signed the agreement saw it as recognising their position as 'sovereign states'.[92] This represented the

---

[84] Quoted from W Partlett, 'Separation of Powers without Checks and Balances: The Failure of Semi-Presidentialism and the Making of the Russian Constitutional System, 1991–1993' in T Borisova and W Simons (eds), *The Legal Dimension in Cold-War Interactions: Some Notes from the Field* (Leiden, Brill, 2012) 129.
[85] ibid.
[86] ibid.
[87] 'Constitution of the Russian Federation, Project Approved by the Constitutional Commission' (in Russian) (21 July 1993) https://constitution.garant.ru/history/active/1022/.
[88] ibid Art 4.
[89] ibid Art 111.
[90] ibid Art 116.
[91] ibid Art 95.
[92] NJ Lynn and AV Novikov, 'Refederalizing Russia: Debates on the Idea of Federalism in Russia' (1997) 27 *Publius* 187, 191.

high-water mark of a constitutional commitment to decentralisation in the organisation of centre-periphery relations in the Russian Federation.

As autumn approached in 1993, there were attempts to reconcile this draft with the one from the Rumiantsev's Constitutional Commission. Both drafts were in virtual agreement on rights provisions and democratic guarantees. The key differences were in the later structural chapters. The Commission's draft included structural provisions that balanced power between the elected President and legislature. Yeltsin's draft concentrated significant power in the office of the President. As the President's conflict with the legislature worsened, the idea of compromise between this draft and the one released by Rumiantsev's Constitutional Commission remained a possibility. But, as we will see in the next chapter, the proper organisation of the state and the powers of the President became caught up in the political emergency of the time. In these conditions, the justifications of the centralised state tradition convinced many that a broadly powerful President was necessary for ensuring reform.

VIII. CONCLUSION

This chapter has examined the history of Russia's Soviet-era democratic movement and its impact on post-Soviet democratic Constitution-making. It shows that Russia did have a strong Soviet-era democratic constitutional movement, exemplified by the thinking of 'rights-protectors' like Andrei Sakharov. This movement's moral commitment to an anti-political form of rights democracy was an important part of a wider international human rights movement that sought to move discussions of democratic reform and the common good away from the domestic organisation of the state to the universal and moral level. This democratic movement did not focus democratic reform on breaking with Russia's long tradition of state centralisation. Instead, it viewed democratic constitutional change as requiring the implementation of universal rights claims in strong, independent courts.

This moral form of anti-politics and the legal Constitution had a powerful influence on how many Russian reformers imagined the creation of a democratic post-Soviet constitutional order in the early 1990s. Some like Oleg Rumiantsev still saw the need for a balanced constitutional order. But, for many others, it obscured the need for a new democratic Russian Constitution to break with Russia's long adherence to state centralisation. This allowed Boris Yeltsin and his liberal supporters – including Vladimir Putin's mentor, Anatoly Sobchak – to argue for a new constitutional order that empowered a strongman President to pursue reform. This powerful President, they argued, was necessary for a democratic order committed to elections, courts and international human rights law. In fact, a popularly elected President would become the guarantor of state unity and this system of rights enforcement. The next chapter will describe how this background set the stage for the adoption of Russia's first post-Soviet Constitution. This background did not make a highly centralised presidential system inevitable. But it certainly helped to justify it when it was proposed at the end of 1993.

3

The Foundation of the Constitutional Dark Arts in Russia

IN LATE SUMMER 1993, after almost a year of smouldering tension between President Yeltsin and the Russian legislature about the pace of market reforms and competing constitutional visions for a democratic Russia, Yeltsin acted. On 21 September 1993, Yeltsin addressed the Russian people and declared that he was dissolving the elected Russian legislature. He justified this decision in the language of the centralised state tradition, stating:

> Russia is in a deep crisis of statehood. Literally all state institutions and political figures are drawn into a fruitless and senseless struggle for destruction. The direct consequence of this is a decline in government power in general. I am sure that all Russian citizens are convinced that in such conditions it is impossible not only to carry out the most difficult reforms, but also to maintain elementary order. It must be said frankly: if we do not put an end to the political confrontation in the Russian government, if we do not restore the normal rhythm of its work, we will not maintain control over the situation, we will not preserve our state, we will not maintain peace in Russia.[1]

Accompanying this speech was a remarkable presidential decree that not only terminated the powers of the Russian legislature but also included a detailed set of rules for a temporary transitional form of governance.[2]

---

[1] Presidential Address of Boris Yeltsin of 21 September 1993 to the Citizens of the Russian Federation 'About the Anti-People, Anti-Constitutional Policy of the Supreme Council, about Changes and Additions to the Current Constitution, about Early Elections of the President and Elections to the Federal Assembly, about the Termination of the Convening of the Congress of People's Deputies and the Dissolution of the Supreme Council of the Russian Federation' (in Russian) (*Yeltsin Centre Online Archive*) www.yeltsin.ru/archive/audio/9020.

[2] Presidential Decree No 1400 of 21 September 1993, 'On Step-by-Step Constitutional Reform in the Russian Federation' (in Russian) (*Yeltsin Centre Online Archive*) www.yeltsin.ru/archive/act/41068.

It included elections for a bicameral parliament as well as a presidentially appointed Election Commission to oversee these elections. This presidential decree explicitly grounded this extraordinary seizure of power on four key ideas from the centralised state tradition: (1) maintaining the unity and integrity of the Russian Federation; (2) bringing the country out of the economic and political crisis; (3) ensuring the security of the Russian Federation; and (4) the restoration of the authority of state power.[3] This decree was justified on realising the popular sovereignty of the Russian people and their personal trust for Yeltsin in the April 1993 referendum result. This populist argument described the unmediated relationship between Yeltsin and the people as having higher legal force than the existing Constitution.

In response to Yeltsin's decree, Russian parliamentary leaders immediately removed Yeltsin for treason and named Yeltsin's Vice President, Alexander Rutskoi, as Russia's new President. The Russian Constitutional Court met late into the night, issuing a conclusion (*zakliuchenie*) finding Yeltsin's decree unconstitutional and approving the decision to remove Boris Yeltsin from the office of the President.[4] Four Justices (Justices Vitruk, Morshchakova, Kononov and Ametistov) dissented, arguing that the Court had acted outside of its legal powers in reaching this conclusion.[5] Russia had two Presidents.

Two weeks later, in the early hours of 4 October, after an attempt by armed supporters of the legislature to seize power, Yeltsin ordered the army to storm the Russian legislature. Muscovites looked on as tanks took up positions across from Parliament in central Moscow. After a heavy bombardment, Russian special forces entered Parliament and arrested Rutskoi and his parliamentary supporters. On 7 October, Yeltsin indefinitely suspended the entire Constitutional Court for 'political activities'.[6]

Operating on the basis of the September 21 decree, the office of the President governed Russia by decree during the months that followed this October revolution. Over this time, Yeltsin banned 14 newspapers

---

[3] ibid 3.
[4] Decision of the Russian Constitutional Court No Z-2 of 21 September 1993 'On the Compliance of the Constitution of the Russian Federation with the Actions and Decisions of the President of the Russian Federation B. N. Yeltsin related to his Decree "On Step-by-Step Constitutional Reform in the Russian Federation" dated No 1400 and Appeal to Citizens of Russia on 21 September 1993' (in Russian) (*Garant*) https://base.garant.ru/1778386/.
[5] ibid.
[6] Presidential Decree No 1612 of 7 October 1993 'On the Constitutional Court of the Russian Federation' (*Garant*) https://base.garant.ru/6303679/.

and a television programme called '600 seconds'.⁷ This censorship was announced in a 'simple administrative note faxed from the Russian Press and Information Ministry'.⁸ Yeltsin and his supporters relied heavily on the arguments of the centralised state tradition in justifying this temporary presidential dictatorship. They repeatedly argued that these extreme actions were necessary to stop civil war and continue reform.

Many Russian liberals supported Yeltsin's actions. Some did so for pragmatic reasons: Yeltsin was the only choice they had to continue reform. Others grounded their support on the deep thread of antipolitical thought in the Russian democratic movement that viewed authoritarianism as necessary for Russia's democratic transition.⁹ These figures viewed compromise with Russia's elected legislature as itself undemocratic. At the 'end of history', they argued, democratic competition needed to be suspended to ensure Russia's market reform and inevitable transition to democracy.¹⁰ They saw Yeltsin as the only leader who could reform Russia and break with the Soviet past. Oleg Rumiantsev would later sum up the logic as reflecting a belief that 'Boris Yeltsin is a talented manager and he can bring Russia out of this crisis'.¹¹ Rumiantsev attributed this to the beginning of a cynical attitude toward 'the basic principles of the constitutional regime'.¹² Many in the West supported Yeltsin. For instance, in the aftermath of the violent dissolution of the legislature, United States Secretary of State Warren Christopher told Boris Yeltsin that the United States President was 'extremely appreciative' of Yeltsin's 'superb handling' of the crisis.¹³

---

[7] CR Whitney, 'Yeltsin Orders Referendum on a New Constitution' *The New York Times* (Moscow, 16 October 1993) www.nytimes.com/1993/10/16/world/yeltsin-orders-referendum-on-a-new-constitution.html.
[8] ibid.
[9] B Sautman, 'The Devil to Pay: The 1989 Debate and the Intellectual Origins of Yeltsin's "Soft Authoritarianism"' (1995) 28 *Communist and Post-Communist Studies* 131.
[10] ibid.
[11] FJ Dresen and WE Pomeranz (eds), 'The Russian Constitution at Fifteen: Assessments and Current Challenges to Russia's Legal Development: Conference Proceedings' (Occasional Paper No 304, Kennan Institute, Woodrow Wilson International Center for Scholars, 2009) 25 www.wilsoncenter.org/sites/default/files/media/documents/publication/op304_russian_constitution_at_fifteen_pomeranz_2010.pdf.
[12] ibid.
[13] 'Secretary Christopher's Meeting with President Yeltsin, 10/22/1993, Moscow' (*George Washington University National Security Archive*, 22 October 1993) https://nsarchive.gwu.edu/document/30737-document-13-secretary-christophers-meeting-president-yeltsin-10221993-moscow.

The dramatic shelling of the parliament in early October 1993 and assertion of presidential dictatorship, however, was not the decisive moment in undermining Russian democracy. Instead, the key decision was when Yeltsin and his team chose to make further changes to his constitutional draft in October and November 1993. These changes contradicted the pledge in Yeltsin's 21 September decree to present a 'single agreed draft' of the Constitution to the people.[14] Yeltsin and his team instead made full use of the constitutional dark arts to create a strongman President that would not face serious any checks and balances from a future parliament.

To do this, Yeltsin and his team altered key provisions detailing the President's relationship with the elected legislature and the executive branch government. These changes weakened the independence of both the Russian legislature and the executive. For instance, the upper house was no longer constitutionally required to be elected; it was now to be 'formed' in a way set by law.[15] Furthermore, a new article was inserted, requiring the government to resign before a newly elected President.[16] Articles 83 and 111 were changed to give the President full management power over the executive branch. This included the ultimate power to appoint the Prime Minister as well as the final say on the resignation of the government (in the event of a legislative no confidence vote).[17]

The Yeltsin team also made a critical change to the constitutional relationship between the central government and the regions. The draft Constitution now included language grounding Russian federalism on 'the unity of the system of state authority'.[18] Moreover, the transitional provisions in the new draft stated clearly that any federal treaty or agreement that had been concluded before the adoption of the Constitution would be subordinated to the text of the 1993 Russian Constitution.[19]

---

[14] Presidential Decree No 1400 (n 2) Art 2.
[15] Art 96.2. Constitution of the Russian Federation (*Council of Europe*) https://rm.coe.int/constitution-of-the-russian-federation-en/1680a1a237.
[16] ibid Art 116.
[17] ibid Arts 111 (allowing the President to dissolve the lower house if they reject a Prime Minister candidate three times) and 117 (allowing the President to reject a first vote of no confidence and dissolve the Duma if a no confidence vote is lodged twice within a three-month period).
[18] ibid Art 5.3.
[19] Ibid Section 2, Art 1.

As Jeffrey Kahn has stated, this provision meant 'the unilateral repeal of the Federation Treaty'.[20]

These changes therefore signalled a clear centralisation of power in the federal centre, reflecting Yeltsin's tightening grip on regional leaders after his decisive victory over the Russian legislature in October 1993. It also reflected the strong influence of authoritarian modernisation thinking and its centralised state justifications on Yeltsin's Constitution-drafting team. As one of Yeltsin's advisers described it, the separate 'branches' of executive, legislative, and judicial power ultimately came from 'the same core, the same trunk'.[21] This strong, stable trunk must be the President. Russia's Constitution therefore had the separation of powers but without any checks and balances on presidential authority.[22]

Alongside this extremely powerful President, the Yeltsin team left in place the broad and abstract constitutional guarantees of individual rights and democracy in the early chapters of the draft Constitution. These provisions closely approximated those in the draft Constitution of Rumiantsev's Constitutional Commission. The preamble continued to affirm the commitment of the 'multi-national Russian people' to individual rights and freedoms and the 'inviolability of the democratic foundations of Russian statehood'.[23] Chapter 1 guaranteed that Russia would be a 'democratic federal law-bound State with a republican form of government'.[24] The initial chapter outlining the 'Fundamentals of the Constitutional Structure' declared that 'the individual and his rights and freedoms' have the 'highest value'[25] in a constitutional order grounded on 'ideological and political pluralism'.[26] Finally, Chapter 2 listed dozens of political and social rights, including the right to freedom of speech, movement, conscience as well as the right to life, housing and a pension.[27]

---

[20] J Kahn, *Federalism, Democratization, and the Rule of Law in Russia* (Oxford, Oxford University Press, 2002) 138.

[21] Quoted from W Partlett, 'Separation of Powers without Checks and Balances: The Failure of Semi-Presidentialism and the Making of the Russian Constitutional System, 1991–1993' in T Borisova and W Simons (eds), *The Legal Dimension in Cold-War Interactions: Some Notes from the Field* (Leiden, Brill, 2012) 130.

[22] ibid.

[23] Russian Constitution (n 15) preamble.

[24] ibid Art 1.

[25] ibid Art 2.

[26] ibid Art 13.

[27] ibid Ch 2.

Drawing on the legacy of the 'rights protectors', individual rights were tied to international law norms and judicial enforcement. For instance, Article 17.1 opened the Russian legal system to international human rights law and standards, stating that individual rights shall be recognised and guaranteed 'according to the universally recognized principles and norms of international law and according to the present Constitution'. Article 15.4 made 'The universally-recognized norms of international law and international treaties and agreements of the Russian Federation' directly enforceable in Russian courts. The implication was clear: not even the President could deny Russians the ability to claim the protection of international human rights in Russian courts.

Finally, the draft Constitution guaranteed that all courts were 'independent' and created a specialised Constitutional Court with broad authority to determine the constitutionality of laws.[28] In particular, the Constitution gave the Constitutional Court the power to invalidate laws as well as the power to interpret provisions of the Constitution in the abstract.[29] It also empowered individual Russian citizens to directly bring rights claims to the Constitutional Court.[30]

The Russian Constitution is therefore a classic example of the hybrid constitutional text of the constitutional dark arts, placing democratic guarantees and individual rights provisions within a centralised constitutional system of presidential domination. This hybrid constitutional text was then put to the Russian people in a December 1993 referendum. This referendum was presented to the Russian people as a *fait accompli*: remarkably, on the same day, Russians not only voted yes or no on the draft Constitution but also were asked to vote for legislative representatives envisioned in the proposed Constitution. The Constitution received a bare majority but its passage was not widely celebrated. On the contrary, most of the reporting focused on the success of a nationalist party (misleadingly called the Liberal Democratic Party of Russia) in the legislative elections that were held at the same time.[31]

Decades later, however, the significance of the adoption of this Constitution can no longer be ignored. The later chapters of Russia's constitutional order have provided the Russian President with key tools

---

[28] ibid Arts 120 and 125.
[29] ibid Art 125.
[30] ibid Art 125.4.
[31] S Schmemann, 'Yeltsin's Reformers Show Weakness in Russian Vote; Constitution is Approved' *The New York Times* (Moscow, 13 December 1993) www.nytimes.com/1993/12/13/world/yeltsin-s-reformers-show-weakness-in-russian-vote-constitution-is-approved.html.

for building and maintaining 'super' or 'hyper' presidential governance.[32] As we will see in the coming chapters, Vladimir Putin used these powers to eliminate checks on his power and build his power. He also used the Constitution to justify this growing power, declaring it as necessary to secure Russia's stable modernisation and sovereignty. This hybrid order has thus played a central role in both creating and maintaining contemporary Russian authoritarianism.

I. RUSSIAN CROWN-PRESIDENTIALISM

The constitutional centralisation in the later chapters of the new Russian Constitution was disguised by an array of democratic institutions, including an elected head-of-state President, a Prime Minister and an elected legislature. This arrangement led many to mistakenly classify Russia as a semi-presidential system.[33] But a close structural-normative reading of these provisions shows that the Constitution departed from French semi-presidentialism. It instead created a centralised 'crown-presidential' system that concentrates power in the hands of the office of the President.[34] This structural analysis reads constitutional provisions not as standalone rules but instead in a way that seeks to understand how they interact with one another to form a constitutional system.

The Russian Constitution combines design ideas from both French and American presidentialism. First, the Constitution gives the head-of-state President *guardian* authority to personally control other branches of power (particularly the legislative branch). This kind of standalone presidential authority is similar to the power of the President in the French semi-presidential system. It draws from a special kind of non-executive authority that the monarch once exercised to unify and coordinate state power. Second, it affords the President *management* authority over day-to-day executive-branch governance. This executive power draws from American presidentialism where the President has broad executive powers over the cabinet (and much of the executive branch bureaucracy). These powers are described in Table 2.

---

[32] W Partlett, 'Crown-Presidentialism' (2022) 20 *International Journal of Constitutional Law* 204.
[33] TJ Colton and C Skach, 'A Fresh Look at Semi-Presidentialism: The Russian Predicament' (2005) 16 *Journal of Democracy* 113, 116–17.
[34] Partlett (n 32).

Table 2 Types of presidential power

	Guardian	Management
Type of power	Personal power	Legal-bureaucratic, executive power
Purpose of power	'**guarantor** of the Constitution of the Russian Federation, the rights and freedoms of man and citizen'.[35] '**takes measures that protect** the sovereignty of the Russian Federation, its independence and state integrity, **maintains civil peace** and harmony in the country'.[36] 'ensures the **coordinated functioning** and interaction of bodies that are part of a single system of public power'.[37]	Determine 'the main directions of domestic and foreign policy'.[38]
Constitutional authority	dissolve the lower house of parliament;[39] determine foreign policy, sign and ratify treaties;[40] issue decrees;[41] give pardons and possess immunity;[42] appoint judges and other public officials;[43] act as Commander in Chief of the Armed Forces.[44]	Appoint and dismiss the Prime Minister and ministry/government;[45] chair meetings of the government;[46] unilaterally form the presidential administration;[47] submit bills to parliament and sign bills;[48] address legislature on the situation in the country and provide the 'guidelines of internal and foreign policy of the State';[49] organise executive branch institutions.[50]

[35] Russian Constitution (n 15) Art 80.3.
[36] ibid.
[37] ibid.
[38] ibid Art 80.2.
[39] ibid Art 84(b).
[40] ibid Art 86.
[41] ibid Art 90.
[42] ibid Art 89(c) and 91.
[43] ibid Art 83.
[44] ibid Art 87.

On their own, these types of presidential power might not be a threat to democratic governance. A head of state President with strong guardian powers but not management ones (as in France) cannot personally dominate everyday politics without majority support in the legislature. Similarly, a President who is simply the head of the executive branch (as in the United States) can be checked by an independent legislative branch. But, when combined, these powers create a 'crown-presidential' system that allows the President to dominate politics by shaping both the content of law and the institutional organisation of Russian politics. This combined authority is an example of what Kim Lane Scheppele describes as a 'Frankenstate', where the 'interaction effects' of 'perfectly reasonable pieces' ultimately leads to the creation of a monster.[51] In this case, the 'monster' is a presidential office that has the power to dominate both formal and informal political ordering. Simultaneously reflecting and bolstering the centralised state tradition, crown-presidentialism creates a kind of permanent state of exception with a sovereign President.

This system provides the President vast rational-legal sovereign authority to assert both formal and informal control over politics while simultaneously justifying this authoritarian project in the language of democracy, rights protection and legality. For instance, the Office of the President can use its vast power over investigative and prosecutorial agencies to justify the prosecution of political opponents. Moreover, the President is placed above the system of separated powers, making it difficult for voters to know who was responsible for a policy failure.[52] This system of 'centralisation without accountability' allows the President to shift accountability for serious policy failures to the executive-branch government or the legislature.[53] It has therefore played a critical role in helping to allow Vladimir Putin to rebuild Russian authoritarianism since 2000. It also undermined the authority of other institutions, weakening the quality and effectiveness of Russian governance.

[45] ibid Art 111, 117.
[46] ibid Art 83(b).
[47] ibid Art 83(i).
[48] ibid Art 84(d) and (e).
[49] ibid Art 84(f).
[50] ibid Art 112.
[51] KL Scheppele, 'The Rule of Law and the Frankenstate: Why Governance Checklists Do Not Work' (2013) 26 *Governance: An International Journal of Policy, Administration, and Institutions* 559, 560.
[52] V Gel'man, *The Politics of Bad Governance in Contemporary Russia* (Ann Arbor, University of Michigan Press, 2022).
[53] J Linz, 'Presidential or Parliamentary Democracy: Does it Make a Difference?' in JJ Linz and A Valenzuela (eds), *The Failure of Presidential Democracy* (Baltimore, Johns Hopkins University Press, 1994) 52 (describing the difficulty of ascribing political accountability in semi-presidential regimes).

II. PRESIDENT AS MONARCH

The Russian Constitution places the President outside and above the system of executive, legislative and judicial power by describing presidential power in its own special chapter of the Constitution and designating the President as the 'head of state' who represents the Russian Federation 'both inside the country and in international affairs' and 'guarantor of the Constitution and individual rights'.[54] This position reflects the anti-politics of the centralised state tradition and its focus on a unifying institution that can ensure civil peace and the common good. A former Chairman of the Russian Constitutional Court Justice described this position:

> [T]he Russian President stands outside the interests of specific political parties or societal groups, as a unique rights-protector and 'lobby' for all the people. The President's interaction with the parliament, which is founded on party representation, should protect the unity of the general government and regional interests. This service of the general will [*obshchenarodnoe sluzhenie*] is found in the president's oath, in which he swears to 'faithfully serve the people'.[55]

These guardian powers are not executive powers but instead draw from the personal powers that monarchs have long exercised to unify the entire constitutional system. This personal authority persists in democratic states but is controversial and is normally limited by law. In some common law states, they are called 'prerogative' powers and there is often much debate about their scope, particularly because of the threat they pose to the rule of law (and legislative power overall).[56]

In Russia, by contrast, the Constitution explicitly gives broad and open-ended guardian powers to the presidency in its position above the system of the executive, legislative, and judicial power. Article 80 of the Russian Constitution describes the general purposes of this guardian authority. It gives the President special guardian powers to safeguard the overall functioning of the system of executive, legislative and judicial power. This includes the power to 'adopt measures to protect the sovereignty of the Russian Federation, its independence and state integrity, ensure coordinated functioning and interaction of all bodies'.[57] Finally, it

---

[54] ibid Art 80.
[55] Marat Baglai, *The Presidents of the Russian Federation and the United States: Role, Elections, and Powers* (in Russian) (Moscow, Norma, 2008) 20–21.
[56] A Twomey, 'The Prerogative and the Courts in Australia' (2021) 3 *Journal of Commonwealth Law* 55.
[57] Russian Constitution (n 15) Art 80.

makes the President the ultimate 'guarantor' of the rights and freedoms of man and citizen.[58]

The Constitution also gives a non-exhaustive list of specific guardian powers. These include the authority to appoint personal representatives (plenipotentiaries),[59] issue decrees,[60] give pardons,[61] dissolve the lower house of parliament,[62] act as Commander in Chief,[63] appoint a wide range of public officials,[64] enjoy immunity from prosecution[65] and personally determine foreign policy through signing and ratifying treaties.[66] It also includes the power to organise 'conciliation procedures to resolve disagreements' between federal and regional authorities and the unilateral power to introduce martial law.[67]

This position also gives the President explicit constitutional authority to personally control parliament. One key example is the President's power to dissolve the lower house of the Russian legislature (the Duma).[68] This power is exercisable when the Duma rejects a presidential appointment to the prime ministerial position three times or when it expresses no confidence in the government.[69] It therefore gives the President significant power to discipline the lower house of the legislature if it seeks to check presidential control of the executive branch. One commentator described this set of rules as undermining 'the parliament's ability to provide an institutional check on the president' and 'coerce adoption of controversial legislation even in the absence of a parliamentary majority'.[70]

In addition, the Constitution also gives the President broad presidential authority over the upper house of the legislature (Federation Council). The Federation Council reflects Russian federalism, including two members from each of Russia's constituent units or 'subjects'.[71] Three constitutional rules interact with one another to give the President

---

[58] ibid Art 80.
[59] ibid Art 83(k).
[60] ibid Art 90.
[61] ibid Art 89(v).
[62] ibid Art 84(b).
[63] ibid Art 87.
[64] ibid Art 83.
[65] ibid Art 91.
[66] ibid Art 86.
[67] ibid Art 85.
[68] ibid Art 84.
[69] ibid Arts 111, 117.
[70] R Moore, 'The Path to the New Russian Constitution: A Comparison of Executive-Legislative Relations in the Major Drafts' (1995) 3(1) *Demokratizatsiya: The Journal of Post-Soviet Democratization* 44, 56.
[71] Russian Constitution (n 15) Art 96.2.

significant power over the upper house. First, the Constitution does not require these members to be elected. Instead, it states that the Federation Council is 'formed' according to rules set by law.[72] Second, and in tandem, the Federation Council comprises two representatives from each of the 'subjects' (or regions) of the Russian Federation: one from the legislative branch and the other from the executive branch.[73] Third, another key provision states that the executive branch is formed into 'a single system of executive power of the Russian Federation'.[74] Because the President is the chief executive officer (see the next section), the President has significant authority over these executive representatives in the upper house.

The Crown-President's rational-legal control of the upper house has important parallels with monarchical practice. It echoes a practice which gave the monarch rational-legal power to create advisory councils of powerful elites that could then be relied upon to ensure the exercise of top-down, monarchical power. For instance, in the 1850 Prussian Constitution, the King appointed the upper house completely and relied on this upper house to govern the nation.[75] These upper houses were not professional, legislative bodies as we understand them in the modern sense; they were advisory bodies that strengthened centralised power.

This presidential power over the upper house further enables the Russian President to dominate the judiciary and other oversight institutions through appointment and dismissal (such as the Constitutional Court, Central Bank, Prosecutor General and Central Election Commission). This is because many of his appointments to these bodies requires the confirmation of the upper house. Control of appointment over the leadership of these oversight institutions allows the President to avoid real accountability. It also allows the President to manipulate elections, for instance by disqualifying candidates or refusing to register political parties.

In addition, the President's guardian powers also include broad decree power which 'must be implemented across the entire territory of Russia'.[76] This legislative-like decree power draws on the monarch's traditional authority to personally make law. This guardian power also includes the authority to create institutions and organise the institutions of the executive branch. Furthermore, the President also has the power

---

[72] ibid Art 96.2.
[73] ibid Art 95.2.
[74] ibid Art 77.
[75] JH Robinson (trans), *Constitution of the Kingdom of Prussia* (Philadelphia, American Academy of Political and Social Science, 1894) Art 68.
[76] Russian Constitution (n 15) Art 90.

to appoint and dismiss plenipotentiary representatives.[77] These representatives approximate the kind of regal representatives that would govern on behalf of the monarch.

These provisions therefore create a rational-legal foundation for other forms of informal power. Most notably, they allow the presidency to link itself with traditional forms of monarchical authority in Russia (the Tsar). Weber described traditional authority as relying on the idea that people obey because 'of the sanctity of immemorial traditions which govern the authority relations'.[78] In Russia's crown-presidential system, the President is the embodied representative of the state and fundamental arbiter and guarantor of the entire system, echoing the traditional role of the Tsar.

The constitutionalisation of guardian authority and its links to traditional authority were intentional. In his struggle for power with the Russian parliament prior to October 1993, Yeltsin and his team had weak rational legal authority. In response, President Boris Yeltsin frequently sought to associate the office of the President with traditional forms of authority. This was frequently done by associating the office of the President with Tsarist symbols and places. For instance, after being elected the first Russian President in 1991, Boris Yeltsin invited the Patriarch of the Orthodox Church to speak at his inauguration. The Patriarch described the President as the 'highest public office in Russia'.[79] Yeltsin also moved his presidential office into the Kremlin, the traditional seat of power in Moscow with ornate halls and orthodox Russian churches. Yeltsin also refused to join a political party when he became President, preferring to describe presidential power as operating above the political fray and the President as representing the whole people.

In describing the Constitution, Yeltsin's advisers did not hide the fact that the Constitution intended to make the President a kind of monarch. Sergei Alekseev, one of the chief drafters of the Constitution alongside Anatoly Sobchak, argued that the new Constitution would be based on Russia's centralising and monarchical history. He explained that the unifying institution 'used to be a monarch, [but] now it's a President.

---

[77] ibid Art 82.
[78] C Matheson, 'Weber and the Classification of the Forms of Legitimacy' (1987) 38 *The British Journal of Sociology* 199, 206.
[79] D Remnick, 'Yeltsin Sworn in as Russian President: Gorbachev, Orthodox Patriarch Speak at Populist's Inauguration' *The Washington Post* (Moscow, 10 July 1991) www.washingtonpost.com/archive/politics/1991/07/11/yeltsin-sworn-in-as-russian-president/533c96df-a858-44a7-8827-eab25130a551/.

Generally speaking, since 1918 we have been moving – not in words but in deeds – toward a constitutional monarchy'.[80] The Constitution's combination of rational legal and traditional authority creates an even stronger basis for the authority of the President. Weber wrote that the most stable systems of authority are not grounded on one type of authority but instead combine different types of authority.[81]

III. PRESIDENT AS CHIEF EXECUTIVE OFFICER

Second, in addition to elevating the President into a crown or Tsar-like position above the system of separated powers (including the executive branch), the Russian Constitution also gives the President broad authority to direct the executive branch implementation of law and policy through the domination of executive power. This legal-bureaucratic form of executive authority gives the President the power to 'determine[] the main directions of the domestic … policy of the state'.[82] The Russian President – which formally is not in the executive branch – can (if he or she chooses to) act as chief executive officer and 'manage' the everyday implementation of the law. A key drafter explained that the President's responsibility 'is the structural integrity of the government. He takes measures, so that the entire government apparatus will work, averts different types of crises, and directly runs the Government'.[83]

This position gives the President authority to determine the general direction of internal state policy[84] and the right to chair the meetings of the Government.[85] Moreover, the President also has the power to decide on the 'structure of the bodies of federal executive power'.[86] This power allows the President power to reshape the legal relationship between powerful executive-branch agencies.

The President also has final authority to determine the composition of the executive-branch government (*pravitelstvo*) by appointing and removing the Chairman of the Government (Prime Minister) and other ministers. The Constitution states that the President shall appoint the

---

[80] Quoted from Partlett (n 21) 128–29.
[81] M Weber, *Theory of Social and Economic Organization* (T Parsons (ed), AM Henderson and T Parsons (trans)) (New York, Free Press, 1947) 388.
[82] Russian Constitution (n 15) Art 80.3.
[83] Quoted from Partlett (n 21) 130.
[84] Russian Constitution (n 15) Art 80.
[85] ibid Art 83(b).
[86] ibid Art 112.

Prime Minister with the 'agreement' of the Duma (the lower house of the legislature).[87] On its own, many have cited this rule as a key check on presidential power. But, read as a system, it is clear that the President has ultimate control over the selection of the Prime Minister. Article 117 states that, if the Duma rejects the presidential candidate three times, 'the President appoints the Prime Minister, dissolves the State Duma, and calls new elections'. Furthermore, the Constitution allows the President to ignore a legislative vote of no confidence in the government and, in the case of a second consecutive no confidence vote within three months, gives the President the choice of either dismissing the government or the legislature itself.[88]

In addition to empowering the President to dominate the federal executive, the President also has vast authority to control executive power in the regions. This control of regional executive power reflects the idea of a 'vertical of power' from the President to the regional executives. A key provision in the chapter on Russian federalism states that 'the bodies of executive authority of the subjects of the Russian Federation shall make up a single system of executive power of the Russian Federation'.[89] This accords with the idea that the President is the guarantor of the 'unity' of the overall system of Russian federalism.[90]

Another important management power is the broad presidential power to organise executive power. As we will see in chapter five, this unilateral power to create, appoint and reorganise institutions is critical in the exercise of presidential management power. This includes the power to 'form' a Presidential Administration and Security Council.[91] Operating in the old buildings of the Soviet Communist Party in central Moscow, officials in the Presidential Administration help to coordinate the personal directives and plans of the President. Moreover, it also encompasses the authority to reorganise the structure of executive branch, enabling the President to control Russia's vast bureaucratic apparatus.[92]

A final set of management powers include the power to submit bills to parliament and sign bills[93] and address the parliament on the situation in the country and to provide the 'guidelines of internal and foreign policy

---

[87] ibid Art 111.
[88] ibid Art 117.
[89] ibid Art 77.2.
[90] ibid Art 5.
[91] ibid Art 83(g) and (i).
[92] ibid Art 112.
[93] ibid Art 84(g) and (d).

of the State'.⁹⁴ The Russian President also has the authority to annul the acts of executive branch officials when they contradict legislation, the Constitution or international law.⁹⁵ Taken together, these powers give the President tremendous power over both the process of legal drafting and implementation (through executive rule-making). Alongside the President's decree power, the President has far-reaching law-making authority.

These management powers help to complement and augment the charismatic authority of the President. Max Weber defined charismatic authority as 'a certain quality of an individual personality, by virtue of which he is set apart from ordinary men and treated as endowed with supernatural, superhuman, or at least specifically exceptional powers or qualities'.⁹⁶ These extraordinary personal abilities then inspire devotion and obedience amongst both the political elite and the people. In particular, people obey and follow the charismatic leader because they believe the individual leader can perform remarkable acts.

Yeltsin made wide use of his charismatic authority in his struggle with the legislative branch in 1992 and 1993. Yeltsin described his leadership as the only way to overcome the Soviet status quo and forge a path of economic and political reform. After being elected President in 1991, Yeltsin frequently appealed to his necessary charismatic authority, declaring that his leadership put the 'interests of the people' above those of a corrupt Communist elite.⁹⁷ He also made heavy use of referendums to ensure popular trust. As we have seen in chapter two, Yeltsin used a 53 per cent vote of popular support in his personal leadership to justify his October 1993 seizure of power.⁹⁸

The management power in the Russian Constitution allows the President to 'routinise' this charismatic authority by affording this office the authority to manage a vast array of challenges.⁹⁹ As we will see in chapter five, this kind of rational-legal authority enables the personalised power of the President. Vladimir Putin has proven particularly adept at using these powers to project an image of a leader who has personally saved Russia from disintegration and weakness. But this image masks

---

[94] ibid Art 84(e).
[95] ibid Art 85.2.
[96] Weber (n 81) 364.
[97] Remnick (n 79).
[98] MC Walker, *The Strategic Use of Referendums: Power, Legitimacy, and Democracy* (New York, Palgrave McMillan, 2003) 83–85.
[99] Weber (n 81) 374 (discussing the routinisation of charismatic authority).

an uncomfortable reality: the significant weakness and incompetence of institutions that are tasked with implementing many of these presidential directives.

IV. JUSTIFYING RUSSIA'S 1993 CONSTITUTION

Read structurally, the 1993 Russian Constitution creates a normative blueprint for a centralised state that rejects a political system of democratic competition and deliberation. It instead values a highly centralised form of presidentialism that draws on the centralised state tradition and its anti-political claim that centralisation is critical to furthering the project of a unified Russian democratic system, rights protection and the common good. Three key arguments were made in support of this centralisation of authority in the office of the President.

First, the centralising provisions in the Russian Constitution were described as ensuring the necessary stability and unity in the pursuit of the common good, which at the time was described simply as 'reform'. Russia was facing a number of challenges in the early 1990s, including economic collapse, increasing demands for territorial autonomy and the breakdown of law and order. Yeltsin described the constitutional draft when it was released to the public in November 1993 as one needed to overcome state weakness and create law-based order. He summed this up by saying that 'We need order, but not the horrible repressive order of the Stalinist camps'.[100] One of the key drafters of the Constitution (Sergei Shakhrai) commented later that a key purpose of the Constitution was to ensure a President who could make 'unpopular decisions' necessary for the continuance of economic and social reforms.[101]

Western leaders expressed support for Russia's new constitutional order in these terms. Elaine Sciolino of the *New York Times* described how the White House saw 'Yeltsin as the country's best hope for democracy, a sort of Russian style Charles de Gaulle delivering his country from chaos by assuming authoritarian powers'.[102] This authoritarian

---

[100] C Bohlen, 'Yeltsin Promotes a Charter that is Very Much His' *The New York Times* (Moscow, 10 November 1993) www.nytimes.com/1993/11/10/world/yeltsin-promotes-a-charter-that-is-very-much-his.html?searchResultPosition=10.
[101] 'Shakhrai: The Constitution Built a New Society Out of Chaos' *BBC News Russian* (11 December 2013) www.bbc.com/russian/russia/2013/12/131211_shakhrai_interview.
[102] E Sciolino, 'Showdown in Moscow; US Supports Move by Russian Leader to Break Deadlock' *The New York Times* (Washington, 22 September 1993) www.nytimes.com/1993/09/22/world/showdown-in-moscow-us-supports-move-by-russian-leader-to-break-deadlock.html.

marketisation – what one book called 'market Bolshevism' – was viewed as inevitably leading to democracy.[103] The White House hoped that the new constitutional rules would 'provide some stability in the relations between the legislative and executive branches, an aspect that has been absent for the last year and a half'.[104] To the extent that these effects were viewed as overly centralising power in the President, many Western scholars saw this as a necessary expedient for introducing economic reforms.[105]

Many Russian liberal reformers also backed the Constitution on this basis. For instance, Mikhail Krasnov, an adviser to President Yeltsin from 1995 to 1998 and one of Russia's leading liberal constitutional law academics, described in a 2018 interview how he viewed the presidential powers in the Constitution as a necessary tool for reform.[106] At the time, he and other liberal reformers were seized 'by euphoria and believed: if we have power, we will choose the president who is needed for reforms'.[107] Looking back 15 years later, he admitted that he failed to take account of the long-term consequences of the Constitution. He concluded that a better path would have been a temporary Constitution that would need to be redrafted once the crisis had passed.

Second, centralisation was justified on the basis that the President was ultimately accountable to the people. One of the main drafters of the Constitution stated that the vast power lodged in the President was rooted in a 'democratic basis: popular sovereignty … The people decide the matter'.[108] Western structural commentary on the Constitution pointed to the presence of elected democratic institutions as evidence that it was ultimately a democratic document. One scholar described the Constitution as the equivalent of the 'Airbus' because it combined provisions from different democratic systems.[109] He commented that the Russian Constitution was the product of 'one of the most extensive transfers of legal ideas in the modern history of law'.[110] Another

---

[103] P Reddaway and D Glinsky, *The Tragedy of Russia's Reforms: Market Bolshevism Against Democracy* (Washington DC, United States Institute for Peace, 2001).
[104] Sciolino (n 104).
[105] A Felkay, *Yeltsin's Russia and the West* (Westport, Praeger, 2002) 4.
[106] T Boiko, 'Imaginary Separation of Powers' (in Russian) (*Everyday Journal*, 27 September 2018) www.ej.ru/?a=note&id=32958.
[107] ibid.
[108] Quoted from Partlett (n 21) 130.
[109] R Sharlet, 'Legal Transplants and Political Mutations: The Reception of Constitutional Law in Russia and the Newly Independent States' (1998) 7 *East European Constitutional Review* 59, 64.
[110] ibid 59.

wrote that the Constitution was the product of a 'constitutional melting pot' that combined 'both French and American features'.[111] Russia's elected institutions were viewed as a clear step away from the Soviet past and toward democracy. United States President Bill Clinton placed the Russian Constitution at the centre of this progressive politics of inevitability: 'the Russian people have eliminated the last vestiges of the old Soviet system and replaced them with new and legitimate institutions that will lay a foundation for continued development of a democratic society'.[112]

As we have seen above, the Constitution did combine institutions from both French and American constitutional presidentialism. But the interaction effects of these different textual provisions were not closely analysed. This misreading led one scholar to describe Russia's first post-Soviet Constitution as a symbolic marker of a 'new beginning'[113] for Russian democracy and 'a crucial component in the establishment of a constitutional society in Russia'.[114] Richard Sakwa argued that Russia's adoption of a Constitution in 1993 was a critical first step away from its authoritarian and communist past: 'The final vestiges of the communist legacy were swept away as the new document promised economic liberalism and the democratic separation of powers'.[115]

Third, the Constitution was justified by the idea that the foundational rights and democratic provisions would limit any excesses of centralisation. In this story, written democratic Constitutions are primarily legal texts that open the domestic order to international human rights law and empower courts to limit public power. This is most notable in rights enforcement, when individuals bring claims against the state on the basis of the Constitution. A common view was expressed by one report which stated that the Russian Constitution represented a 'clear break' with its predecessors because 'Gone are the references to the supremacy of the Communist Party and the requirement that the citizens comply with standards of socialist conduct. Instead, the Constitution contains

---

[111] RR Ludwikowski, "'Mixed" Constitutions: Product of an East-Central European Constitutional Melting Pot' (1998) 16 *Boston University International Law Journal* 41.

[112] TL Friedman, 'On the Russian Vote, Clinton Accentuates the Positive' *The New York Times* (14 December 1993) www.nytimes.com/1993/12/14/world/the-russian-vote-on-the-russian-vote-clinton-accentuates-the-positive.html.

[113] B Ackerman, 'The Rise of World Constitutionalism' (1997) 83 *Virginia Law Review* 771, 786.

[114] DD Atchison, 'Notes on Constitutionalism for a 21st-Century Russian President' (1998) 6 *Cardozo Journal of International and Comparative Law* 239, 351.

[115] R Sakwa, 'The Struggle for the Constitution in Russia and the Triumph of Ethical Individualism' (1996) 48 *Studies in East European Thought* 115, 131.

specific sections devoted to civil rights, the division of powers'.[116] The implication was that these rights would now allow rights challenges to the actions of the Russian state.

The Constitution's commitment to international human rights law was also cited as a critical part of its democratic potential. An analysis of the new Russian Constitution, for instance, speculated that the powers of the President 'may ultimately be checked by what is perceived by international law as appropriate, even if it is not formally checked by structures established in the Russian Constitution'.[117] Another suggested that 'international law may serve as a basis for human rights and democracy that may have a stabilizing influence on Russia'.[118]

Rights advocates supported the Constitution on this legalist basis. For instance, Sergei Kovalev described his belief in the transformative power of the legal guarantees in the Constitution in his resignation letter to Boris Yeltsin.[119] He described how he supported Yeltsin in the 'tragic days' of the autumn of 1993 on the basis that Yeltsin's action would overcome the 'crisis of legitimacy' and 'create a basis for the rule of law in Russia'.[120] He admitted that the 1993 Constitution 'confers enormous powers on the President' but that it also places enormous legal responsibilities on the President. Those include the responsibility to act as 'guarantor of the rights and liberties of citizens' and 'to maintain law and order throughout the country'.[121] As we will see in chapter four, Kovalev would ultimately resign his post as Russia's first ombudsman because of Yeltsin's unwillingness to play this enlightened dictator role.

V. CONCLUSION

This chapter revises our understanding of Russia's post-Soviet constitutional order. Rather than a Western-inspired liberal democratic Constitution which would fail, Russia's 1993 Constitution was a hybrid document that guaranteed democracy and rights but in a constitutional

---

[116] Dresen and Pomeranz (n 11) 3.
[117] ML McClure, 'An Analysis of the New Russian Constitution' (1995) 4 *Journal of International Law and Practice* 601, 605.
[118] GM Danilenko, 'The New Russian Constitution and International Law' (1994) 88 *The American Journal of International Law* 451, 470.
[119] 'Sergei Kovalev Resignation Letter to Boris Yeltsin 1996' (*George Washington University National Security Archive*, 23 January 1996) https://nsarchive.gwu.edu/document/24413-sergei-kovalev-resignation-letter-boris-yeltsin-1996-translation.
[120] ibid.
[121] ibid.

system of highly centralised presidential power. By placing the Russian President in a constitutional position that is simultaneously above the other branches of public power and able to direct executive power, Yeltsin (and his supporters) continued Russia's long adherence to the anti-politics of the centralised state tradition. The Office of the President replaced the position of the Communist Party or the Tsar. Centralisation was no longer justified as necessary to vindicate the vanguard role of the Party or the traditional authority of the Tsar; now it was necessary for representing the unified will of the people and continuing Russian reform. The 1993 Constitution therefore did not break with the centralisation of the Soviet and Tsarist past; instead, it continued this tradition by giving centralisation a new purpose.

The use of the constitutional dark arts in 1993 Russia was clearly shaped by the anti-political legalism of Russia's democratic movement. But it was not inevitable. Instead, there were possible moments of compromise that were bypassed in 1993 that would have led to a different outcome. Even after seizing power in October 1993, Yeltsin could have built political checks on the concentration of power into the Russian constitutional state by creating a 'single agreed draft' that incorporated the balanced state ideas of the Constitutional Commission's draft. But he and his supporters' belief in the need for a powerful elected President to continue reform helped to allow this centralised constitutional system to be justified in the dominant name of rights and democracy.

The next four chapters will describe how this centralised constitutional system has shaped Russian politics since 1993. This centralised system has changed over time. Depending on who was President, Russian politics has taken on different forms, from personalism to managerialism to imperialism. Despite these different manifestations, each shares a key similarity: they were not systems of accountable democratic governance. On the contrary, they were centralised systems of top-down governance that have struggled to effectively govern Russia.

4

The Personal President (1994–99)

IN DECEMBER 1994, as the breakaway government in Russia's southern province of Chechnya increasingly asserted control, President Boris Yeltsin decided to act. Pushing the guardian authority of the President to the limits, he refused to ask the upper house of the Russian legislature to declare a state of emergency. Instead, he issued a presidential decree instructing the Russian military to use 'all means at the state's disposal' to restore constitutional order in Chechnya and subdue 'illegal armed groups'.[1] Two days later, Russian armed forces entered Chechnya and Russian warplanes began to bomb the Chechen capital, Grozny. This war would last two years and prove to be a human rights and military disaster.

The way President Yeltsin waged the First Chechen War is just one example of the highly personalised and dictatorial style of anti-politics that President Boris Yeltsin built out of Russia's new crown-presidential constitutional system. Yeltsin and his team justified the broad use of the guardian authority of the President – and particularly its extensive decree power – as necessary to deliver Russia from its crisis and ensure Russian economic and political reform. They therefore aggressively pushed these powers, seeing the President as a kind of reformist 'bulldozer' that could overcome the pressing challenges facing post-Soviet Russia.[2] Critical to this anti-politics was the 'end of history' belief that building a laissez-faire, market system and small state would inevitably foster Russian democracy.[3] As one of Yeltsin's key advisers, Anatoly Chubais,

---

[1] Presidential Decree No 2166 of 9 December 1994, 'On Measures to Suppress the Activities of Illegal Armed Groups on the Territory of the Chechen Republic and in the Zone of the Ossetian-Ingush Conflict' (in Russian) (Yeltsin Centre Online Archive) www.yeltsin.ru/archive/act/41002/.
[2] D Kurnosov, 'Beware of the Bulldozer: What We Can Learn from Russia's 1993 Extra-Constitutional Constitution-Making' (*Verfassungsblog*, 7 January 2022) www.verfassungsblog.de/beware-of-the-bulldozer/.
[3] T Snyder, *The Road to Unfreedom: Russia, Europe, America* (New York, Penguin, 2019) (discussing the politics of inevitability).

said: 'In order to have a democracy in society, there must be a dictatorship in power'.[4]

This 'bulldozer' approach to governance did not foster full-scale authoritarianism. Instead, Yeltsin allowed space for criticism and debate in the media and in civil society. He also used the power of the presidency to shrink the size of the state and transfer economic and political power to a new class of business oligarchs and regional leaders. These checks on presidential power did not, however, mean Russia was a democracy. In fact, there was little real popular accountability in 1990s Russia. Most notably, in 1996, Yeltsin made self-interested use of his broad presidential powers to secure his re-election.

The Russian Constitution therefore helped to create a system of 'pluralism by default', where political competition emerges 'not because leaders are especially democratic or because institutions or societal actors are particularly strong, but because the government is too fragmented and the state too weak to monopolise political control'.[5] This decree-based approach form of personalistic governance drastically undermined rule of law and the effectiveness of the Russian state. Without effective state power, powerful private interests were free to operate with little accountability, generating vast corruption and economic inequality.

This chapter will describe how Yeltsin's personalised style of governance (mis)managed two key challenges facing Russia in the 1990s: centre-periphery relations and market reform. It will then turn to the weakness of both popular and legal accountability in limiting the excesses of this system. It will recount how Yeltsin drew on his constitutional authority to recover from a single digit approval rating and win the 1996 presidential election. Meanwhile, the majority of the Constitutional Court deferred to broad assertions of presidential authority, instead choosing to protect individuals from the consequences of state dysfunction. Finally, the international community was largely unwilling to hold Russia accountable for its rights abuses in Chechnya.

I. CENTRE-PERIPHERY RELATIONS

Persistent demands for autonomy (and sometimes outright independence) from Russia's regions were a critical political challenge of the

---

[4] D Hoffman, 'Yeltsin's "Ruthless" Bureaucrat' *The Washington Post* (Moscow, 21 November 1996) www.washingtonpost.com/archive/politics/1996/11/22/yeltsins-ruthless-bureaucrat/d8236b02-fa5e-4777-b29a-97cd72d63913/.

[5] L Way, *Pluralism by Default: Weak Autocrats and the Rise of Competitive Politics* (Baltimore, John Hopkins University Press, 2015) 2.

time. The most extreme example was Chechnya, which declared formal independence from the Russian Federation in 1991 and formed its own military.[6] Other regional governments, such as Tatarstan, sought to pressure Moscow to negotiate by declaring itself a 'sovereign state' that was the 'subject of international law'.[7] Many of these regions also refused to send tax payments to Moscow. President Yeltsin relied heavily on the personalised, guardian powers of the presidency and the justifications of the centralised state tradition to respond to these demands.

A. The First Chechen War

To address the situation in Chechnya, President Yeltsin aggressively drew on the guardian powers of his office. In December 1994, almost exactly a year after the Russian Constitution had been adopted, President Yeltsin ordered the Russian armed forces into Chechnya without declaring a state of emergency (which would have constitutionally required the assent of the upper house of the legislature).[8] Instead, he commenced this military action unilaterally on the basis of a series of presidential decrees.[9] These decrees – one of which was unpublished and therefore unavailable to the public – operated on the basis that the President possessed full legal authority to manage the internal military operation without the participation of the legislature.

These decrees formed the entire legal regulatory framework for the military operation in Chechnya. For instance, one decree appointed a representative, Nikolai Yegerov, to negotiate on behalf of President Yeltsin.[10] Another ordered the General Prosecutor not to prosecute any Chechen fighters who voluntarily handed in their weapons.[11] Another

[6] SAA Shah, 'Genesis of the Chechen Resistance Movement' (2004) 24(4) *Strategic Studies* 84.
[7] Commission on Security and Cooperation in Europe, US Helsinki Commission, 'Report on the Tatarstan Referendum on Sovereignty' (21 March 1992) 1, www.csce.gov/publications/report-tatarstan-referendum-sovereignty/.
[8] Art 102. Constitution of the Russian Federation (*Council of Europe*) https://rm.coe.int/constitution-of-the-russian-federation-en/1680a1a237.
[9] See generally Valery Baranov, 'Use of Internal Troops of the Ministry of Internal Affairs of the Russian Federation within the Country (in the Southern Federal District): Legal, Political and Moral Aspects' (in Russian) (2006) 3 *Herald of the St Petersburg University Ministry for Internal Affairs* 103 www.cyberleninka.ru/article/n/ispolzovanie-vnutrennih-voysk-ministerstva-vnutrennih-del-rossiyskoy-federatsii-vnutri-strany-v-yuzhnom-federal-nom-okruge-pravovye/viewer.
[10] Presidential Decree No 2136 of 30 November 1994 'About Egerove N.D.' (in Russian) (Yeltsin Centre Online Archive) www.yeltsin.ru/archive/act/40982.
[11] Presidential Decree No 2142 of 1 December 1994, 'About Certain Measures for the Strengthening of Order in the North Caucasus' (in Russian) (Yeltsin Centre Online Archive) https://yeltsin.ru/archive/act/40986/.

unpublished decree from 30 November 1994 even provided for a start time for a series of emergency military measures in Chechnya (6 am on 1 December).[12] It also provided for the creation of a group to lead actions to disarm and liquidate armed groups and introduced a state of emergency on the territory of the republic. Finally, it established a mechanism for coordinating the activities of federal executive authorities and security forces in the implementation of these measures.

This unpublished decree, however, was never implemented and was soon rescinded. Instead, Yeltsin published a new (public) decree on 9 December 1994.[13] The decree that ultimately led to military action was only one page and simply instructed the Ministry of Defence to 'use all means available to the state to ensure state security, legality, rights and freedoms of citizens, public order, crime control, disarmament all illegal armed groups'.[14] The decree based its authority on Article 80 of the Constitution and its requirement that the President safeguard 'the sovereignty of the Russian Federation, its independence and state integrity'.[15] The decree also drew support from the finding of the presidentially appointed Security Council that 'illegal armed formations' in Chechnya had violated Article 13.5 of the Constitution banning 'activities aimed at violating the integrity of the Russian Federation, undermining the security of the state, creating armed formations, inciting national and religious hatred'. The implication of this decree was clear: there was no need to negotiate a special state of emergency with the legislature for the President to unilaterally act to resolve the situation. One commentator summed up this decree as the 'order of the supreme commander and guarantor of the Constitution to restore constitutional order in Chechnya'.[16] Two days later, on 11 December 1994, the Russian military entered Chechnya and commenced a bloody war to regain control of the breakaway province.

This unilateral approach reflected the Yeltsin team's long-standing, anti-political distrust of political negotiation and their belief that a

---

[12] Presidential Decree No 2137c. The decree is unpublished so the detail here is as described in the Decision of the Russian Constitutional Court No 10-P of 31 July 1995 N 10-P, 'In the Case of Verifying the Constitutionality of Decree of the President of the Russian Federation of November 30, 1994 N 2137 "On Measures to Restore Constitutional Legality and Order on the Territory of the Chechen Republic"' (in Russian) (*Konsultant Plus*) www.consultant.ru/document/cons_doc_LAW_7552/.
[13] Presidential Decree No 2166 (n 1).
[14] ibid.
[15] ibid.
[16] See R Sharlet, 'Transitional Constitutionalism: Politics and Law in the Second Russian Republic' (1996) 14 *Wisconsin International Law Journal* 495, 509.

sovereign President was necessary to tackle the pressing problems facing post-Soviet Russia. This approach, however, did not produce an efficient and decisive response. Instead, it led to a disastrous military campaign, one that was poorly planned and carried a high human toll. Memorial, a leading human rights group set up by Andrei Sakharov, played a critical role in exposing the rights violations and mismanagement of the Chechen war. This effort was led by a former Yeltsin supporter, Sergei Kovalev, who was part of a team that personally documented the terrible cost of the Chechen invasion. This included, he argued, the death of 25,000 civilians, killed by 'indiscriminate bombing and artillery or mortar fire'.[17] When Yeltsin agreed to a ceasefire in 1996, little had been achieved beyond civilian casualties and rights abuses. Yeltsin's personalised Presidency had not proven to be an effective or decisive force in delivering Russia from its crisis.

B. Ad Hoc Federalism

Yeltsin also relied on the President's vast guardian authority to *personally* negotiate individualised bilateral arrangements with regions that were seeking more autonomy. These negotiations drew on the constitutional authority of the President to 'represent[] the Russian Federation within the country'.[18] This 'parade of treaties' with regional leaders took an asymmetrical and extra-legal approach to decentralisation that reflected the haphazard implementation of Yeltsin's call for regional leaders to 'take as much sovereignty as you can swallow'.[19] It ultimately gave Russia's regional executives different powers and privileges depending on their relative negotiating position and power with the President.

The process of deal-making started with the ethnic republics and then turned to other regions in 1995 and 1996. The regions that had resources and power were prioritised over those that were not. The treaty with Tatarstan, which set the model for others, was grounded on a highly personalised process of negotiation and was not 'subject to ratification either by the Federation Council or by the Tatar legislature' and 'entered

---

[17] S Kovalev, 'Death in Chechnya' *The New York Review* (8 June 1995) www.nybooks.com/articles/1995/06/08/death-in-chechnya/.
[18] Art 80.4.
[19] J Kahn, *Federalism, Democratization, and the Rule of Law in Russia* (Oxford, Oxford University Press, 2002) 157.

into force seven days after the signing ceremony'.[20] This and other bilateral treaties also contained provisions that included serious legal and constitutional ambiguities.[21]

Yeltsin's desire to personally manage centre-periphery relations also shaped his legislative reforms. Despite the Constitution stating that the Federation Council was 'selected', the first Federation Council of 1993 had been directly elected.[22] In 1995, Yeltsin pushed through a legislative change that cancelled elections and specified that the Federation Council would now include two representatives from each subject: the head of the executive branch (often called a governor) and the speaker or chair of the regional legislative branch.[23]

This change reflected Yeltsin's desire to personally work with the heads of the regions. As Jeffrey Kahn wrote, Yeltsin was aiming 'for a less cantankerous body of law-makers, who by the very nature of their dual appointment, would behave more like a part-time legislature'.[24] In reality, however, it created another legislative check on presidential power at the federal level as the regional leadership used their national office to protect their own interests. This was particularly true after the 1996 election when Yeltsin's popularity waned and regional leaders increasingly protected their own interests against those of the centre.

This personalistic approach to managing centre-periphery relations undermined Russia's fragile rule of law. The personalised bilateral agreements between the President and the regions were of dubious legal status and led to contradictory and conflicting laws. Jeffrey Kahn described how these 'bilateral executive-driven negotiations had the effect of eroding conceptions of a federal civic identity, a unified legal space, and fiscal burden-sharing'.[25] Furthermore, the law granting regional heads a seat in the Federation Council only worsened corruption by giving regional leaders blanket immunity from prosecution. In addition, the absence of a unified legal space increased the difficulties of the centre in implementing its policies across Russia's vast space. Often this included attempts by the centre to lessen the social impacts of economic reforms on the Russian population.

[20] ibid 155.
[21] ibid 156.
[22] ibid 255.
[23] Federal Law No 192-FZ of 5 December 1995 'On the procedure for forming the Federation Council of the Federal Assembly of the Russian Federation (in Russian) (*Garant*) https://base.garant.ru/1518431/.
[24] Kahn (n 19) 255.
[25] ibid 188.

II. ECONOMIC REFORM

The central economic challenge in 1990s post-Soviet Russia was market reform. Emerging from the 1993 crisis, Yeltsin and his team remained committed to the rapid privatisation of state-owned assets. This policy was underpinned by the 'Washington consensus' and the idea that the only way to organise economics at the 'end of history' was through 'extensive market de-regulation, privatisation and liberalisation'.[26] This approach to economics was strongly advocated by international financial institutions such as the World Bank and the International Monetary Fund.

To carry out this policy, Yeltsin did not negotiate new legal frameworks for this market economy. Instead, he relied on his decree power and executive branch institutions run by close personal associates. For instance, a key player in Russian economic reform was the Committee for the Management of State Property, initially led by Yeltsin's close personal adviser, Anatoly Chubais. This executive branch Committee had been created as part of the 1991 Russian Law on Privatization of State and Municipal Enterprises.[27] It became central in implementing President Yeltsin's radical market reform plans.

Perhaps the most problematic example of this reform process was the 1995 transfer of some of Russia's largest state-owned energy companies to powerful businessmen in a program that would come to be known as 'loans for shares'.[28] This plan had initially been proposed by the new class of ruthless oligarchs seeking to secure more wealth and power. It was also in the interests of the presidential administration, which desperately needed money and media support to win the 1996 presidential election (see next section). As a result, a group of powerful oligarchs negotiated a series of insider deals to loan the government money in return for shares in the largest state-owned companies.

The process was structured in this way to circumvent law. The Russian legislature had recently passed a law prohibiting the sale of state-owned blocks of shares in companies producing strategically important

---

[26] K Cowling and PR Tomlinson, 'Post the "Washington Consensus": Economic Governance and Industrial Strategies for the Twenty-First Century' (2011) 35 *Cambridge Journal of Economics* 831, 831.

[27] See GG Angelov, 'Legal Framework of Privatization in Russia' (1993) 2 *Minnesota Journal of International Law* 207, 211–212.

[28] D Hoffman, *The Oligarchs: Wealth and Power in the New Russia* (New York, Public Affairs, 2011) 309–13.

products.²⁹ This ban included companies engaged in oil extraction, refining and marketing. To avoid this law, Yeltsin issued a 40-page presidential decree that set up an auction process to regulate this loans for shares transfer.³⁰ Everyone involved knew these loans would never be paid back; these auctions were the *de facto* sale of some of Russia's largest hydrocarbon assets. This process was justified as necessary for 'provid[ing] sources for covering the federal budget deficit and the efficient use of blocks of shares owned by the federal government'.³¹

This decree contained a number of different sections that purported to regulate the auction process. These sections included both a set of 'rules' for the auction as well as four appendices. The rules stated that the buyer that offered the highest loan to the government would win a block of shares. Despite this detail, however, the rules did not set up an independent oversight committee to run the auctions. Instead, the decree delegated vast authority to the 'State Committee for Property Management' to manage the process.³² When it became clear to Chubais – now Deputy Prime Minister for Economic Policy – how corrupt the process was, he commented that he would 'support this process at any cost'.³³

It came at a very high cost to the Russian state. Without strong legal regulation, insiders rigged the outcomes in favour of one bank.³⁴ This 'insider' process meant that state assets were given away for a small fraction of their worth. In one auction, a Western oil analyst calculated that the successful bidder had paid the equivalent of two cents a barrel for the hydrocarbon reserves, when the going rate internationally was $4 or $5 a barrel.³⁵ This kind of insider privatisation was typical of Yeltsin's decree-based privatisation process. It fuelled skyrocketing inequality and triggered an almost 50 per cent drop in GDP between 1992 and 1995.³⁶ Finally, it reflected a personalistic, crony style of economic policy that failed to recognise the critical importance of robust legal protections in allowing market reform to contribute to broader economic growth.³⁷

---

[29] Federal Law of March 31, 1995 N 39-FZ 'On the Federal Budget for 1995' (*Garant*) https://base.garant.ru/10104182/.
[30] Presidential Decree No 889 of 31 August 1995, 'On the procedure for transferring federally owned shares as collateral in 1995' (Garant) https://base.garant.ru/10104673/.
[31] ibid Article 1.
[32] ibid Rules section. Article 1.
[33] Quoted from Hoffman (n 28) 310.
[34] ibid 309–11.
[35] M Bivens and J Bernstein, 'The Russia You Never Met' (1998) 6 *Demokratizatsiya* 613, 628.
[36] Y M Brudny, 'In Pursuit of the Russian Presidency: Why and How Yeltsin Won the 1996 Presidential Election' (1997) 30 *Communist and Post-Communist Studies* 255, 256–57.
[37] K Pistor, *The Code of Capital: How the Law Creates Wealth and Inequality* (Princeton, Princeton University Press, 2019).

III. EFFECTIVENESS

Taken together, these two examples show how President Boris Yeltsin aggressively pushed the broad powers of the Russian President to pursue a personalistic form of governance that operated without the participation of other institutions. This decree-based form of governance was repeatedly justified as necessary to decisively solve threats to Russia's territorial integrity and reform the Russian economy. In reality, it did the opposite, further undermining the unity of the Russian system and fostering a highly corrupt and inefficient economic system with spiralling economic inequality.

These problems therefore contributed to a dysfunctional state that failed to secure many of the key promises of centralisation. Lacking resources and an effective set of public institutions, the Russian state was unable to actually implement many of its directives or decrees. To attempt to overcome these problems of implementation, President Yeltsin made frequent use of 'assignments' that included instructions that, in some cases, were issued to the courts or even state-owned companies.[38] Many of these too were left unimplemented. A leading researcher on Russian presidential power writes that there are clear 'limits' on presidential decree power because they 'depend[] on the cooperation of other players in the political arena'.[39] Yeltsin's personalistic style undermined this cooperation.

Meanwhile, the Russian state itself grew increasingly and perilously weak. The state was not only unable to regain control of Chechnya or effectively build a market economy. It also was unable to carry out even the basic function of collecting taxes. In 1994, for instance, less than 6 per cent of Russians actually filed income tax returns.[40] This failure to collect tax perilously weakened the financial position of the Russian state. It also reflected the reality that many people were not being paid. Wage arrears grew from 614 million dollars on 1 January 1994 to 5.3 billion dollars on 3 June 1996.[41] With spiralling inflation, the Russian economy increasingly relied on barter in the 1990s. Meanwhile, crime

---

[38] F Burkhardt, 'Institutionalising Authoritarian Presidencies: Polymorphous Power and Russia's Presidential Administration' (2021) 73 *Europe-Asia Studies* 472, 493–94.

[39] TF Remington, *Presidential Decrees in Russia: A Comparative Perspective* (New York, Cambridge University Press, 2014) 4.

[40] J Alm and J Martinez-Vazquez, 'Russian Tax Morale in the 1990s' (2005) 98 *Proceedings of the Annual Conference on Taxation and Minutes of the Annual Meeting of the National Tax Association* 287, 287.

[41] Brudny (n 36) 256.

grew by an amazing 21.5 per cent since 1992; the murder rate alone grew by 27.4 per cent, while drug-related crimes increased by 62.7 per cent during the same period.[42] Stephen Holmes describes how this kind of state dysfunction allows a 'pathological' private sector to operate with impunity and outside of legal regulation.[43]

IV. POPULAR ACCOUNTABILITY

Yeltsin's personalist style of governance was deeply unpopular. One year before the 1996 presidential elections, Yeltsin's approval rating was in the single digits. Moreover, the parties that supported the Yeltsin administration had performed poorly in the 1995 parliamentary elections. Pro-Yeltsin parties such as Our Home Russia and the Bloc of Ivan Rybkin, received only 11.2 per cent of the vote. By contrast, the legislative opposition and, notably, the Communist Party of the Russian Federation – a party that had reformed at the Russian level after the collapse of the Soviet Union – was in a far stronger position. In fact, its growing alliance with the nationalist movement meant that the Communist Party of the Russian Federation, the Agrarian Party, and Working Russia received 31.2 per cent of the vote in the 1995 election.[44]

Yeltsin appeared to have little chance of re-election in 1996. In response, his team considered a number of options. Some advisers like Yegor Gaidar floated the idea of finding another candidate to run for re-election. Others – reflecting the strong strain of liberal authoritarianism in Yeltsin's team – advised Yeltsin to cancel the elections altogether.[45] Neither was a realistic option: Russia's crown-presidential system relied on popular legitimacy and winning elections. Yeltsin ultimately had little choice but to go forward with the elections.

In response, Yeltsin and his team deployed the powers of the President to win the election. For instance, Yeltsin expanded his practice of signing bilateral treaties with regional leadership to ensure that these would become a tool in his re-election.[46] Regional leaders knew that these treaties were far more likely to be honoured if Yeltsin was re-elected in 1996.

---

[42] ibid 257.
[43] S Holmes, 'What Russia Teaches Us Now' (*The American Prospect: Ideas, Politics, and Power*, 19 December 2001) www.prospect.org/world/russia-teaches-us-now/.
[44] Brudny (n 36) 256.
[45] ibid 255.
[46] Kahn (n 19) 162.

For that reason, they had strong incentives to use their own regional administrative resources in Yeltsin's favour.

Moreover, Yeltsin's 'loans for shares' scheme (described above) was a critical tool in the re-election. This vast privatisation scheme gave a group of wealthy businessmen strong incentives to ensure that Yeltsin won the 1996 election.[47] One writer described how this program 'was the weld between the tycoons and the Kremlin, the embrace of wealth and power'.[48] These oligarchs used their control over television and print media to attack Yeltsin's opponent: Gennady Zyuganov of the Russian Communist Party. Arguing that the Communists would bring Russia back to the Soviet period, oligarch-owned television showed the 'the horrors of the communist era … in the weeks leading up to the election'.[49]

This strategy was also combined with a new campaign that focused on reaching the voters who had personally supported Yeltsin in the April 1993 referendum. As a result, Yeltsin's team sent him to campaign in

> regions where he received a vote of confidence in the 25 April 1993 Referendum (i.e. 50 per cent or more support on the question No. 1) but where support for the liberal and centrist parties fell below 50 per cent in the December 1995 parliamentary election.[50]

This focus on 1993 also triggered a change in messaging which framed the election as involving the question of whether Russians wanted to 'return to the political and economic system of the Communist era'.[51] Finally, Yeltsin relied on the symbolic power of his decree power to secure support. In the months before the election, he issued 39 decrees that promised to pay overdue wages and pensions, to increase subsidies to the military-industrial complex, and to restore the money lost in the hyperinflation of 1992.[52] The combined used of this authority helped to ensure that Yeltsin won the election.

Yeltsin had therefore successfully deployed the vast powers of the presidency to manufacture a victory in the 1996 election. This win, however, did not suggest a more effective system of public accountability. Instead, the Russian state remained unable to respond to the demands of its citizens in the wake of the 1996 election. Moreover, it did not suggest

---

[47] D Hoffman, *The Oligarchs: Wealth and Power in the New Russia* (New York, Public Affairs, 2011).
[48] Ibid 309.
[49] Brudny (n 36) 260.
[50] ibid 262.
[51] ibid 260.
[52] ibid 262–63.

robust popular support. Yeltsin's popularity quickly waned and private interests continued to dominate politics.

V. DOMESTIC LEGAL ACCOUNTABILITY

Russia's dysfunctional system of personalised presidential power faced significant legal scrutiny during this period in the Russian Constitutional Court. Both the upper and lower houses of the legislature frequently challenged the President's broad assertions of presidential power in Court. In addition, Russian citizens also filed thousands of personal claims in the Court for violations of their constitutional rights.

The Court considering these claims had been expanded in the 1993 Constitution. After a period of new appointments by President Yeltsin, it finally returned to work on 6 February 1995. This reconstituted Court restarted in a precarious position. President Yeltsin and many in his team viewed it with suspicion because of its actions in the October crisis of 1993. In response, Vladimir Tumanov, a new Yeltsin appointee and the Chairman of the Court, adopted a cautious approach that sought to avoid high-stakes confrontations with the President.[53] This caution led to deference to the arguments of powerful Russian state actors. This deference was justified in the language of the centralised state tradition.

One of the first cases the Court considered was a legislative challenge to Yeltsin's use of the presidential decree power to wage war in Chechnya.[54] Drawing on the arguments of the balanced state tradition, the upper and lower house of the Russian legislature argued that the series of presidential decrees ordering military operations in Chechnya were unconstitutional. First, they argued that this military action could not be carried out through a decree; it required the declaration of a formal state of emergency approved by the Federation Council.[55] Second, they argued that these presidential decrees directly contradicted existing legislation.[56] Allowing the President to proceed in the face of law, they argued, was a violation of the separation of powers guaranteed in Article 10 of the Constitution. Third, they argued that the decrees violated key human rights guarantees in Chapter 2 of the Constitution.

---

[53] A Trochev, *Judging Russia: The Role of the Constitutional Court in Russian Politics, 1990–2006* (Leiden, Cambridge University Press, 2008) 119.
[54] Decision of the Russian Constitutional Court (n 12).
[55] Russian Constitution (n 8) Art 102(c).
[56] WE Pomeranz, 'Judicial Review and the Russian Constitutional Court: The Chechen Case' (1997) 23 *Review of Central and East European Law* 9, 17.

This rights challenge was supported by many of the human rights advocates who had supported Yeltsin in 1993. In fact, the leading human rights organisation that had been founded by Sakharov himself, Memorial, had carefully documented how 'civilians in the Chechen Republic suffered from indiscriminate fire by federal troops and indiscriminate bombing throughout the armed conflict'.[57] Sergei Kovalev, a former adviser to Sakharov and supporter of Yeltsin in 1993, testified in front of the Court. He described the decrees as 'pure hypocrisy' and accused Yeltsin of 'using a guillotine to cure one's dandruff'.[58]

In response, President Yeltsin's legal team – led by key constitutional drafter Sergei Shakhrai – justified the decrees on the basis of the broad textual powers of the Russian President in Chapter 4 of the Constitution and the arguments of the centralised state tradition.[59] Shakhrai argued that the Constitution granted the President broad, free-standing authority as protector of the territorial integrity of the Russian state and Commander in Chief of the Russian armed forces to act in this situation. Furthermore, he argued that the laws that the decrees contradicted were Soviet-era laws and no longer relevant in post-Soviet Russia. Since there was no new federal law on a state of emergency, he argued, the President was not acting in contravention of law.

In the end, 11 (out of the 19) Justices on the Court upheld President Yeltsin's actions in Chechnya as constitutional.[60] This majority decision Court chose to sidestep the human rights issues. In particular, it decided that it was only able to 'resolve questions of laws, not the ensuing application of these laws, and, therefore, human rights violations did not fall within its jurisdiction'.[61]

In justifying Yeltsin's broad exercise of presidential decree power, the majority of the Court drew heavily on the arguments of the centralised state discourse. In a key early section, the Court described the 'extraordinary situation' in the Chechen Republic as 'threaten[ing] to develop into a civil war' and therefore endangering Russian territorial integrity.[62] The Court argued that the integrity of the Russian state was a foundational

---

[57] Memorial Human Rights Centre, 'A Chain of Wars, A Chain of Crimes, A Chain of Impunity: Russian Wars in Chechnya, Syria, and Ukraine' (*Novaya Gazeta Europe*, Report, 25 February 2023) www.novayagazeta.eu/articles/2023/02/24/a-chain-of-wars-a-chain-of-crimes-a-chain-of-impunity-en.
[58] Quoted from Pomeranz (n 56) 23–24.
[59] ibid 23–24.
[60] Decision of the Constitutional Court of the Russian Federation (n 12).
[61] ibid.
[62] ibid.

constitutional value that protected the rights and freedoms of citizens in Chechnya. The Court also cited the importance of territorial integrity to the United Nations Charter which did not allow the right to self-determination to lead to the 'dismemberment' of sovereign states.[63]

The Court then turned to the President's vast authority as guarantor of Russian territorial integrity. This power, it argued, could be found in the constitutional provisions directing the President to safeguard 'the sovereignty' and 'integrity' of Russia.[64] It also cited the President's position as the Commander-in-Chief of the Russian Armed Forces, and broad power to issue decrees[65] which must be implemented by the government.[66] Taken together, these provisions afforded the President direct constitutional authority to immediately and unilaterally act in the event of a threat to the integrity of the Russian state. In effect, the Court recognised the President as a kind of sovereign dictator who can act to counter threats to the state. This position, the Court further explained, was not just about ensuring state stability, it was also 'an important condition for the equal legal status of all citizens, regardless of their place of residence, and one of the guarantees of their constitutional rights and freedoms'.[67]

The Court also argued that the decree did not contradict any laws. It did not violate the Soviet-era law 'On a State of Emergency' because this law was not suited to the unique nature of the conflict. The Court explained further that other existing Russian laws for defence and security contained 'gaps, inconsistencies, and outdated provisions'.[68] In these areas of contradiction, the Court argued, the 'direct application' of the constitutional norms giving the President authority to protect state integrity were particularly 'important'.[69] This interpretation effectively gave the President significant implied legislative power to operate by decree when law did not clearly regulate the matter.

The dissenters relied heavily on the justifications of the balanced state tradition. Justice Vitruk, for instance, argued that Yeltsin's assertion of presidential power violated the separation of powers in Article 10.[70]

---

[63] ibid.
[64] Russian Constitution (n 8) Art 80.2 and Art 82.
[65] ibid Art 90.
[66] ibid Art 114(g).
[67] Decision of the Constitutional Court of the Russian Federation (n 12).
[68] ibid.
[69] ibid.
[70] Dissenting Opinion of Justice Vitruk in Russian Constitutional Court Decision No 10-P of 31 July 1995 (in Russian) (*Konsultant Plus*) www.consultant.ru/document/cons_doc_LAW_7552/2ca2c3f2000a8e3a39fdc6945f0bb1591d64571f/.

He argued that the majority judgment 'means an unlawful expansion of the powers of the President as head of state at the expense of the powers of the federal parliament and the federal government'.[71] He also criticised the inconsistencies and inefficiencies of Yeltsin's decree-based approach.[72] Justice Morshchakova argued that key parts of the 9 December decree unconstitutionally violated individual rights.[73] Justice Kononov argued that the presidential decrees did not adequately balance the need for territorial integrity with the more fundamental protection of individual rights and liberty.[74] The Court, he argued, incorrectly subordinated the interests of the individual to those of the state, including 'sovereignty, territorial integrity, constitutional order, state security and other state interests.'[75] Finally, former Court Chairman, Valery Zorkin, also dissented, questioning why the President did not just work with the legislature and introduce martial law.[76] The decision to bypass the legislative process altogether, he argued, 'is the path not to the rule of law, but to arbitrariness and tyranny'.[77]

The Court faced another important challenge to a broad assertion of presidential power in 1998.[78] This case involved the meaning of Article 111.4 of the Constitution which gives the President the power to dissolve the lower house and call new elections if the lower house rejects the presidential candidate three times. A group of deputies from the lower house of the legislature (the State Duma) argued that the President of the Russian Federation should not be able to submit the same candidate for the Chairman of the Government of the Russian Federation three times before having the right to dissolve the Duma. 'Submitted candidates' in in Part 4 of Article 111 of the Constitution of the Russian Federation, they argued, must mean different persons.

[71] ibid.
[72] ibid.
[73] Dissenting Opinion of Justice Morshchakova in Russian Constitutional Court Decision No 10-P of 31 July 1995 (in Russian) (*Konsultant Plus*) www.consultant.ru/document/cons_doc_LAW_7552/73c3cd9f9c782941a15398949dc193e41b9678c0/.
[74] Dissenting Opinion of Justice Kononov in Russian Constitutional Court Decision No 10-P of 31 July 1995 (in Russian) (*Konsultant Plus*) www.consultant.ru/document/cons_doc_LAW_7552/65174409027f1b0f80dcca6370e77fdb707928cc/.
[75] ibid.
[76] Dissenting Opinion of Justice Zorkin in Russian Constitutional Court Decision No 10-P of 31 July 1995 (in Russian) (*Konsultant Plus*) www.consultant.ru/document/cons_doc_LAW_7552/f43c90f3261665e6ee1e816ae1f6955f98e2351b/.
[77] ibid.
[78] Decision of the Russian Constitutional Court No 28-P of 11 December 1998, 'In the Case of the Interpretation of the Provisions of Part 4 of Article 111 of the Constitution of the Russian Federation' (in Russian) (*Konsultant Plus*) www.consultant.ru/document/cons_doc_LAW_21423/.

The majority of the Court drew on the arguments of the centralised state tradition in deciding that the President has the authority to propose the same candidate three times. It based this decision on the Constitution's unified form of popular sovereignty, arguing that the only source from which the different branches of government draw their power 'is the multinational people of the Russian Federation'.[79] It described how the preamble requires 'civil peace and harmony' and this requires the President – who embodies the unified sovereignty of the people – to be able to ensure the 'coordinated functioning and interaction of government bodies'.[80] Without this power, the Court concluded, the ability of the President to maintain the 'stability' of the constitutional system 'governed by the rule of law' would be endangered.

Justice Vitruk again dissented, arguing that the ability to appoint the same person three times in a row clearly violates the separation of powers in Article 10.[81] In so doing, he drew on the reasoning of the balanced state tradition and argued that the State Duma can only 'act[] as a means of check, a certain counterbalance' in the event that the President is required to propose different candidates each time.[82] In another dissenting opinion, Justice Luchin questioned the extent to which there is a 'mechanism' of 'checks and balances' present at all if the President is able to appoint the same candidate three times in a row.[83] He then concluded that 'Only the presentation of different candidates for the Chairman of the Government of the Russian Federation can serve as a justification for such a constitutional sanction as the dissolution of the State Duma'.

The continuing influence of the centralised state tradition for the majority of the Court also shaped how it understood rights more broadly. A 1997 case considered the constitutionality of a legislative provision requiring a company to first pay wages to individuals before making tax payments to the state.[84] Rather than deferring to the legislator

---

[79] ibid.
[80] ibid.
[81] Dissenting Opinion of Justice Vitruk in Decision of the Russian Constitutional Court No 28-P of 11 December 1998 (in Russian) (*Konsultant Plus*) www.consultant.ru/document/cons_doc_LAW_21423/91744d32101fc2f2b5969a16fe57e597295697cb/.
[82] ibid.
[83] Dissenting Opinion of Justice Luchin in Decision of the Russian Constitutional Court No 28-P of 11 December 1998 (in Russian) (*Konsultant Plus*) www.consultant.ru/document/cons_doc_LAW_21423/be0f284f54e9033849d86b5e4c0d42a413df1c96/.
[84] Decision of the Russian Constitutional Court No 21-P of 23 December 1997, 'In the Case of Verifying the Constitutionality of Paragraph 2 of Article 855 of the Civil Code of the Russian Federation and Part Six of Article 15 of the Law of the Russian Federation

(as the Court often did in cases of ambiguity), the Court struck down the legislative requirement. The Court argued that taxes should take priority because they are an important source of 'revenue through which the observance and protection of the rights and freedoms of citizens, as well as the implementation of the social function of the state must be ensured'.[85]

The Court's deference to the centralised state did not mean, however, that the Court always rejected individual rights claims. When it considered cases that did not involve significant presidential or central interests, the Court often sought to protect individual Russians facing the bureaucratic lawlessness of the Yeltsin system. To do this, the Court expanded its own power not just to review federal laws but also regional laws that violated individual rights.[86] Much of this jurisprudence focused on creating a more predictable and stable market system by protecting the property rights of Russian individuals and corporations. This kind of 'constitutional economics'[87] often sought to protect individuals from vague laws that allowed discrimination.[88] This jurisprudence could also be seen as enabling the centre, by ironing out the inequities and dysfunctionality of the centralised state system. The second Chairman of the Court, Marat Baglai, explained on Russian TV that the Court could not simply 'throw citizens in the waves of the raging sea of liberalism'.[89]

Finally, the Court was also willing to enter into contested areas to protect individual rights. In 1999, it considered whether the death penalty could be applied to an individual that was not convicted in a jury trial.[90]

"On the Fundamentals of the Tax System in the Russian Federation" in Connection with the Request of the Presidium of the Supreme Court Russian Federation' (in Russian) (*Konsultant Plus*) www.consultant.ru/document/cons_doc_LAW_17252/92d969e26a4326c5d02fa79b8f9cf4994ee5633b/.

[85] ibid.

[86] Trochev (n 53) 159.

[87] See, eg P Barenboim et al, *Constitutional Economics* (in Russian) (Moscow, YustitsInform, 2006).

[88] Trochev (n 53) 177.

[89] ibid 158.

[90] Decision of the Russian Constitutional Court No 3-P of 2 February 1999, 'In the Case of Verifying the Constitutionality of the Provisions of Article 41 and Part Three of Article 42 of the Code of Criminal Procedure of the RSFSR, Paragraphs 1 and 2 of the Resolution of the Supreme Council of the Russian Federation of July 16, 1993 "On the Procedure for Enacting the Law Russian Federation "On Amendments and Additions to the Law of the RSFSR "On the Judicial System of the RSFSR", the Criminal Procedure Code of the RSFSR, the Criminal Code of the RSFSR and the Code of the RSFSR on Administrative Offenses" in Connection with the Request of the Moscow City Court and Complaints from a Number of Citizens' (*Konsultant Plus*) www.consultant.ru/document/cons_doc_LAW_21949/.

The claimant argued that a non-jury trial that resulted in a death penalty verdict would violate his right to life under Article 20 of the Russian Constitution. The Constitutional Court accepted this argument but stopped short of abolishing the death penalty. Instead, it suspended the death penalty until jury trials had been introduced in all constituent entities of the Federation.

Taken together, therefore, the centralising structural provisions of the 1993 Constitution helped to bolster the influence of the arguments of the centralised state tradition in the jurisprudence of the post-1993 Constitutional Court. This commitment did not, however, stop a consistent minority who were committed to the balanced state tradition. It also did not stop the Court from expanding its own jurisdiction to protect individual Russians rights from the many inequities of the often dysfunctional and arbitrary Russian state. Political scientists have referred to this jurisprudence as a 'pragmatic' response by a Court seeking to avoid a confrontation with the President but also seeking to secure its power in the Russian constitutional system.[91] This jurisprudence is also consistent with the centralised state tradition and the idea that the Court should defer in cases involving centralised or presidential power.

VI. INTERNATIONAL LEGAL ACCOUNTABILITY

International rights organisations also failed to emerge as a powerful check on the growing personalisation of Russian presidentialism and its excesses. This was not because they accepted the arguments of the centralised state tradition or believed that Yeltsin would be able to personally guarantee Russian democratic reform. Instead, the international community hoped that engaging with Russia and bringing it into key international right tribunals and institutions would transform Russia's poor human rights record over time.

A good example of this kind of wishful thinking is Russia's relationship with the Council of Europe. In the 1990s, Russia made a formal request to join the Council of Europe. The Council requires any new member to show a strong commitment to 'pluralist democracy'.[92] This

---

[91] A Trochev and PH Solomon Jr, 'Authoritarian Constitutionalism in Putin's Russia: A Pragmatic Constitutional Court in a Dual State' (2018) 51 *Communist and Post-Communist Studies* 201, 202–04.
[92] Council of Europe, Committee of Ministers, 'Declaration on the Future Role of the Council of Europe in European Construction' (CM(89)PV1, 5 May 1989) https://rm.coe.int/1680535ad9.

condition is aimed at encouraging any prospective members to reform themselves before they join the Council.

A lawyers' report that considered the conformity of Russia with the Council's standard of pluralist democracy concluded that although Russia 'has embarked upon the road towards democracy' it has 'not yet fully reached the goal of that journey and the obstacles which lay ahead are great and manifold'.[93] As to the rule of law, it concluded that 'the rule of law is not established in the Russian Federation'.[94] It concluded that that 'the Russian Federation does not yet fulfil the conditions of membership as laid down in Article 3 and 4 of the Statute of the Council of Europe'.[95]

Two additional Committees also considered Russia's eligibility for membership. The Committee on Legal Affairs and Human Rights echoed the lawyers report, concluding that Russia did not yet meet the standards required for membership.[96] The Committee on Political Affairs and Democracy, by contrast, was far more willing to look past Russia's problems and argued for accession. Although the report admitted problems with Russian democracy, it concluded that 'integration is better than isolation; cooperation is better than confrontation'.[97] It ultimately saw Russian membership in the Council as encouraging pluralist democracy.[98]

This position of the Committee on Political Affairs and Democracy ultimately prevailed and Russia was accepted into the Council of Europe in 1996. As Jeffrey Kahn has noted, it was the decision of the Parliamentary Assembly that 'Russia should be invited to become a member of the Council because it did *not* meet the requirements of membership'.[99] This failure to apply its conditions in the *hope* that membership would improve the protection of rights inside Russia over time was an early example of the unwillingness of the international

---

[93] Council of Europe, 'Report on the Conformity of the Legal Order of the Russian Federation with Council of Europe Standards' (AS/Bur/Russia (1994) 7, 28 September 1994).

[94] ibid.

[95] ibid § VI, ¶ 13.

[96] Council of Europe, Committee on Legal Affairs and Human Rights, 'Report of the Committee on Legal Affairs and Human Rights on the Human Rights Situation in Chechnya' (AS/Jur (1995) 22, 29 June 1995) 7, ¶ 30.

[97] ibid § 6, ¶ 103(xii).

[98] Council of Europe, Committee on Political Affairs and Democracy, 'Report of the Political Affairs Committee (PACE) on Russia's Request for Membership of the Council of Europe' (Report 7443 (1996), 2 January 1996).

[99] J Kahn, 'The Origins of Russian Membership in the Council of Europe and the Seeds of Russia's Expulsion' (2024) 14(1) *Notre Dame Journal of International and Comparative Law* (advance) https://scholarship.law.nd.edu/ndjicl/vol14/iss1/4/.

community to aggressively seek to hold the Russian state to account for its abuses. More broadly, it reflected the disregard of international rights institutions for the problems of state centralisation and their inevitable consequences on rights protection.

VII. CONCLUSION

This chapter revises our understanding of the 1990s. During the 1990s, President Boris Yeltsin drew on the broad guardian powers of the President in the 1993 Russian Constitution to unilaterally tackle the most pressing political and economic challenges of the time. This approach was justified as necessary for a decisive set of reforms. Although it generated pluralism and destroyed the old Soviet economic system, it did not effectively reform Russian economics or build a 'partial' democracy.[100] Instead, it created a system of 'pluralism by default' characterised by corruption, weak popular accountability and rights abuse.

The failure of Yeltsin's reform agenda shows the problems of decree-based, personalised governance in fostering real economic and political reform. Among other things, it ignored the central role of comprehensive legal regulation and institutional development in promoting economic and political reform. Real reform, it turned out, could not be not a one-man job. The next chapter will show how Yeltsin's hand-picked successor for President, Vladimir Putin, would tackle the problems facing Russia. It will show how President Putin drew on not just the guardian powers of the presidency but also its management power in rebuilding Russian authoritarianism.

---

[100] M McFaul, *Russia's Unfinished Revolution: Political Change from Gorbachev to Putin* (Ithaca, Cornell University Press, 2001) 338–72 (discussing Russia's incomplete transition to partial democracy).

5

The Managerial President (2000–08)

IN AUGUST 2000, as the largest submarine disaster in Russian history was unfolding, newly elected President Vladimir Putin was on holiday. As the situation worsened, Putin was heavily criticised in the media for ignoring the unfolding crisis.[1] Meanwhile, at a meeting with government officials, a mother of one of the men in the submarine began screaming at member of the Russian government and was forcibly sedated and removed from the room.[2] Putin would later come to the site of the disaster and address the grieving mothers. His remarks were criticised by the media for failing to show empathy with the scale of the tragedy. Six months after Putin's election, it was a major crisis for the new President.[3]

The Kursk tragedy is an important reminder of the uncertain early months of Putin's presidency. At the time, Putin was largely unknown to the Russian people, possessing little charismatic appeal and no ability to shape media coverage.[4] He also inherited the dysfunctional Russian state of the 1990s, struggling to exercise effective authority over his top officials. For instance, one commentator suggested that Putin had been deliberately misled by top military officials, who claimed that the submarine was being lifted from the sea floor and had collided with a NATO submarine.[5] At the time, the success of Putin's presidency looked in doubt.

---

[1] I Traynor, 'Putin Aims Kursk Fury at Media' *The Guardian* (Moscow, 25 August 2000) www.theguardian.com/world/2000/aug/25/kursk.russia2.

[2] I Traynor, 'Grieving Mother Silenced with a Syringe' *The Guardian* (25 August 2000) www.theguardian.com/world/2000/aug/25/kursk.russia3.

[3] Z Barany, 'The Tragedy of the Kursk: Crisis Management in Putin's Russia' (2004) 39 *Government and Opposition* 476, 490.

[4] K Sonin, 'How the Putin Phenomenon Happened by Accident' *The Moscow Times* (20 March 2024) www.themoscowtimes.com/2024/03/20/how-the-putin-phenomenon-happened-by-accident-a84544 (describing how Putin 'does not possess any qualities that would distinguish him from other Russian politicians, other than the office he holds').

[5] A Monaghan, 'The *Vertikal*: Power and Authority in Russia' (2012) 88 *International Affairs* 1, 9.

Putin's ability to overcome this setback and dominate Russian politics relied heavily on the constitutional provisions centralising power in the President. Putin was a lawyer by training and, in the months prior to the presidential election in 2000, he explicitly signalled his intention to draw on the constitutional authority of the President in a pre-election statement that became known as his 'Millenium Manifesto'.[6] Describing Russia as at a turning point in its history, Putin argued that Russia needed to fully implement its 1993 constitutional order. Russian law, he argued, was currently in a desperate state of disunity, with laws at both the federal and regional level that do not comply with the Constitution. He demanded that Russia's legal officials – judges, prosecutors and the justice ministry – unite under presidential leadership to restore 'the federal centre's capabilities, the country's manageability, and Russia's integrity'.[7]

Putin therefore did not break with Russia's constitutional system to rebuild Russian authoritarianism. On the contrary, he did the opposite: Putin and his administration directly drew on the vast sovereign authority given to the President in the later chapters of the Constitution. In particular, they drew on the President's broad management power to create a set of dependent institutions that would help to secure centralised presidential power. In building this system, Putin and his team justified the consolidation of power on the effectiveness of technocratic and centralised authoritarian modernisation.

This managerial project of presidential dominance therefore broke with Yeltsin's understanding of authoritarian modernisation. The sovereign President was no longer a free market bulldozer at the 'end of history'. Instead, the President was the central institution in restoring what Putin described as Russia's historical need for a strong state. He argued explicitly in the Manifesto that Russia should no longer engage in the 'mechanical copying' of other countries but instead face 'Russian realities'.[8] A 'strong state' reflected Russia's unique historical identity, serving as a 'source and guarantor of order, and the initiator and main driving force of any change'.[9] By a strong state, Putin meant a state organised around a powerful President who could manage Russian politics.

---

[6] V Putin, 'Russia on the Brink of a New Millenium' (in Russian) (*Nezavisimaya Gazeta*, 30 December 1999) www.ng.ru/politics/1999-12-30/4_millenium.html.
[7] ibid.
[8] ibid.
[9] ibid.

To create this managerial President, Putin and his team focused on institution-building, streamlining the Presidential Administration and creating a ruling party (United Russia) to win elections. They also reorganised the executive branch and appointed technocrats to a government that would solve problems through planning. Finally, they passed new laws and encouraged judges to enforce legal unity. This new legal-bureaucratic, management style enhanced the power of the President but created a new principal-agent problem: how to ensure that lower-level officials were actually implementing centrally formulated policy.[10] Meanwhile, accountability remained weak as elections, courts and international law remained unable to check the centralisation of power and its inevitable curbing of individual rights.

I. PRESIDENTIAL INSTITUTION-BUILDING

The managerial presidency drew heavily on the unilateral institution-building authority of the Russian President. For instance, Article 83(i) of the Russian Constitution gives the office of the President exclusive power to 'form' a Presidential Administration (PA). The PA had been first set up by a Yeltsin decree in the early 1990s and was frequently reformed during the 1990s.[11] Yeltsin never successfully built an effective legal-bureaucratic system through the PA.

Under Putin, by contrast, the PA became the nerve-centre of the managerial activities of the President. Drawing on his experience in Yeltsin's PA, Putin used his unilateral presidential authority over the PA to streamline its organisation.[12] A critical change was the creation of a new department called the Directorate of Domestic Politics (DDP).[13] The DDP unified the departments previously covering domestic policy, political planning, and public relations and culture.[14] The DDP was put

---

[10] V Gel'man, *The Politics of Bad Governance in Contemporary Russia* (Ann Arbor, University of Michigan Press, 2022) 73–75.

[11] F Burkhardt, 'Institutionalising Authoritarian Presidencies: Polymorphous Power and Russia's Presidential Administration' (2021) 73 *Europe-Asia Studies* 472, 487–88.

[12] Presidential Decree No 1013 of 6 March 2000, 'On the Formation of the Administration of the President of the Russian Federation' (in Russian) (*Konsultant*) www.consultant.ru/document/cons_doc_LAW_27408/.

[13] ibid.

[14] C Pallin, 'Russia's Presidential Domestic Policy Directorate: HQ for Defeat-Proofing Russian Politics' (2017) 25 *Demokratizatsiya: The Journal of Post-Soviet Democratization* 255.

in charge of the entire political system, including 'elites, society, parties, regions, and civil society'.[15] It also coordinated the President's relationship with the legislature, business groups, NGOs and Russia's regional leadership (through control of the President's personal representatives). The DDP was also involved in a vast information gathering project to understand public concerns and opposition, including the study of petitions made by ordinary Russians and extensive polling. This sociological study of the population was described as helping to construct more effective policy outcomes. The leader of one of the leading state survey groups described this work as constantly studying 'content on social networks and in the blogosphere' in order to understand and solve Russia's problems.[16]

In addition to this organisational change, President Putin used his broad appointment authority to more than double the number of staff with security service backgrounds (*siloviki*) in the PA.[17] This new group of appointees shared Putin's belief in the benefits of centralised authority. Their training led them to see a unified, top-down command structure as the only way to effectively protect state security. Taken together, these changes transformed the PA into a powerful tool of presidential authority and ultimately 'made the president more powerful'.[18]

Putin also relied on his broad authority in Article 112 to reorganise the existing system of federal executive bodies to increase presidential control early in his first term. For instance, in 2000, Putin issued a decree that streamlined the organisation of federal executive institutions.[19] One of the most important changes placed the Federal Security Service under the direct control of the President.[20]

He also relied on his broad presidential appointment powers to control the key Ministers who oversaw Russia's vast bureaucracy. This started with control over the Prime Minister. Although the President formally must receive approval for his Prime Minister appointment from

---

[15] ibid 262.
[16] A Pertsev and M Solopov, 'What Putin Reads: Vital Policymaking in Russia Relies on Sociological Research Conducted by the Secret Service. Here's How it Works' (*Meduza*, 17 July 2020) www.meduza.io/en/feature/2020/07/17/what-putin-reads.
[17] ibid 483 (from 21 per cent in the 1990s to a mean of 52 per cent in the 2000s).
[18] Burkhardt (n 10) 499.
[19] Presidential Decree No 867 of May 17 2000, 'On the Structure of Federal Executive Bodies' (in Russian) (*Konsultant Plus*) www.consultant.ru/document/cons_doc_LAW_272 33/2011a123b16a58aa919bb52261df7e3ee94ca6e3/.
[20] E Schneider, 'The Russian Federal Security Service under President Putin' in S White (ed), *Politics and the Ruling Group in Putin's Russia* (New York, Palgrave Macmillan, 2008).

the lower house, the President can ultimately dismiss this legislative body for failing to approve his appointment three times[21] and has the power to chair governmental meetings.[22] Putin relied on this appointment power to appoint loyal, technocratic ministers to key ministries. A good example was Alexei Kudrin, a highly regarded economist who is a close associate of Vladimir Putin and who was appointed Finance Minister in May 2000. Technocratic appointments like Kudrin were described as a key component of the presidentially led Russian state's ability to 'manage' Russia's stable development. The government was no longer a small team of reformers focused on implementing radical market change. Instead, it was oriented toward stabilising Russia's market economy by managing its key companies.

Putin himself was a devoted acolyte of centralised technocratic management. Putin's dissertation at St Petersburg's Mining Institute focused heavily on the techniques of management and strategic planning. In that dissertation, Putin wrote that long-range planning was necessary and beneficial even under 'under conditions of change, especially rapid change caused by circumstances beyond one's own control'.[23]

Putin and his team described this management planning style as a superior form of governance, one that responds to the demands of the public but without the damaging, partisan struggle for power that characterises pluralistic democracies. This system, they argued, does not need a mobilised electorate; on the contrary, it is one that studies what is needed and solves problems and 'gets things done'. Underlying this idea is that the bureaucracy creates a 'a value-neutral "science" of public opinion, as practised by a category of professional experts with specific competences who can help leader solve the people's real problems'.[24] Putin himself frequently described this legal-bureaucratic management in anti-political language, as a system rooted in rational planning that develops effective centralised plans for the development of the country. This justification was not just aimed at the general population; in many cases, it was also used to appeal to a Russian elite who saw this as effective and competence governance after the turbulence of the 1990s.

---

[21] Article 111. Constitution of the Russian Federation (*Council of Europe*) https://rm.coe.int/constitution-of-the-russian-federation-en/1680a1a237.
[22] ibid Article 83.
[23] Igor Danchenko and Clifford Gaddy, 'The Mystery of Vladimir Putin's Dissertation' (Brookings Institution, 30 March 2006) www.brookings.edu/wp-content/uploads/2012/09/Putin-Dissertation-Event-remarks-with-slides.pdf.
[24] CJ Bickerton and CI Accetti, *Technopopulism: The New Logic of Democratic Politics* (Oxford, Oxford University Press, 2021) 66–67.

As part of this system, Putin used the guardian authority of the President to issue broad guidelines for policy change that the executive branch must implement. For instance, in a speech on 5 September 2005, Putin introduced the National Priority Projects of Russia. To implement these projects, Putin signed a decree creating a 'Council for Implementing Priority National Projects'.[25] This body was tasked with implementing the broad policy directives outlined by the President and had vast power itself to formulate normative acts to that end.[26]

As a whole, this new state-centred form of managerial governance remained committed to democratic legitimacy. It was justified as creating a kind of 'managed' or 'sovereign' democracy. Managed democracy was described as 'a semi-authoritarian regime tasked with conducting necessary structural reforms'.[27] The practice, one supporter explained, is formally justified by the 'backwardness of democratic institutions', and the need to implement certain 'modernization projects' for the benefit of the people and the state. Another term to describe this form of governance was 'sovereign democracy', which more specifically engaged with the need for one sovereign institution – the President – to direct the way in which Russian 'democracy' developed.[28] In both, however, politics was engineered in a way that advanced the partisan interests of the President and his team. Although they broke with the free market ideology of the 1990s, these concepts continued the Yeltsin-era, centralised state commitment to the necessity of authoritarian methods for ensuring Russian democracy and modernisation.

II. DICTATORSHIP OF THE LAW

Another critical tool in Putin's presidential managerialism was increased presidential attention to lawmaking. Breaking with the personalised governance of the Yeltsin years, Putin now called for a 'dictatorship of

---

[25] Presidential Decree No 1226 of 21 October 2005 (in Russian) (*Garant*, 21 October 2005) https://base.garant.ru/5478944/.
[26] H Oversloot, 'Reordering the State (Without Changing the Constitution): Russia under Putin's Rule, 2000–2008' (2007) 32 *Review of Central and East European Law* 41.
[27] AP Tsygankov, *The Strong State in Russia: Development and Crisis* (New York, Oxford University Press, 2012) 133.
[28] M Lipman, 'Putin's "Sovereign Democracy"' (*Carnegie Endowment for International Peace*, 15 July 2006) https://carnegiemoscow.org/2006/07/15/putin-s-sovereign-democracy-pub-18540.

the law'.[29] To do this, Putin sought to draw heavily on the broad constitutional powers in Article 85 that gave the President the explicit authority to submit bills to Parliament and to determine Russian domestic policy. These powers were not, however, unlimited. The presidential administration did not always get its way in this legislative process. At times, it was sometimes forced to negotiate or compromise on the details of legislation, particularly when powerful executive ministers or interests disagreed on key details.[30]

In calling for this legal 'dictatorship', Putin was not signalling a commitment to a liberal rule of law. Instead, he was drawing on an understanding of law that had its roots in the late Soviet period and which he had learned both at law school and in the KGB. In the early 1980s, the short-lived leadership of Yuri Andropov – the former KGB chief – had attempted to use legality as a way to educate and control society.[31] The term 'dictatorship of the law' had then been explicitly used by Valery Zorkin in the 1990s to criticise Yeltsin's circumvention of the hostile legislature. Worried about the personalisation of power in the hands of President Yeltsin, Zorkin and his colleagues openly called for a 'dictatorship of law' as a necessary element of a strong form of centralised Russian statehood.[32]

In using this terminology in the early months of his presidency, therefore, Putin had two key objectives. First was to secure the cooperation of legal elites and judges for a project of restoring legal unity and recentralising power in Moscow. In his first month as acting President, Putin spent a great deal of his time delivering speeches to key members of the legal elite about the importance of legal uniformity. On 13 January 2000, he spoke at the Law Faculty of St Petersburg State where he had studied under Anatoly Sobchak. Putin explained that

> For people like me who are now engaged in the construction of a new Russian state, we know that this project must be founded on the principles that have for decades been developed within the walls of the Faculty of Law of the University of St. Petersburg.[33]

---

[29] J Kahn, 'Vladimir Putin and the Rule of the Law in Russia' (2008) 36 *Georgia Journal of International Law* 511, 524.

[30] B Noble, 'Authoritarian Amendments: Legislative Institutions as Intraexecutive Constraints in Post-Soviet Russia' (2020) 53 *Comparative Political Studies* 1417.

[31] R Horvath, *The Legacy of Soviet Dissent: Dissidents, Democratisation and Radical Nationalism in Russia* (New York, Routledge Curzon, 2005) 83–85.

[32] A Trochev, *Judging Russia: The Role of the Constitutional Court in Russian Politics, 1990–2006* (Cambridge, Cambridge University Press, 2008) 141–42.

[33] Quoted from F Hill and C Gaddy, *Mr Putin: Operative in the Kremlin* (Washington DC, Brookings Institution Press, 2013) 50.

Eight days later, he delivered a speech to Russia's equivalent of the FBI, declaring that law enforcement must be central in eliminating two threats to the Russian state: terrorism and economic crime.[34] The subtext was clear: legal reform and unity was necessary to rebuild the Russian state and ensure internal security.

He also linked this legal strategy with past reforms. On January 24, Putin urged the heads of regional federal court systems to end their dependency on regional power structures and work closely with the Kremlin. He linked this centralising mission with Czar Alexander II's period of 'Great Reforms'.[35] Finally, in a 31 January speech to the Ministry of Justice, Putin asked officials to work with him to unify the Russian legal system by striking down regional laws that conflicted with the federal Constitution. He argued that this legal reform would reflect Russia's commitment to 'legality and the state' and explained that:

> our traditional approach to law and the Russian state was not born in 1917 or even in 1991. And therefore, whatever we may be doing today – judicial reform or nation building – we must remember the age-old Russian tradition of fairness and justice.[36]

Second, the office of the President actively introduced legislation that would modernise Russia's formal legal system. In his first term, Putin oversaw the introduction of ten new legal codes. These reforms streamlined the legal system, including a new tax code that introduced a 13 per cent flat tax that would be easier to collect. Some of these changes advanced individual rights. Most notably, the legislature introduced a Criminal Procedure Code that that greatly expanded access to jury trials while limiting prosecutorial power and the amount of time for pretrial detention.[37] These reforms created the legal framework for a more efficient and stable economic system that would generate tax revenue more efficiently. They also allowed the Office of the President to more systematically project its power.

III. RECENTRALISING POWER IN MOSCOW

These institutional and legal tools were critical in Putin's effort to manage a critical check on presidential power: Russia's regional

---
[34] ibid.
[35] Quoted from W Partlett, 'Putin's Artful Jurisprudence' (2013) 123 *National Interest* 35.
[36] ibid.
[37] Kahn (n 28) 542–52.

governors. To achieve this, Putin deployed both his decree and lawmaking authority. First, Putin used his decree power to replace Yeltsin's system of presidential representatives in each region and instead appoint a presidential representative under Article 83(k) of the Russian Constitution to seven newly created and much larger super-districts.[38] The decree delegated the management of these representatives to the PA.[39] This streamlined form of control was intended to ensure that the Presidency could better exercise its 'constitutional powers'.[40]

Second, the Putin administration introduced legislation that reformed the upper house of the legislature (Federation Council).[41] This legislation repealed the old system created by Yeltsin where regional executive and legislative leaders also served as deputies in the Federation Council. As described in the previous chapter, this dual status had given regional elites immunity from prosecution and power to block presidential legislation and appointments.

To reverse these effects, the Putin administration's law forbid regional governors from automatically sitting in the Federation Council.[42] This law was bitterly opposed by the regional leadership. After a series of compromises and the use of the lower house (Duma) to override the opposition of the upper house, however, the Office of the President prevailed.[43] Each regional chief executive was now required to appoint an executive delegate to the Federation Council (as long as this choice was not vetoed by a vote of two-thirds of the members of their regional parliaments). Regional assemblies were also required to choose one 'delegate' to sit in the Federation Council. No longer formally sitting in the upper house, these reforms gave the President power to threaten the formal prosecution of regional chief executives.[44] Regional chief executives were left with the right to sit in a largely advisory State Council that

---

[38] J Kahn, 'What is the New Russian Federalism?' in A Brown (ed), *Contemporary Russian Politics: A Reader* (Oxford, Oxford University Press, 2001) 374.
[39] Presidential Decree No 849 of 13 May 2000 'On the Plenipotentiary Representative of the President of the Russian Federation in the Federal District" (in Russian) (*Garant*) https://base.garant.ru/12119586/.
[40] ibid.
[41] Federal Law No 113-F3 of 5 August 2000 'On the procedure for forming the Federation Council of the Federal Assembly of the Russian Federation' (in Russian) (*Konsultant Plus*) www.consultant.ru/document/cons_doc_LAW_28087/.
[42] J Kahn, *Federalism, Democratisation, and the Rule of Law in Russia* (Oxford, Oxford University Press, 2002).
[43] ibid 253.
[44] C Ross, 'Putin's Federal Reforms and the Consolidation of Federalism in Russia: One Step Forward, Two Steps Back!' (2003) 36 *Communist and Post-Communist Studies* 29.

gave them only 'limited input into policy making'.[45] In 2004, presidential control increased again when a new law cancelled direct elections for regional executives and empowered the President to effectively appoint regional governors.[46]

Finally, as part of his appeal to judges and prosecutors, the presidential administration embarked on a major campaign to bring regional charters and republican Constitutions into line with the Russian Constitution. This included a set of presidential decrees that called on 'the republics of Altai, Bashkortostan and Ingushetiya in addition to Amur, Smolensk and Tver oblasts, to bring their regional laws into accordance with the Russian Constitution and federal legislation.[47] The Russian Constitutional Court responded quickly to this signal, deciding that the declarations of sovereignty of many regions were incompatible with the sovereignty and Constitution of the Russian Federation.[48] These changes made the Russian Federation more uniform and ended the extravagant powers that some regional leaders had enjoyed during the 1990s.

IV. CONTROLLING THE OLIGARCHS

These tools also afforded the President power to control the powerful business oligarchs who had accumulated vast wealth and influence in the 1990s. Putin did not want to reverse the privatisation of the 1990s. But he did expect that these oligarchs would respect the authority of the President. As with the governors, this required the disciplining power of law. First, the Putin administration used its control over the Russian Prosecutor General to open criminal cases against two leading media oligarchs, Vladimir Gusinsky and Boris Berezovsky. Both men had angered Putin with their media coverage of the Kursk disaster and were

---

[45] ibid 40.
[46] Federal Law No 159-FZ of 11 December 2004 'On Amendments to the Federal Law "On General Principles of Organization of Legislative (Representative) and Executive Bodies of State Power of the Subjects of the Russian Federation"' (in Russian) (*Konsultant Plus*) www.consultant.ru/document/cons_doc_LAW_50659/. (requiring the proposed candidate to be confirmed by the regional legislature but this was largely a foregone conclusion because of the powers that the President had over the regional legislatures, including dissolution).
[47] Ross (n 43) 42.
[48] See, e.g. Decision of the Russian Constitutional Court 7 June 2000 'On the case of verifying the constitutionality of certain provisions of the Constitution of the Altai Republic' (in Russian) (*Garant*) https://base.garant.ru/12119810/.

seen as a threat to the power of the President.[49] Seeing the likelihood of conviction, both fled the country and relinquished control of their media empires to the Russian state.

Putin also sent a clear message to the remaining oligarchs that as long as they paid taxes and did not criticise the Kremlin, he would refrain from prosecuting them for any past (or continuing) corruption. Scholars have described how this strategy creates a kind of informal contract where corruption is tolerated 'in exchange for effective implementation of central directives and a share of the proceeds'.[50] The threat of criminal sanctions are a powerful incentive for ensuring elite cohesion, summed up in the well-known phrase 'for my friends, everything. For my enemies, the law.'[51]

In order to enforce this informal contract, Putin has used not just his control over the prosecutorial elite. He has also deployed the President's vast rational-legal power to reshape the executive branch by creating an agency that would monopolise the gathering of sensitive (and potentially incriminating) financial information. In 2001, Putin signed a presidential decree creating a wholly new financial intelligence gathering unit called Russian Financial Monitoring Agency (RFM).[52] RFM was automatically entered into the specified list of federal executive agencies and immediately consolidated control over the patchwork of local and federal institutions that had handled financial information gathering. Putin entrusted this institution to one of the most loyal members of his team, Viktor Zubkov.

This new agency quickly built an effective presidential monopoly over financial intelligence gathering in the Russian Federation. Moreover, in Russia's vast legal-bureaucratic apparatus, RFM has never had any institutional legacies or personal loyalties other than those given to it by Putin and his closest associates.[53] These characteristics have enabled RFM to become a critical institution in enabling Putin's control over the Russian business elite. In particular, RFM helps to anchor a 'vertical of

---

[49] M Goldman, 'Putin and the Oligarchs' (2004) 83 *Foreign Affairs* 33, 36–37, 41.

[50] K Darden, 'The Integrity of Corrupt States: Graft as an Informal State Institution' (2008) 36 *Politics and Society* 35, 42.

[51] Quoted from W Partlett, 'Putin's Artful Jurisprudence' (2013) 123 *National Interest* 35, 36.

[52] Presidential Decree No 1263 of 1 November 2001 N 1263, 'On the Authorized Body for Combating the Legalization (Laundering) of Proceeds from Crime and the Financing of Terrorism' (in Russian) (*Garant*) https://base.garant.ru/5168397/.

[53] F Hill and CG Gaddy, *Mr Putin: Operative in the Kremlin* (Washington DC, Brookings Institution Press, 2013) 182.

impunity' or 'protection racket', one that tacitly allows corrupt behaviour by leading elites and then offers protection from prosecution to those who remain loyal.[54] After setting up a presidential monopoly over financial information, the leadership of RFM has also sought to expand RFM's legal powers of financial surveillance. This expansion of power quickly translated into a massively increased flow of financial information. According to the leading international body regulating financial crime and money laundering,

> By January 2005, the FIU had received 3 million messages from reporting institutions (including about 1.8 million STRs). In 2006, the database volume doubled, when the FIU received another 6.1 million messages (of which 3.8 million STRs). By April 2007, the database had accumulated about 14 million messages.[55]

This system of loyalty was tested in 2003, when Mikhail Khodorkovsky, the chairman and CEO of Russia's largest oil-producing company, began funding opposition parties and independent media critical of the Kremlin. In response, Khordorkovsky was immediately jailed and his oil company was seized.[56] The message to other oligarchs was clear: follow the rules or face devastating legal consequences.

V. EFFECTIVENESS

The use of the vast rational-legal authority of the managerial presidency to build supportive institutions and make new laws clearly enhanced the institutional power of the Office of the President. As we have seen, this new more stable set of institutions – most notably the PA – built a far more potent President that allowed Putin to use law to weaken those who sought to check his power. Key elites were either loyal to the President or faced the possibility of legal prosecution.

These managerial tools were also important in allowing Putin to build his personal, non-legal authority. This was clear in his deliberate

---

[54] BW Ickes and CG Gaddy, 'Protecting Putin's Protection Racket' (*Brookings*, 11 November 2009) www.brookings.edu/blogs/up-front/posts/2009/11/11-putin-deripaska-gaddy (arguing that 'Financial information is the nuclear weapon of Russia's thoroughly opaque corporate elite').
[55] Financial Action Task Force, 'Second Mutual Evaluation Report: Anti-Money Laundering and Combating the Financing of Terrorism – Russian Federation (20 June 2008) 59 www.fatf-gafi.org/content/dam/fatf-gafi/mer/MER%20Russia%20ful.pdf.coredownload.pdf.
[56] Goldman (n 48).

construction of charismatic authority. Putin is an unlikely charismatic leader: He is short of stature and, in comparison with Yeltsin, is not a compelling public speaker. As Konstantin Sonin describes him, 'he never made an impression on anyone until he gained power'.[57] Once he was noticed, Sonin explains, his only 'apparent charm' was the 'product of his office, not his personality'.[58] The authority of the presidential office and particularly the streamlined PA were critical in building Putin's non-legal, charismatic power. In fact, Putin used his legal background to enable the PA to build a media image portraying him as a charismatic, action man who has singlehandedly saved Russia from the humiliations and collapse of the 1990s. This media image has proven successful, quickly helping to build a cult of personality around President Putin.[59]

This media control has also allowed Putin and his team to exploit traditional forms of authority. Putin and his team increasingly compared the President with earlier forms of traditional authority, particularly from the Tsarist period. To stress this link, Putin moved the presidential inauguration to the Grand Kremlin Palace to create more links with the Tsarist past. Putin also makes frequent reference to history to justify the centralisation of power.[60]

Putin's systematic use of the rational-legal, constitutional authority of Russia's crown-presidential Constitution to build his non-legal authority shows that rational-legal authority of constitutional law is not always opposed to informal and personal forms of charismatic or traditional authority. On the contrary, when combined, this authority provides the President a powerful basis for dominating politics. In describing the different types of legitimate authority, Max Weber wrote that charismatic, traditional and rational types of authority are almost always combined.[61] This is the case, he argued, because the willingness to obey is often best secured on a multiplicity of grounds. In Russia, the President is obeyed not just because this institution exercises the rational-legal authority in the Constitution but also because the *person* in that office (Vladimir Putin) possesses both traditional and charismatic power.

[57] Sonin (n 4).
[58] ibid.
[59] DS Hutcheson and B Petersson, 'Shortcut to Legitimacy: Popularity in Putin's Russia' (2016) 68 *Europe-Asia Studies* 1107, 1111.
[60] W Partlett, 'Putin's Past: The Return of Ideological History and the Strongman' (*American Historical Association, Perspectives on History*, 7 December 2022) www.historians.org/research-and-publications/perspectives-on-history/january-2023/putins-past-the-return-of-ideological-history-and-the-strongman.
[61] M Weber, *Theory of Social and Economic Organization* (T Parsons (ed), AM Henderson and T Parsons (trans)) (New York, Free Press, 1947) 388.

Although this centralisation of power was justified as strengthening the Russian state, it had a mixed record in enhancing the overall effectiveness of the state. Putin's legal reforms have helped to ensure a more stable economy. The Russian economy doubled in size over the first decade of 2000s and living standards greatly improved. This growth is a reflection of rising hydrocarbon prices as well as a more efficient legal system. For instance, after simplifying the tax code, the Russian state was better able to collect taxes.

But the Russian state still remained weak. The vast private corruption that had emerged in the 1990s was not eliminated by Putin's centralising reforms. On the contrary, as described above, corruption became an important way of ensuring presidential control over powerful individuals. By some measures, official corruption actually grew worse in Putin's second term as public officials used their authority for personal benefit.[62] One example was the 'Three Whales' case, which allegedly involved high level individuals in Putin's inner circle.[63] This allegation was seemingly strengthened when this investigation was closed down after Putin took personal control of the case.

This continued corruption was not the only problem. Despite the legal-bureaucratic reforms, the centre still lacked the ability to control its agents. One analyst describes how 'the potential for the exercise of the president's authority was "sapped" by the bureaucratic machinery and the need to delegate'.[64] For instance, he describes how in 2006 Putin signed a decree firing a number of security service generals but two months later, the generals were still in office.[65] This raises an uncomfortable truth for Russia's managerial system: its centralised planning is often better at projecting the image of policy-making than actually implementing any real policy changes.

In sum, the continuing weakness of the Russian state reflects what Fabian Burkhardt calls a 'paradox' of presidential power. Putin's use of rational-legal authority to institutionalise Russian power has helped to increase the institutional authority of the Office of the President and increase Putin's own *personal* authority. But it has not strengthened other institutions of the Russian state. On the contrary, growing centralisation has done the opposite. In fact, the institutionalisation of the presidency

---

[62] L Holmes, 'Corruption and Organised Crime in Putin's Russia' (2008) 60 *Europe-Asia Studies* 1011, 1023.
[63] K Rothrock, 'Three Whales after 20 Years' (*Meduza*, 25 August 2021) www.meduza.io/en/feature/2021/08/25/three-whales-after-20-years.
[64] Monaghan (n 5) 19.
[65] ibid 10.

has created a new problem: how to effectively monitor and steer the institutions that implement centralised policy.[66] Often the only way to solve these problems is through manual control by the President. Vladimir Gelman places this principal-agent problem at the centre of Russia's system of bad governance.[67]

VI. POPULAR ACCOUNTABILITY

Although it had a mixed record in restoring the effectiveness of the state, this new managerial President proved to be a highly effective way to evade real electoral accountability and win elections. The key players in this process were the 'political technologists' who viewed 'politics as artifice, manipulation, engineering or programming.'[68] They used a range of methods to win elections. They worked with media outlets to manipulate public information and discredit opposition candidates.[69] They also worked with the Central Election Commission to set 'targets for election turnout' and determine 'which candidates should be allowed to run'.[70]

Another critical institution in the management of elections was the creation of a ruling party named United Russia. Formed by the PA from existing party structures, United Russia became a potent tool for furthering the power of the Russian President over the elected legislature. It was successful almost immediately, securing a majority in Russia's lower house (Duma). Its success was not due to any particular policy position. Instead, United Russia reflected the anti-politics of the constitutional system more generally.[71]

Its success was drawn from its close association with the popularity of Vladimir Putin, becoming his personal 'party of power'. Although Putin never formally joined the Party during this period, its leaders described it as part of Putin's attempt to create a strong, united Russia. As Andrei Klimov, deputy chair of the United Russia group in the Duma, stated: 'Mr Putin did not appear by chance … Russia needed someone like him who could unite

---

[66] Burkhardt (n 10) 473–74.
[67] Gel'man (n 9) at 56–57.
[68] A Wilson, *Political Technology: The Globalisation of Political Manipulation* (Cambridge, Cambridge University Press, 2023) 3.
[69] See, eg A Wilson, *Virtual Politics: Faking Democracy in the Post-Soviet World* (New Haven, Yale University Press, 2005).
[70] Pallin (n 13) 277.
[71] N Rosenblum, *On the Side of Angels: An Appreciation of Politics and Partisanship* (Princeton, Princeton University Press, 2008) 46.

society'.[72] This anti-political approach has allowed United Russia to adopt a wide number of different ideological positions; this flexibility has allowed it to co-opt any challenge from the left or the right. Dmitry Medvedev later admitted that United Russia does not have a clear party platform, instead describing the party as one that finds compromise between competing interests in public debate.[73] It therefore replicated Putin's own lack of left-right partisan commitments. A key poller, Yuri Levada, has commented that Putin is 'a mirror in which everyone, Communist or democrat, sees what he wants to see and what he hopes for'.[74]

These legal and institutional mechanisms would prove critical in dominating Russian politics. Popular legitimacy remained the key pillar of state authority. In particular, presidential elections have provided an opportunity to show the popularity of the leader to both the Russian people and the world. They therefore feed into the central claim of the constitutional dark arts that this centralised system is democratic.[75] Ivan Krastev and Stephen Holmes describe elections in Russia as 'a central, load-bearing institutional pillar of Putin's regime'.[76]

In sum, the managerial President was able to use its power to manipulate the 'supply side' of democratic politics and ensure that the 'entire party and political system is engineered and scripted'.[77] Opposition voices were either co-opted, marginalised or prosecuted. It created a kind of 'staged democracy ... in which the Kremlin is the director, casting the roles'.[78] The vast powers of the Russian President therefore had succeeded in transforming elections from a method of accountability to one that enables centralised power.

VII. DOMESTIC LEGAL ACCOUNTABILITY

The new managerial President transformed the domestic legal landscape. Because it was now squarely controlled by PA, the legislature no

---

[72] N Buckley, 'Putin's Managed Democracy' (*Financial Times*, 27 June 2006) www.ft.com/content/39682de4-053d-11db-9b9e-0000779e2340.

[73] Andrey Vinokurov and Ivan Sukhov, Interview with D Medvedev, 'There Are No Ideal Parties' (*Kommersant*, 1 June 2021) www.kommersant.ru/doc/4837620.

[74] Quoted from S White and I McAllister, 'The Putin Phenomenon' (2008) 24 *Journal of Communist Studies and Transition Politics* 604, 615.

[75] ibid 36.

[76] I Krastev and S Holmes, 'Putinism under Siege: An Autopsy of Managed Democracy' (2012) 23(3) *Journal of Democracy* 33, 34.

[77] A Wilson, *Political Technology: The Globalisation of Political Manipulation* (Cambridge, Cambridge University Press, 2023) 3.

[78] Quoted from Buckley (n 71).

longer brought claims to the Constitutional Court seeking to invalidate the centralisation of power. Individual Russians, however, continued to file claims challenging the constitutionality of the increasing centralisation of power in the office of the President.[79]

The Court also changed in composition and leadership during this period. In 2002 and 2003, two of the clearest proponents for interpreting the Constitution in line with the balanced constitutional tradition (Morshchakova and Vitruk) left the Court. Moreover, in 2003, Valery Zorkin was elected Chairman of the Court. Despite some concern about this appointment because of his opposition to Yeltsin in the early 1990s, Zorkin quickly emerged as a Chairman who was willing to support a powerful presidency. In fact, in a series of public speeches and appearances, he described the need for a strong presidency to stop Russia from disintegrating.[80] Zorkin would emerge as a leading voice of the centralised state tradition in constitutional interpretation more generally.

The Zorkin-led Court therefore continued to defer to broad interpretations of presidential power, relying on the broad constitutional descriptions of presidential power and the arguments of the centralised state tradition. The most high-profile challenge was filed by a number of Russian citizens to the constitutional validity of a law giving the President the authority to effectively appoint regional executives.[81] This challenge centred on one of the foundational constitutional principles in the Russian constitutional system: Article 3's guarantee of popular sovereignty.

In 1996, the Russian Constitutional Court had decided a case in broad terms about the importance of popular sovereignty to the Russian constitutional order.[82] In this case, the claimant had argued that provisions in

---

[79] Trochev (n 31) 159 (describing how 37,733 individual complaints were received by the Court between 1995 and 2006).

[80] ibid 141.

[81] Resolution of the Constitutional Court of the Russian Federation of 21 December 2005 N 13-P, 'In the Case of Verifying the Constitutionality of Certain Provisions of the Federal Law "On the General Principles of the Organization of Legislative (Representative) and Executive Bodies of State Power of the Subjects of the Russian Federation" in Connection with Complaints from a Number of Citizens' (*Konsultant Plus*, 21 December 2005) www.consultant.ru/document/cons_doc_LAW_57388/. See also W.E. Pomeranz, 'President Medvedev and the Contested Constitutional Underpinnings of Russia's Power Vertical' (2009) 17 *Demokratizatsiya* 179.

[82] Decision of the Russian Constitutional Court N 2-P of 18 January 1996, 'On the Case of Verifying the Constitutionality of a Number of Provisions of the Charter (Fundamental Law) of the Altai Territory' (in Russian) (*Konsultant Plus*) www.consultant.ru/document/cons_doc_LAW_23036/.

a regional Constitution were unconstitutional because they provided for the regional executive to be elected by the regional legislature rather than the people. The claimant argued that these provisions violated Article 3's guarantee of popular sovereignty and Article 10's separation of powers. The Court agreed. It reasoned that the provision giving the legislature (and not the people) the power to elect the President violated the principle of popular sovereignty which holds that the people 'exercise their power directly'.[83] Reading the popular sovereignty requirement together with another provision enshrining the right of citizens to elect their representatives,[84] the Court stated that 'the highest official who forms the executive body receives his mandate directly from the people and is responsible to them'.[85] The regional Constitution violated this principle by turning the legislature into a kind of 'electoral college' that 'replaces the direct expression of the will of voters'. This way of electing the executive, therefore, was unconstitutional because 'the federal structure of the Russian Federation is based on the unity of the system of state power' and therefore 'government bodies in the constituent entities of the Russian Federation are formed on the same principles as federal ones'.[86]

This 1996 judgment about the constitutional importance of direct popular sovereignty in electing regional executives provided strong grounds for a challenge to the 2004 federal law empowering the President to appoint regional executives. The challengers argued that this law giving the Russian President the power to appoint a regional executives undermined their right to exercise their popular sovereignty and choose their chief executive. The logic was simple: if government bodies at the federal and regional level were formed on the same principles, then regional executives must be elected as well.

A majority of the Court, however, rejected this argument. Reading the Constitution through the centralised state tradition, it saw the 'unity' of state power differently than the claimants. The Court stressed that the 'unity of the system of state power' in Article 5.3 empowered the elected President to create a top-down vertical of power where regional executives are responsible to the President.[87] This unified vertical was not a violation of popular sovereignty because the President is 'the direct representative of all the people of the Russian Federation' and therefore

---

[83] Russian Constitution (n 20) Art 3.
[84] ibid Art 32.
[85] Decision of the Russian Constitutional Court (n 81).
[86] ibid.
[87] ibid.

is the highest representative of the people's will. It therefore concluded that the federal legislator 'at each specific stage of development of its statehood' has broad power to 'ensure the unity of the system of state power and the delimitation of jurisdiction and powers between state bodies authorities of the Russian Federation and state authorities of the constituent entities of the Russian Federation'.[88] This discretion is further supported, it reasoned, because direct election is not 'the only acceptable mechanism for the formation of all public authorities at each level of its organization'.[89] In support, it described how members of the upper house are not directly elected.

The Court also considered the decree power of the President. Although legislation was an important new part of the managerial presidency, decrees still remained a common tool of presidential power. In an important 2001 case, the Court considered a challenge to a presidential decree regulating pensions that the legislature claimed was unlawful because it contradicted a series of laws on how pensions were to be paid.[90] The Court held that a presidential decree was valid not just when law was silent but also where the law was contradictory or 'in disharmony'. In this case, the different legal regimes were conflicting and the President, as the guarantor of the system, had the power to regulate this area by decree.[91] This confirmed a legal position that had been mentioned but not broadly discussed in the 1995 Chechen War case: presidential decrees were a critical source of legal norms in areas of contested legislative norms.

The Court not only continued to uphold major challenges to the further centralisation of power in the office of the President. It also took an active role in centralising power in the centre by striking down provisions in regional Constitutions declaring sovereignty. This could be traced directly to President Putin's rhetoric about a dictatorship of the law. As a Constitutional Court justice told a leading researcher: 'We struck down the key clauses of seven constitutions of the republics in June 2000 only after President Putin announced his crackdown on recalcitrant regions; we would not have been brave enough to do this under Yeltsin.'[92]

---

[88] ibid.
[89] ibid.
[90] Decision of the Constitutional Court of the Russian Federation N 9-P of 25 June 2001, 'On the Case of Verifying the Constitutionality of Decree of the President of the Russian Federation of September 27, 2000 N 1709 "On Measures to Improve the Management of State Pension Provision in the Russian Federation" in Connection with a Request from a Group of Deputies of the State Duma' (in Russian) (*Konsultant Plus*, 25 June 2001) www.consultant.ru/document/cons_doc_LAW_32258/.
[91] See Trochev (n 31) 130.
[92] ibid 146.

Finally, despite this centralising role, the Court continued to actively protect individuals and their rights amidst the problems of a dysfunctional state. In particular, the Court expanded its activities in the areas of economics and socio-economic rights. For instance, the Court constitutionalised the 'freedom of contract' on the basis of Article 8's guarantee of the freedom of economic activity.[93] The Court also sought to protect individual Russians from the chaos of privatisation by reading the Civil Code to protect the property interests of 'bona fide purchasers'.[94] The Court therefore continued to attempt to secure its power in the system while upholding the centralisation of power in the President.

VIII. INTERNATIONAL LEGAL ACCOUNTABILITY

Russia's membership in the Council of Europe allowed thousands of cases to be brought by Russian litigants against the Russian state in the European Court of Human Rights (ECtHR). These cases, however, failed to limit the centralisation of power in the office of the President and its rights abuses. Sometimes this was a practical matter. In 2008, for instance, individual claims against Russia made up more than a quarter (28 per cent) of the overall number of cases filed in the ECtHR.[95] The sheer number of these cases led to a serious challenge for the ECtHR in resolving these cases in a timely manner. The ECtHR acknowledged the backlog of cases as 'alarming' and stated that it was actively seeking ways of overcoming it.[96] To make matters worse, the Russian government itself has often withheld needed documents in a way that furthers slows the resolution of the case.[97]

In the cases that did reach the ECtHR, Russia frequently lost. Russia responded by complying with the monetary demands of these cases

---

[93] ibid 166.
[94] See, eg Decision of the Russian Constitutional Court No 6-P of April 21, 2003, 'In the Case of Verifying the Constitutionality of the Provisions of Paragraphs 1 and 2 of Article 167 of the Civil Code of the Russian Federation in Connection with Complaints from Citizens OM Marinicheva, AV Nemirovskaya, ZA Sklyanova, RM Sklyanova and VM Shiryaev' (in Russian) (*Konsultant Plus*) www.consultant.ru/document/cons_doc_LAW_41943/.
[95] European Court of Human Rights, Council of Europe, 'Annual Report 2008' (Strasbourg, 2009) 11 www.echr.coe.int/documents/d/echr/annual_report_2008_eng.
[96] ibid 35.
[97] O Solvang, 'Russia and the European Court of Human Rights: The Price of Non-Cooperation' (2008) 15(2) *Human Rights Brief* 14, 14.

but generally refused to make real meaningful change in line with the recommendations of the ECtHR.⁹⁸ In *Musayev et al v Russia* (2007), the ECtHR stated that 'no meaningful result whatsoever' had been achieved in the task of identifying and prosecuting the individuals responsible six years after the 'cold-blooded execution of more than 50 civilians' in a village outside of Grozny.⁹⁹ In its unanimous decision, the seven-judge panel said that 'the astonishing ineffectiveness of the prosecuting authorities in this case could only be qualified as acquiescence in the events'.¹⁰⁰

This kind of criticism was common. The Parliamentary Assembly of the Council of Europe accused Russia of 'unacceptable delays of implementation' and 'important systemic problems'.¹⁰¹ Sometimes this was a deliberate attempt by the Russian state to evade accountability. In other cases, it was a reflection of the dysfunctionality of Russia's centralised system. In a 2007 report, Vladimir Lukin, the Commissioner for Human Rights of the Russian Federation, worried that the execution of court decisions was so poor in Russia that they were becoming a kind of 'legal fiction'.¹⁰² He criticised the widespread perception 'not only in society but also in government bodies' that legal judgments were merely 'non-compulsory recommendations'.¹⁰³

IX. CONCLUSION

This chapter revises our understanding of Putin's first two terms as President. President Putin did not break with the Russian constitutional order in asserting his power. Instead, he used the full range of his constitutional authority to build a legal-bureaucratic system that allowed him to dominate Russian politics. This constitutional authority also allowed him to accumulate non-legal authority as a charismatic populist leader

---

⁹⁸ 'Update on European Court of Human Rights Judgments against Russia regarding Cases from Chechnya' (*Human Rights Watch*, 20 March 2009) www.hrw.org/news/2009/03/20/update-european-court-human-rights-judgments-against-russia-regarding-cases-chechnya.
⁹⁹ *Musayev et al v Russia* App nos 57941/00, 58699/00 and 60403/00 (ECtHR, 31 March 2008).
¹⁰⁰ ibid.
¹⁰¹ Parliamentary Assembly, Council of Europe, 'Implementation of Judgments of the European Court of Human Rights' (Res No 1516, 2006), https://assembly.coe.int/nw/xml/XRef/Xref-XML2HTML-en.asp?fileid=17472&lang=en.
¹⁰² V Lukin, 'Report of the Ombudsman for Human Rights in the Russian Federation for 2007' (*Rossiskaya Gazeta*, 14 March 2008) http://perma.cc/5ZJX-8WE2.
¹⁰³ ibid.

who acted in the interests of the people. The constitutional powers of the President were critical in allowing Putin to recover from the uncertain, early months of his Presidency.

The managerial President was justified as a new form of Russian antipolitics: a project of rebuilding the authority of the Russian state centred around a highly powerful office of the President. This managerialism did create a more effective form of legal regulation and stabilised the economy. But this system was not able to reverse the institutional weakness and corruption of the broader Russian state apparatus. These deeper problems continued to generate poor quality governance.

While relying on the rational-legal powers of the presidency, Putin also had to respect those that limited his power. The most important was Article 81 which stated that one person could not serve more than two terms in a row. This ultimately forced him to step down from the presidency. The following chapter will describe how Putin's decision to give up the presidency but remain Prime Minister impacted Russia's centralised constitutional system.

6

The Constrained President (2008–12)

ON 17 MARCH 2011, the United States, France and Britain introduced a broadly worded resolution to the United Nations Security Council authorising the use of 'all necessary measures' to protect civilians in an escalating civil war in Libya.[1] After much speculation, new Russian President Dmitry Medvedev directed the Russian ambassador to abstain from the vote.[2] A few days later, Prime Minister Vladimir Putin criticised this decision, describing the Resolution to be 'deficient and flawed' and 'reminiscent of a medieval call for a crusade'.[3] President Medvedev immediately responded that Putin's description of the UN resolution on Libya was 'unacceptable' and could 'lead to a clash of civilisations'.[4] Soon after, Putin backed down, stating 'it is the Russian president who is in charge of foreign policy and there can be no divergence'.[5]

This episode challenges the conventional story that President Dmitry Medvedev was an ineffectual puppet of Vladimir Putin with no independent power of his own. This chapter will instead show that the vast rational-legal authority of the President did matter during this period. This constitutional order shaped Putin's careful moves to place both legal and non-legal constraints on the ability of President Medvedev to use the power of the President against him. It also enabled President

---

[1] United Nations Security Council Resolution 1973, UN Doc S/RES/1973 (17 March 2011) www.un.org/securitycouncil/s/res/1973-%282011%29.
[2] Ann Larssen, 'Russia: The Principle of Non-Intervention and the Libya Case' in Dag Henriksen and Ann Larsen (eds), *Political Rationale and International Consequences of the War in Libya* (Oxford, Oxford University Press, 2016) 77–78.
[3] 'Putin Likens UN Libya Resolution to Crusade Call' *Ria Novosti* (21 March 2011) http://en.ria.ru/russia/20110321/163126957.html.
[4] 'Medvedev Rejects Putin "Crusade" Remark over Libya' *BBC News* (21 March 2011) www.bbc.com/news/world-europe-12810566.
[5] B Whitmore, 'Battle Lines Being Drawn?' *Radio Free Europe/Radio Liberty* (22 March 2011) www.rferl.org/articleprintview/2346539.html.

Medvedev to make decisions that contradicted Prime Minister Putin. This freedom was particularly clear in the foreign policy realm, where the Russian President has significant personal, guardian power under Article 86. Russia's constitutional system also constrained Putin as Prime Minister, as he himself repeatedly backed down from direct and public confrontation with President Medvedev.

For this four-year period, therefore, Russia had two power centres. A constrained President with broad rational-legal authority (Medvedev) and a strong Prime Minister with significant personal, non-legal authority (Putin). Often, they agreed on policy. When they did not, Putin had to rely on his non-legal authority to constrain President Medvedev. This shows that the rational-legal powers of Russian crown-presidentialism do not *always* yield presidential domination. In the short term at least, this vast presidential authority can be constrained by the non-legal power of another official in the system. It is unlikely, however, that Putin could have continued to constrain a determined President Medvedev if he had remained President for another six-year term until 2018.

Despite the reality of a constrained presidency for this four-year period, the constitutional system was still committed to an anti-political form of centralised management. This was shown in constitutional amendments increasing the length of the presidential term. and the broadening influence of the centralised state tradition in Russian constitutional discourse. Meanwhile, both popular and legal accountability for the abuses of centralisation remained weak.

I. THE COMPLIANCE PULL OF THE PRESIDENTIAL TERM LIMIT

Before analysing the constitutional politics of this period, it is important to explore why Vladimir Putin stepped down from the presidency. He was not in a position like Yeltsin who was deeply unpopular and too unhealthy to remain in office. On the contrary, in the year proceeding the 2008 election, Putin's personal popularity was extremely high. One poll showed 86 per cent of Russians approved of President Putin.[6] Many also were speculating whether Putin would seek to exploit legal loopholes that would allow him to serve a third term as President.[7] One possibility

---

[6] JA Cassiday and ED Johnson, 'Putin, Putiniana and the Question of a Post-Soviet Cult of Personality' (2010) 88 *The Slavonic and East European Review* 681, 683.

[7] C Lowe, 'Russian Loophole Offers Putin Chance of Third Term' *Reuters* (Moscow, 16 November 2007) www.reuters.com/article/uk-russia-putin-analysis-idUKL1638698 920071116.

included stepping down from the presidency for a short period and then running again in 2008. Furthermore, the December 2007 elections to the State Duma produced a supermajority for the United Russia party, which could have amended the Constitution to allow Putin a third term. Finally, extra-constitutional options were also available. In late 2007, a movement called on Putin to remain Russia's 'national leader'.

But, in a suggestion of the normative pull of the term limit rule in Article 81, Putin decided to step down from the presidency. This was a remarkable moment in Russian history. It was one of the only times in history that a healthy and powerful Russian leader had ever voluntarily stepped away from the supreme public office. But, as we will see in the next section, Putin took counter-measures to protect himself (and his supporters) from the broad formal powers of a new President Medvedev.

Despite these precautions, Putin's decision to step down from the presidency did introduce significant uncertainty into the system about who was in charge. Many lower-level officials were uncertain who was actually in charge.[8] Moreover, Putin was careful not to publicly contest the authority of President Medvedev, particularly in the area of foreign policy. The years between 2008 and 2012 thus witnessed an uneasy coexistence between two power centres in Russian politics.

II. CONSTRAINING THE NEW PRESIDENT

Russia's formal constitutional system continued to afford vast rational-legal authority to the Office of the President. But newly elected President Dmitry Medvedev faced a number of obstacles in exercising this authority. These obstacles stemmed from Vladimir Putin's careful steps in the final months of his presidency to strengthen the office of the Prime Minister. More importantly, they included Putin's deliberate decision to continue to cultivate his non-legal authority through the personal loyalty of high-level officials and his popularity with the Russian people.

Putin carefully chose his presidential successor in order to ensure that the new President would be someone who shared many of his views and had long been a loyal subordinate. Putin's choice, Dmitry Medvedev, had deep personal ties to Putin and had long been part of Putin's team.

---

[8] A Baturo and S Mikhaylov, 'Reading the Tea Leaves: Medvedev's Presidency through Political Rhetoric of Federal and Sub-National Actors' (2014) 66 *Europe-Asia Studies* 969.

Both men agreed on policy solutions to many of the problems that Russia faced.[9] Moreover, Putin had long been a mentor and patron of Medvedev. One clear example of this hierarchical relationship is that Medvedev uses the more formal form of 'you' (Вы, 'vy') when addressing Putin, while Putin addresses Medvedev with the more informal you 'ty' (ты).[10] This close relationship – sometimes referred to as 'the tandem' – was a central feature of Medvedev's 2008 presidential campaign, which emphasised 'continuity and stability' with the Putin presidency.[11]

Putin also went to great lengths to increase the powers of his future office, the Prime Minister. This included subordinating a number of powerful ministers to the Prime Minister and not the President.[12] He also abolished 'the obligation for presidential counter-signature for some types of governmental documents'.[13] Putin also transferred direct legal control over the Russian Financial Monitoring Agency (*Rosfinmonitoring*) from the office of the President to the office of the Prime Minister.[14] This change signalled how important the control of financial information was in controlling public officials and the business elite. Continued access to this information, including any financial activity of Dmitry Medvedev himself, would afford Putin significant non-legal authority.

Putin also worked hard to make significant changes to the by-laws (*reglamenty*) under which the government worked to increase his power. Most importantly, Putin repeatedly complained about the institution of interdepartmental coordination. To combat the need to cooperate with other ministers and departments, he introduced changes that significantly

---

[9] A Monaghan, 'The Russian *Vertikal*: The Tandem, Power and the Elections' (Russia and Eurasia Programme Paper REP 2011/01, Chatham House, June 2011) www.chathamhouse.org/sites/default/files/19412_0511ppmonaghan.pdf.

[10] A Osborn, 'Dmitry Medvedev's Russia Still Feels the Cold Hand of Vladimir Putin' *The Telegraph* (Moscow, 7 March 2010) www.telegraph.co.uk/news/worldnews/europe/russia/7386448/Dmitry-Medvedevs-Russia-still-feels-the-cold-hand-of-Vladimir-Putin.html.

[11] R Coalson, 'Medvedev Marks a Year in the Kremlin, But Does He Rule?' (*Radio Free Europe/Radio Liberty*, 7 May 2009) www.rferl.org/a/Medvedev_Marks_A_Year_In_The_Kremlin_But_Does_He_Rule/1623372.html.

[12] O Kryshtanovskaya, 'The Tandem and the Crisis' (2011) 27 *The Journal of Communist Studies and Transition Politics* 407, 411; O Kryshtanovskaya and S White, 'The Sovietization of Russian Politics' (2009) 25 *Post-Soviet Affairs* 283.

[13] F Burkhardt, 'Institutionalising Authoritarian Presidencies: Polymorphous Power and Russia's Presidential Administration (2021) 73 *Europe-Asia Studies* 472, 490.

[14] Decree of the Russian President No 1274, 'Questions of the Structure of Federal Organs of Executive Power' (in Russian) (*Konsultant*, 24 September 2007) www.consultant.ru/document/cons_doc_LAW_71250/.

centralised power in the office of the Prime Minister. Notably, this included rescinding a requirement to avoid departmental sign offs, allowing him to make policy decisions in 'an expedited manner'.[15]

Taken together, these changes created the strongest Prime Minister in post-Soviet Russian history. These moves alone were not enough to consolidate his position, however, because the President had the authority to remove the Prime Minister. Furthermore, the President also had the formal authority to reshape the structure of the executive government or countermand many of these changes. Putin therefore had to rely on his non-legal authority.

Putin thus made sure to formally move important military and defence matters into the control of individuals loyal to Putin such as Sergei Ivanov and Igor Sechin.[16] Putin also kept officials who were loyal to him in the presidential administration after he had stepped down. Putin did not just seek to maintain control over presidential and executive branch officials. He also became the formal head of the United Russia party for the first time, which gave him power over a number of parliamentary and regional officials. This afforded Putin control over a party that controlled both houses of the Federal Parliament, most of the governors, regional parliaments, the heads of municipalities and deputies in local councils. Overall, this tactic reflected Stalin's old saying that 'cadres decide everything'. It also relied on Weber's insight that authority could not be exercised without 'the existence and continual functioning' of a loyal administrative staff.[17]

Putin also continued to actively cultivate his personal popularity with the Russian people. This popularity underpinned his non-legal, charismatic authority. Despite no longer being President, Putin himself continued to hold a live call-in show that he had started as President in 2001. This show – called Direct Line – allows Russians to send in their questions or complaints directly to Vladimir Putin. A select few of the submissions are able to speak with Putin directly. The 'direct' interaction between these Russian citizens and Putin often includes a live video feed from citizens in a small Russian village who complain about poor

---

[15] D Butrin, 'All power to the lawyers and financiers' *Kommersant* (Moscow, 25 November 2009) www.kommersant.ru/doc/1280439. See also S Fortescue, 'The Policymaking Process in Putin's Prime Ministership' in L Jonson and S White (eds), *Waiting for Reform under Putin and Medvedev* (New York, Palgrave Macmillan, 2012) 119.
[16] Kryshtanovskaya (n 12) 411.
[17] M Weber, *Theory of Social and Economic Organization* (T Parsons (ed), AM Henderson and T Parsons (trans)) (New York, Free Press, 1947) 389.

roads or a crumbling school. Putin then moves to personally solve the issue, scolding the local officials for inaction. Each year, Putin has extended the length of the show, demonstrating his stamina and powers of concentration.

Direct Line not only shows Putin as the active strongman. It also projects the image of Putin as a master of the details of implementation, a leader who is able to get things done when Russian institutions are increasingly paralysed or ineffective. This is visually emphasised by panning television shots of subordinates, who are fielding, classifying and compiling all submissions. Putin himself commented that Direct Line is both a 'powerful sociological survey' and 'an opportunity to convey to the Russian people both my position and the position of the country's leadership on some key issues'.[18] The continued use of this forum as Prime Minister therefore reflected Putin's understanding that his popularity was a powerful non-legal form of leverage in any potential struggle for power with President Medvedev.

III. IMPACT ON DOMESTIC POLICY

These tactics successfully allowed Prime Minister Putin to take a leading role in managing domestic politics. One of the most pressing problems facing Russia during this period was the global financial crisis. Between June 2008 and January 2009, the Russian stock market dropped by 70 per cent.[19] In response, Prime Minister Putin personally oversaw a large economic stimulus plan which played an important role in ending the debt crisis.[20] This stimulus drew heavily on the reserves that had been accrued under Putin's presidency.

In implementing this response, Putin ensured that he was portrayed as an effective man of action who could solve the challenges of the time. A good example of this kind of public image work was in a small industry town south of St Petersburg called Pikalevo.[21] Pikalevo had been badly affected by the global crisis and unhappy workers blocked a major

---

[18] 'The BBC spoke about the new format of Putin's Direct Line' *Vedomosti* (21 May 2018) www.vedomosti.ru/politics/news/2018/05/21/770171-pryamoi-linii.

[19] K Stoner-Weiss, 'Russia and the Global Financial Crisis: The End of "Putinism"?' (2009) 15 *The Brown Journal of World Affairs* 103, 104.

[20] N Robinson, 'Russia's Response to Crisis: The Paradox of Success' (2013) 65 *Europe-Asia Studies* 450, 459.

[21] 'Putin "Settled" the Problems of a Number of Enterprises Live' (in Russian) *RIA Novosti* (Moscow, 3 December 2009) www.ria.ru/20091203/196899157.html.

road to protest unpaid salaries. In response, Putin compared the three plant owners to cockroaches, accusing them of greed. In a staged televised meeting, he ordered a powerful oligarch, Oleg Deripaska, to sign an agreement intended to help restart the Pikalevo factories. Putin also ridiculed the board members for their inability to make the necessary decisions without his intervention: 'You have made thousands of people hostage to your ambitions, your lack of professionalism – or maybe simply your trivial greed'.[22]

Although Putin made wide use of his executive, management powers as Prime Minister, Medvedev did not withdraw from domestic policy-making. On the contrary, Medvedev drew on the guardian powers of the presidency to outline an ambitious set of modernisation reforms. He made this policy most clear in a policy statement 'Forward Russia' released in 2009. It set out a new policy focused on 'modernizing the economic, political, and social life of the country, and curbing corruption'.[23] He also used his State of the Union speech to call for economic, social, and political modernisation on the basis of democratic values. In making these arguments, Medvedev hoped to set a new tone for the Russian political system.

These grand reforms largely failed. A good example was Medvedev's attempt to modernise the police. From the beginning, these reforms were blocked by powerful members of the Russian security services who opposed any real accountability for the police. In fact, Medvedev had no choice but to rely for implementation on 'Ministry of the Interior officials who were the least interested actors when it came to genuine change'.[24] The only real change was a largely symbolic name change: the police were stripped of their Soviet-era name 'militia (*militsiya*)' and were instead called 'police (*politsiya*)'. Medvedev faced similar barriers in his attempts to fight corruption.[25]

Some of these failures could be attributed to the systemic problems of centralisation. President Medvedev was far more forthright about these problems of implementation than Putin had been in his first two terms.

---

[22] O Zagoruyko, 'Russia's Putin Raps Tycoons in Crisis-Hit Town' *Reuters* (5 June 2009) www.reuters.com/article/russia-putin-idUSL445098320090604.
[23] JL Black, *The Russian Presidency of Dmitry Medvedev, 2008–2012: The Next Step Forward or Merely a Time Out?* (Abingdon, Routledge, 2015) 15.
[24] V Gel'man, *The Politics of Bad Governance in Contemporary Russia* (Ann Arbor, University of Michigan Press, 2022) 90.
[25] C Humphries, 'Kremlin Says Russia Losing Battle on Corruption' *Reuters* (Moscow, 15 July 2010) www.reuters.com/article/us-russia-medvedev-corruption-idUSTRE66D 42W20100714.

In 2009, Medvedev criticised the government 'for its failure to implement more than 30 per cent of measures announced to address the financial crisis'.[26] At the end of 2010, Medvedev complained that the President was so involved in operational questions of implementation that it had little time for strategy. Medvedev complained that 'he often found himself signing orders that would not change anything: nor bring about anything new, but simply reiterate an instruction already issued'.[27] Also information was not passed up the chain of command. For instance, after a terrorist attack in 2011, it came to light that plans from 2010 to increase security had simply been ignored.[28]

The failure of his domestic initiatives could also be attributed to Putin's continuing control over the domestic implementation of policy. Particularly in the early years of his presidency, Medvedev remained a 'president without a team' who worked himself 'within the Putin leadership team'.[29] This significantly limited the ability of Medvedev to exercise his vast constitutional prerogatives.

Although Medvedev's power was constrained, his reformist approach did allow him some small victories. An important one relied on the President's legal authority to dismiss executives who no longer commanded the confidence of the President.[30] In September 2010, he dismissed Moscow mayor Yuri Luzhkov before the end of his term despite Putin reportedly wanting Luzhkov to remain in office until the end of his term.[31] Luzhkov had emerged as a symbol of corruption, accused of fleeing Moscow for Austria during August's devastating forest fires and caring more about his bees than the city's smog-choked residents. In addition, Luzhkov faced accusation that his wife's $2.8 billion fortune had been acquired thanks to her husband's job.[32]

Although Medvedev's own power as President was constrained, both Medvedev and Putin remained normatively committed to further

---

[26] A Monaghan, 'The *Vertikal*: Power and Authority in Russia' (2012) 88 *International Affairs* 1, 11.
[27] ibid 10.
[28] ibid 11.
[29] Kryshtanovskaya (n 12) 409.
[30] Federal Law N 184-FZ of October 6, 1999 "On the General Principles of Organization of Legislative (Representative) and Executive Bodies of State Power of the Subjects of the Russian Federation" (Konsultant Plus) www.consultant.ru/document/cons_doc_LAW_14058/.
[31] A Kolesnikov, 'Putin and Medvedev: A Split in the Tandem?' (*Open Democracy*, 5 January 2011) www.opendemocracy.net/en/odr/putin-and-medvedev-split-in-tandem/.
[32] L Harding, 'Russian President Fires Moscow Mayor after Weeks of Feuding' *The Guardian* (Moscow, 29 September 2010) www.theguardian.com/world/2010/sep/28/russia-president-fires-moscow-mayor.

centralising authority in the Office of the President. This included constitutional change. In 2008, President Medvedev pushed through a constitutional change that expanded presidential power by extending the presidential term from four to six years for future Presidents.[33] This was justified by both Medvedev and Putin as providing additional stability to the system. In reality, it gave the Russian electorate less ability to hold the Russian President to account.

IV. IMPACT ON FOREIGN POLICY

Although Putin was able to constrain Medvedev's domestic policy-making power through his non-legal authority, he was less successful in limiting Medvedev's power over foreign policy. This difference can be traced in large part to the constitutional position of the President. In foreign policy President Medvedev had more constitutional power to carry out policy. The Constitution gives the Russian President broad personal authority in this area, notably stating that the President is the representative of the Russian state[34] and giving the President the unilateral authority to determine foreign policy and both sign and ratify treaties.[35] In addition, foreign policy decision-making did not rely on domestic implementation by the Prime Minister or executive ministers.[36]

Foreign policy also showed more clearly the importance of constitutional powers because the policy instincts of Medvedev and Putin diverged more clearly in this area. Putin had a far more adversarial and conspiratorial view of the West, expressed perhaps most clearly in a major speech in Munich speech a year before leaving the Presidency. Medvedev, by contrast, was younger and more interested in cooperation and integration into the world. He therefore placed more emphasis on European security issues (as exemplified by his proposed European Security Treaty) and a desire to improve relations with the United States.

The first foreign policy flashpoint took place early in Medvedev's term of office. In early August 2008, while the world's attention was focused on the Beijing Olympic games, the Russian military entered Georgia.

---

[33] Luke Harding, 'Russian vote paves way for early Putin comeback' *The Guardian* (14 November 2008) www.theguardian.com/world/2008/nov/14/russia-putin.
[34] Art 80.4. Constitution of the Russian Federation (*Council of Europe*) https://rm.coe.int/constitution-of-the-russian-federation-en/1680a1a237.
[35] ibid Art 86.
[36] VA Pacer, *Russian Foreign Policy under Dmitry Medvedev, 2008–2012* (London, Routledge, 2016).

Putin immediately took the lead, cutting short his stay at the Beijing Olympics and flying directly to the capital of Russian North Ossetia, Vladikavkaz. Putin's personal intervention was immediately controversial and he immediately backed away. Putin's visit was removed from the official account of the war.[37] Furthermore, when the French President Sarkozy sought to negotiate a cease-fire to end the Georgia conflict, Putin refused to negotiate. Instead, Medvedev accepted this intervention and negotiated a cease-fire.[38] Putin's decision to step back was significant, suggesting clearly that he did not want to openly usurp or challenge a clear area of presidential authority.

In the years that followed, President Medvedev was able to use his presidential authority to implement his less confrontational foreign policy approach. Medvedev pursued a 'multivectoral' policy that sought to cooperate with the West for a number of reasons, including to facilitate Russia's technological and economic modernisation.[39] This cooperation even included a search for 'areas of cooperation with the North Atlantic Treaty Organisation' rather than areas of difference.[40] Furthermore, Medvedev's Military Doctrine stated that relations between Russia and NATO should be 'developed'.[41]

This new approach transformed relations with Europe. President Medvedev was the first Russian leader to propose a European security agreement.[42] This more positive attempt to engage with the West reflected a definite shift in tone from the Putin presidency of 2000 to 2008. One scholar described how an Eastern European ambassador said that 'there was a different attitude coming from Moscow' during the Medvedev period as Medvedev 'tried to bring something new to the table'.[43]

This more cooperative approach also reshaped Russian relations with the United States, which had been particularly bad since the United States invasion of Iraq. Using his position as President, Medvedev was able to move relations on to a more stable footing, negotiating and signing a 'New Strategic Arms Reduction Treaty'.[44] As well as reducing

---

[37] Kryshtanovskaya (n 12) 408.
[38] Pacer (n 36) 35–36.
[39] GM Hahn, 'Medvedev, Putin, and Perestroika 2.0' (2010) 18 *Demokratizatsiya* 228, 252.
[40] Pacer (n 36) 191.
[41] ibid 191.
[42] ibid 117.
[43] ibid.
[44] Staff, 'US Senate approves nuclear arms control treaty with Russia' *The Guardian* (23 December 2010) www.theguardian.com/world/2010/dec/22/us-senate-new-start-approved.

the number of strategic nuclear weapons held by each side, this treaty restored a verification regime. This treaty also reflected a good working relationship between Medvedev and United States President Barak Obama, who had called for moving beyond a Cold War mentality and initiating a 'reset' policy that would reshape relations.

Medvedev's approach also shaped Russia's accession to the World Trade Organisation (WTO). Vladimir Putin had a complicated relationship with Russian accession to the WTO. After initially appearing to support WTO membership in his first term, Putin had soured on the idea in his second term.[45] In June 2009, Putin had stated that Russia would only join the WTO as part of the Customs Union of the Eurasian Economic Community.[46] This appeared to be an attempt to slow down or halt Russia's accession to the WTO. President Medvedev disagreed and argued that it would be 'simpler and more realistic' for Russia to join on its own.[47] It was Medvedev, not Putin, who prevailed. In December 2011, after 18 years of talks, Russia was invited to join the WTO.[48] This reflected an essential difference between Putin and Medvedev; Putin prioritised integration within the countries of the former Soviet Union, while Medvedev prioritised Russia's broader engagement with the world.

Finally, perhaps the clearest and most dramatic example of Medvedev exerting his foreign policy independence was in the Libyan crisis. As Libyan dictator Muammar Gaddafi threatened to use overwhelming military force against rebel forces inside Libya, the United States, France and Britain called for a United Nations Security Council Resolution that would protect civilians. As described at the beginning of this chapter, Medvedev directed the Russian Ambassador to not to block this resolution. Putin clearly disagreed but ultimately backed down from a confrontation with Medvedev on this issue.

In foreign policy, therefore, Medvedev was able to use the powers of the President to implement a much more cooperative approach to the outside world. This had yielded strong personal relationships with Western leaders. This was particularly true with the Obama administration which had

---

[45] A Aslund, 'Why Doesn't Russia Join the WTO?' (2010) 33(2) *The Washington Quarterly* 49.

[46] SM Patrick, 'A Rocky Start to Russian WTO Membership' (*Council on Foreign Relations*, 22 August 2012) www.cfr.org/blog/rocky-start-russian-wto-membership.

[47] A Smolchenko, 'Medvedev Backs Away from Joint WTO Bid' *The Sydney Morning Herald* (11 July 2009) www.smh.com.au/world/medvedev-backs-away-from-joint-wto-bid-20090711-dg9y.html.

[48] 'Russia Becomes WTO Member after 18 Years of Talks' *BBC News* (16 December 2011) www.bbc.com/news/business-16212643.

invested heavily in a close personal relationship with Medvedev. Putin's return to the presidency in 2012 dramatically changed the tone of diplomatic negotiations. One researcher described how conversations after the return of Putin were 'louder, more strident' and this had made it far 'more difficult' to get things done on security issues.[49]

Overall, Medvedev's rhetoric and use of the guardian power of the office of the President had changed the tone of Russian politics. In foreign policy, this new tone had yielded real policy successes. Domestically, this tone had been less successful. But the increased space in the system raised expectations that Russia's managed presidential system was opening up. This helps to explain the series of unprecedented protests that took place in late 2011 to early 2012 in response to Putin's decision to once again return to the presidency. Putin's return suggested Russian politics was not slowly democratising after all.

V. POPULAR ACCOUNTABILITY

During this period, elections continued to be managed in a top-down way by the presidential administration. Dmitry Medvevev's election to the presidency in 2008 was a direct product of this kind of management. In fact, the Council of Europe described the election as 'not fair' and a 'more of a plebiscite' rather than an election.[50] The Council pointed in particular to the broad use of state media to support Medvedev.

President Medvedev did, however, attempt to open up this system by restoring elections for regional leaders after they had been abolished in 2004. In bringing back regional elections, however, the devil was in the details. Vladimir Putin wanted elections that would include a presidential filter that would allow only presidentially approved candidates to run for election. President Medvedev, in his final state of the union address, made no mention of this presidential filter and later made it known he was opposed.[51]

In his final months as President, Medvedev introduced a bill into the Duma that did not include a presidential filter. Putin repeated his call for a presidential filter to be introduced into the bill. He was joined by other

---

[49] Pacer (n 36) 165.
[50] L Harding, 'Russian Election Not Free or Fair, Say Observers' *The Guardian* (Moscow, 3 March 2008) www.theguardian.com/world/2008/mar/03/russia.eu.
[51] E Teague, 'Russia's Return to the Direct Elections of Governors: Re-Shaping the Power Vertical?' (2014) 3 *Region: Regional Studies of Russia, Eastern Europe, and Central Asia* 37, 41.

regional governors who warned of regional separatism. This ultimately led to a compromise, which included a 'municipal filter' requiring the support of a percentage of the deputies and heads of municipalities in their regions.[52]

But, despite this victory, it was clear that neither Putin nor Medvedev wanted real popular accountability. Regional elections were reintroduced as part of Russia's managed system of 'electoral authoritarianism'.[53] These regional elections could help to serve as 'laboratories' for electoral management strategies that could be used for the more important national and presidential elections.[54] These elections were also controllable by the President: The municipal filter itself gave significant power to United Russia to block problematic candidates.[55] Furthermore, the system continued to be underpinned by anti-politics, shown clearly when Medvedev announced that he would not be running again for President in 2012 and that the people should support Putin's candidacy.[56] This decision had been made behind closed doors, without popular accountability.

VI. DOMESTIC LEGAL ACCOUNTABILITY

Although this four-year period produced the most political pluralism in Russia since the 1990s, the Constitutional Court continued to be unable to place any real limitations on the power of the President. The Court's position in the Russian system only grew weaker. In May 2008, the Court moved from Moscow to St Petersburg. Although strongly opposed by the leader of the Constitutional Court Chairman Valery Zorkin, the Court had little choice but to move once Vladimir Putin signed a decree in late 2007 requiring the move to take place by 21 May.[57] The forced relocation meant the Court was no longer in the

---

[52] ibid 46.
[53] R Smyth and R Turovsky, 'Legitimising Victories: Electoral Authoritarian Control in Russia's Gubernatorial Elections' (2018) 70(2) *Europe-Asia Studies* 182, 182–84.
[54] ibid 183.
[55] C Ross, 'Regional Elections in Russia: Instruments of Authoritarian Legitimacy or Instability?' (2018) 4 *Palgrave Communications* 1.
[56] S Williams and A Smolchenko, 'Putin Set to Return as Russian President' *The Sydney Morning Herald* (Moscow, 25 September 2011) www.smh.com.au/world/putin-set-to-return-as-russian-president-20110924-1kr3f.html.
[57] 'V. Putin signed a decree on moving the Constitutional Court to St. Petersburg' (in Russian) *RBK* (24 December 2007) www.rbc.ru/spb_sz/24/12/2007/5592c0f09a79473b7f4ba261 (implementing a law requiring the Court to move).

heart of the Russian political system. More importantly, the move meant that the Court lost a large number of experienced members of their Secretariat, who had played a critical role in helping to manage its caseload.[58] This reduced the capacity of the Court to respond to the vast numbers of individual complaints that it received.

Second, the Russian President introduced a series of changes to the Law on the Constitutional Court that brought the Court further under the control of the President. In 2009, an amendment stripped the Court of the ability to elect its own Chairman. Instead, this power was given to the President and the upper house.[59] In 2010, an amendment allowed the upper house of the legislature (on the proposal of the President) to 'terminate the powers of the Chairman or Deputy Chairman' of the Court.[60]

Third, dissenters on the Court who had interpreted the Constitution in line with the balanced state tradition were now increasingly marginalised. In 2009, Justice Anatoly Kononov resigned from the Court seven years before the end of his term after being condemned by the majority of his colleagues for criticising Russia's rule of law.[61] In the same year, Justice Vladimir Yaroslavtsev gave an interview to the Spanish newspaper El Pais, describing Russia's legislative bodies as 'paralysed' and calling the Government 'authoritarian'.[62] He was promptly removed from a leadership role.

As its institutional position continued to erode, the majority of the Russian Constitutional Court continued to defer to presidential interests in high profile cases. A decision of the Constitutional Court involving the rights of a key Putin opponent – Vladimir Kara-Murza – is a good example.[63] Kara-Murza challenged a provision in a federal law barring dual citizens (or those who have a residence permit of a foreign state)

---

[58] A Dzmitryieva, 'Case Selection in the Russian Constitutional Court: The Role of Legal Assistants' (2017) 6(3) *Laws* 12.

[59] A Trochev and PH Solomon Jr, 'Authoritarian Constitutionalism in Putin's Russia: A Pragmatic Constitutional Court in a Dual State' (2018) 51 *Communist and Post-Communist Studies* 201, 204.

[60] Federal Constitutional Law N 7-FKZ of 3 November 2010, 'On Amendments to the Federal Constitutional Law "On the Constitutional Court of the Russian Federation"' (in Russian) (*Konsultant Plus*) www.consultant.ru/document/cons_doc_LAW_106383/.

[61] C Schimizzi, 'Russia Judges Resign after Criticizing Lack of Judicial Independence' *Jurist* (3 December 2009) www.jurist.org/news/2009/12/russia-judges-resign-after-criticizing/.

[62] The Telegraph (London), 'Judges forced out for criticising Kremlin' *Sydney Morning Herald* (4 December 2009).

[63] Decision of Russian Constitutional Court No 797-O-O 4 December 2007 'On the refusal to accept for consideration the complaint of citizen Vladimir Vladimirovich Kara-Murza about the violation of his constitutional rights' (in Russian) (*Konsultant Plus*) www.consultant.ru/document/cons_doc_LAW_73638/.

from running for election. He argued that this law unconstitutionally burdened his constitutional right to run for office and be elected in Article 32.2 of the Constitution.[64]

In rejecting his claim, the Court reasoned that the legislature limited this right in order to pursue the legitimate goal of protecting 'the foundations of the constitutional system of the Russian Federation'.[65] It accepted the argument that dual citizenship can lead to a conflict of interests in the execution of public powers in elected positions. In reaching this outcome, the Court did not address whether the restriction was *necessary* to achieving this goal by, for instance, considering whether there were any less restrictive means. This might include, for instance, requiring dual citizens who are elected to public office to take an oath of office or to renounce their foreign citizenship to hold public office.

The Court's refusal to consider the *necessity* of the restriction was typical of its overall approach. In fact, one Russian law professor has described the Court's approach to rights limitation cases as a form of 'reverse proportionality' which 'consists of restricting human rights in all cases where their implementation may encroach too seriously on the public interest'.[66] In this deferential approach, the Court considers rights claims by simply asking whether the restriction is rationally related to a legitimate government interest. This approach ignores the clear requirement in international human rights law that rights be limited in a way that is not just related to a public interest but that is proportionate and necessary to achieving this interest.

The Court did not just limit itself to advancing the justifications of the centralised state tradition in judicial decisions. The Chairman of the Court, Valery Zorkin, also made these justifications in a series of interviews and articles in Russia's official state newspaper, *Rossisskaya Gazeta*.[67] These extra-curial statements argued that the Constitution should be interpreted on the basis of Russia's need for centralised, presidential authority. For instance, in a 2008 interview, he explained that the Russian Constitution was a 'living document' that must be 'considered in its context'.[68] For Zorkin, this context includes Russia's 'fundamental

---

[64] ibid.
[65] ibid.
[66] S Belov, 'Values of the Russian Constitution in the Text and Practice of Constitutional Interpretation' (2019) 131(4) *Comparative Constitutional Law* 68, 79–81.
[67] All of these articles are available in Russian at 'Valery Zorkin' (*Rossisskaya Gazeta*) https://rg.ru/authors/Valerij-Zorkin.
[68] A Zakatnova, 'Zorkin: Our Constitution Turned Out to Be Very Good and Effective' (in Russian) *Rossisskaya Gazeta* (12 December 2018) www.rg.ru/2008/12/12/zorkin.html.

reality' which includes 'authoritarian elements' that can ensure Russia's stable 'transition' from 'a lawless past to a new democracy'.[69]

The authoritarian elements in Russia's historical legacy, he argued, were also necessary to avoid the collapse of the Russian state.[70] In fact, Zorkin repeatedly argued that Russia must rely on its own unique legal tradition of using law to ensure agreement and unity while avoiding chaos, disintegration, and weakness. These arguments drew heavily on emotional claims about the likelihood of state disintegration without centralised presidential power.[71] This kind of unified state, he argued, would then ensure Russia's democratic development and would lead to a strong state.[72]

Zorkin also made these kinds of arguments in response to current events. For instance, he wrote two articles that responded to the popular protests that swept Russia in the wake of Putin's decision to return to the presidency in late 2011. The first, published exactly 18 years after the adoption of the Russian Constitution, suggested that the protest movement threatened to throw Russia back into 'national catastrophe'.[73] Zorkin argued the protestors were on the threshold of repeating President Yeltsin's mistake from 1993: believing that the end (democracy) justifies the means (illegality). Yeltsin's decision to break with legality for democracy, he argued, was a 'deep tragedy for the country: bloody street clashes, the military destruction of Parliament ... and ... the deepest cut of all was to the respect for law, without which democracy is simply not possible'.[74] To avoid this outcome, he called on the opposition to abandon its disregard for legality and embark upon a legal reform strategy marked by 'heroic moderation'.[75]

In a second article a month later, Mr Zorkin significantly expanded this argument.[76] He condemned a 'creeping move' towards an international system where some foreign governments – and here we can clearly

[69] ibid.
[70] V Zorkin, 'The World Is Neither Getting Better Nor Worse' (in Russian) (*Rossisskaya Gazeta*, 22 August 2006) www.rg.ru/2006/08/22/zorjkin-statja.html.
[71] A Soboleva, 'Values Underpinning Court Decisions: Valery Dmitrievich Zorkin against Tamara Georgievna Morshchakova' (in Russian) (*Novaya iustitsiya*, 2009) 1 www.hse.ru/data/2010/06/08/1219671266/Soboleva_new_copy.pdf.
[72] For more on these articles and their relationship to foreign policy, see W Partlett, 'Valery Zorkin's State and Revolution' (*Brookings*, 13 February 2012) www.brookings.edu/articles/valery-zorkins-state-and-revolution/.
[73] V Zorkin, 'The Constitution of the Russian Federation is one of the main achievements of the post-Soviet era' (in Russian) *Rossiisskaya Gazeta* (12 December 2011) https://rg.ru/2011/12/11/zorkin-site.html.
[74] ibid.
[75] ibid.
[76] V Zorkin, 'The world system has entered a phase of profound transformations,' *Rossisskaya Gazeta* (in Russian) (24 January 2012) https://rg.ru/2012/01/25/zorkin-site.html.

infer the United States – believe that they are justified in undermining other countries' sovereignty and system of legality in the name of democratic revolution. Perhaps signalling his support for Putin's harder line, Zorkin cited the example of Libya. The destruction of Libya's 'extremely defective' system of legality by the international community, he argued, had led to an even worse outcome, a 'chaotic intertribal warfare' and 'the total destruction of the basis for the legal regulation of life'.[77] Applying these lessons to Russia's domestic situation, Zorkin argued that the opposition has no extra-legal 'right to revolution'.[78] He argued instead that the opposition should pursue its goals through the 'mechanisms and procedures for the democratic resolution of conflicts'.[79]

The centralised state tradition also further cemented itself in Russian constitutional discourse by appearing in the constitutional law textbooks. One of the most influential was a textbook authored by Marat Baglai, the second Chairman of the Russian Constitutional Court, and which has been published more than 13 times and is frequently used in Russian law classes.[80] This book describes the 1993 Russian Constitution through the lens of the centralised state tradition.

The book explains that the Constitution provides a solution to the dangers of dual power by ensuring unity and harmony.[81] The basis of this unity, it explains, can be found in popular sovereignty. Citing Article 3, it describes how people are a unified and undivided whole.[82] The separation of powers, it argues, must be understood through the idea of the 'preservation of the constitutional principle of unified state power'.[83] The key institution in maintaining this unity, it argues, is the Russian President. The book describes the vast guardian authority of the Russian President by equating it with the authority of a hereditary monarch. It states that the President is responsible for 'constitutional order, the stability and continuity of the mechanism of power, and representing the state in international affairs'.[84] The President is the symbol of the state and official representative of the people. The President 'cements' state power by solving crises and conflicts between the organs of state power.[85]

---

[77] ibid.
[78] ibid.
[79] ibid.
[80] Marat Baglai, *Constitutional Law of the Russian Federation: A Textbook for Universities* (in Russian) 13th edn (Moscow, Norma, 2018).
[81] ibid 122.
[82] ibid.
[83] ibid 151.
[84] ibid 473.
[85] ibid.

This guardian authority, the book explains, naturally affords the President a number of 'sole powers' that are not executive, legislative or judicial. These discretionary or 'prerogative' powers are so great, it holds, that we see the President in 'unstable' contexts 'develop into dictatorship or authoritarianism'.[86] In those contexts, the President becomes a kind of 'uncrowned monarch'.[87] Relying on the anti-political rationale of the constitutional dark arts, he argues that 'Strong presidential power does not undermine the democratic character of a law-based state- on the contrary, in certain circumstances it is the only possible instrument for protecting constitutional order'.[88] During Russia's 'transitional stage', the book argues, this reflects the necessary presence of 'authoritarian elements' in the Russian Constitution.[89]

The book also clearly describes the management powers of the President, describing control over the executive-branch government to be an 'undoubted priority' of presidential power. It stresses how the President is completely free to organise the government and exercises vast power over the implementation of law.[90] This includes vast power over the heads of the regional subjects as well as to appoint federal judges.[91] Finally, the President has vast power to form powerful presidential institutions such as the State Council and the Security Council.

Finally, the book explains that unity is critical for understanding Russian federalism. 'Any attempts by a subject of the Russian Federation to claim sovereign status contradicts the Constitution and common sense'.[92] It argues that federalism must yield to the fundamental unity of the state, which is 'one of the foundations of Russian constitutional structure'.[93] The centralised state tradition therefore was growing in influence not just in Russian Constitutional Court decisions but also in Russian constitutional discourse.

VII. INTERNATIONAL LEGAL ACCOUNTABILITY

The opening of the Russian constitutional system to the international legal system continued to be unable to protect individual rights

---
[86] ibid 475, 480–81, 490.
[87] ibid 475.
[88] ibid.
[89] ibid 20.
[90] ibid 498.
[91] ibid 500.
[92] ibid 146–47.
[93] ibid 147.

when they threatened the interests of the President. Inside Russia, the Constitutional Court often cited international law but in a selective and incomplete way that favoured state interests. The case above involving Vladimir Kara-Murza is a good example.[94] In that case, the Court cited international human rights law for the proposition that individual rights are not absolute and therefore can be limited.[95] It pointed to the fact that key international human rights law allow for reasonable restrictions on the right and opportunity of every citizen to be elected in periodic elections. In so doing, however, it failed to apply the full proportionality test taken from international human rights law. Most importantly, the Court did not examine whether the Russia law was *proportionate* and therefore necessary to a legitimate state purpose.[96] It instead applied a much more deferential test that assumed the restriction was related to the preservation of Russian sovereignty.

The opening of the Russian legal system to international law also helped to further strengthen the centralised state discourse in Russia. It did so by triggering a national backlash that allowed Russian leaders to argue that the international human rights tribunals were improperly interfering in Russian sovereignty. A key moment was when the European Court of Human Rights (ECtHR) overturned a Russian Constitutional Court decision. The case involved Konstantin Markin, a Russian military serviceman who was denied parental leave because parental leave was available only to female military personnel.[97] He brought a claim to the Russian Constitutional Court alleging that he had been discriminated against on grounds of sex.

After losing his claim in the Russian Constitutional Court, Markin was successful in 2010 (and in a follow up decision by the Grand Chamber in 2012) in the ECtHR. The ECtHR held that there had been a violation of Article 14 which prohibits discrimination on the basis of numerous

---

[94] Decision of the Russian Constitutional Court (n 63).
[95] *Clerfayt v Belgium*, European Court of Human Rights (2 March 1987) https://hudoc.echr.coe.int/eng#{%22itemid%22:[%22001-57536%22]}.
[96] ibid para 52.
[97] Decision of the Russian Constitutional Court No 187-O-O of 15 January 2009 'On the refusal to accept for consideration complaints from citizen Konstantin Aleksandrovich Markin regarding violation of his constitutional rights by the provisions of Articles 13 and 15 of the Federal Law "On State Benefits for Citizens with Children", Article 10 and 11 of the Federal Law "On the Status of Military Personnel", Article 32 of the Regulations on the Procedure for Military Service and paragraphs 35 and 44 of the Regulations on the Assignment and Payment of State Benefits to Citizens with Children' (in Russian) (*Konsultant Plus*) www.consultant.ru/document/cons_doc_LAW_87365/.

grounds, including sex.⁹⁸ In reaching its decision, the ECtHR came into open conflict with the Russian Constitutional Court by rejecting the Russian Constitutional Court's argument that the decision to discriminate based on gender was objective and reasonably justified.

There was a furious backlash to this case in Russia. Constitutional Court Chairman Valery Zorkin discussed the limits to complying with the ECtHR. He also floated the idea of introducing legal mechanisms to protect national sovereignty by permitting national authorities not to execute ECtHR judgments if they would be contrary to the Russian Court's judgments.⁹⁹ President Medvedev immediately drew on the language of sovereignty, stating that 'we will never surrender that part of our sovereignty, which would allow any international court or any foreign court to render a decision, changing our national legislation'.¹⁰⁰ This sovereigntist backlash further reinforced the centralised state tradition. It also further highlights the deep legitimacy problems in using international human rights law to limit the power of elected domestic institutions.

VIII. CONCLUSION

This chapter complicates the common understanding of the four-year Medvedev presidency. During this period, the Russian President was more constrained than it ever had been. With careful use of his accumulated non-legal authority, Putin had successfully secured his position. But, despite Putin's careful counter-measures, the constitutional powers of the presidency mattered and allowed President Medvedev to execute policy positions that Putin clearly did not agree with. This impact was most clear in foreign policy. Moreover, the tone that Medvedev had set as President had a significant impact on the development of the political system.

There was evidence that Medvedev would have preferred to remain President and further consolidate his position. According to Alexei Kudrin, Medvedev had 'wanted to be nominated again. He [Medvedev]

---

⁹⁸ *Konstantin Markin v Russia* App no 30078/06 (ECtHR, 22 March 2012).
⁹⁹ A Ferris-Rotman, 'Russia Could Shun European Rights Court – Top Judge' *Reuters* (Moscow, 23 November 2010) www.reuters.com/article/us-russia-court-rights/russia-could-shun-european-rights-court-top-judge-idUSTRE6AL5IW20101122/.
¹⁰⁰ Quoted from WE Pomeranz, 'Uneasy Partners: Russia and the European Court of Human Rights' (2012) 19(3) *Human Rights Brief* 17, 19.

underlined it, as a matter of fact, at every meeting'.[101] In the end, however, Putin's deliberate attempts to maintain his non-legal, charismatic authority had allowed him to return. Medvedev hinted at the importance of this charismatic, personal authority when he explained that 'Prime Minister Putin is now unquestionably the most authoritative politician in our country and … his rating is somewhat higher'.[102] He went on to say that 'The choice is made by the people, and these are not empty words – that's absolutely the way it is'.[103]

Medvedev had been forced to step aside because did not have the time to secure his own power. Over time, however, the vast rational legal authority of the President would have allowed even a leader like Medvedev the ability to build a team of supporters around him and entrench his power. As one commentator described it,

> Putin simply had to return to the presidency as the formal competences of the post of the prime minister were too weak to sustain de facto leadership while Medvedev occupied the presidency as de jure leader backed by the institutionalised Presidential Administration.[104]

The following chapter will consider the impacts on the Russian political system of Putin's return to the presidency in 2012.

---

[101] Leonid Parfenov, Interview with Alexey Kudrin, Former Russian Finance Minister (*Kommersant*, 22 January 2012) www.kommersant.ru/doc/1856438.
[102] 'Vladimir Putin Is More Popular Than Me, Says Medvedev' *BBC News* (30 September 2011) www.bbc.com/news/world-europe-15124345.
[103] ibid.
[104] Burkhardt (n 13) 490.

7

The Imperial President (2012–the Present)

IN JANUARY 2020, President Vladimir Putin unexpectedly announced a process of constitutional reform. He described those changes as improving the quality of 'state governance' and 'strengthening' Russian democracy.[1] The Chairman of the State Duma later said that the amendments gave 'concrete meaning to the norm of the social state in Russia'.[2] Six months later, during the final referendum vote on the amendments, President Putin reiterated that the changes will 'strengthen our nationhood and create conditions for the progressive development of our country for decades to come'.[3] Seven months later, the process was over and Russia formally made the most significant changes to its Constitution since its adoption in 1993.

Despite making almost 200 changes to the Constitution, these changes were not a fundamental break with the past.[4] Instead, Putin and his team introduced these amendments to cement the creeping, sub-constitutional centralisation of power in the Office of the President that had taken place since 2000. They then described this increasingly powerful imperial President as a way to improve Russian democracy and rights protection. In particular, the changes were justified as a way to improve the quality of Russian *social* rights protection, a tacit acknowledgment

---

[1] V Putin, 'Presidential Address to the Federal Assembly' (*President of Russia*, 15 January 2020) http://en.kremlin.ru/events/president/news/62582; 'Putin Remains Coy on Future Political Plans' *VOA News* (4 February 2020) www.voanews.com/a/europe_putin-remains-coy-future-political-plans/6183678.html.

[2] 'Viacheslav Volodin: Russia's Strength is Not Oil and Gas, But Vladimir Putin' (*The State Duma*, 12 March 2020) www.duma.gov.ru/en/news/48036/.

[3] M Rodionov, 'Constitutional Changes Are the "Right Thing" for Russia: Putin' *Reuters* (Moscow, 6 July 2020) www.reuters.com/article/us-russia-putin-constitution/constitutional-changes-are-the-right-thing-for-russia-putin-idUSKBN2460OD..

[4] Matthew Luxmoore, 'The Putin Constitution: How Will It Change Russia' *RFE/RL* (Moscow, 1 July 2020) www.rferl.org/a/the-putin-constitution-how-will-it-change-russia/30699899.html.

of the ongoing problems of the provision of social services in Russia. In addition, this imperial President was also described as necessary for protecting Russia's unique, imperial identity against external threats.

Domestically, Vladimir Putin used the powers of the imperial President to close off any space even for managed politics, pushing through laws associating political opposition with hostile foreign influence. Internationally, he used this authority to enter into a far more adversarial relationship with the West, climaxing in the full-scale invasion of Ukraine. This imperial presidency has not solved any of the broader structural problems that underpin Russian governance; if anything, it has worsened these problems. Moreover, Putin has used this power to turn elections and courts into institutions that do little more than legitimise presidential power. Finally, international legal accountability has been eliminated as Russia left the Council of Europe and shut down key human rights organisations such as Memorial.

I. THE CLOSING OF RUSSIAN POLITICS

Putin's return to the presidency in 2012 signalled a clear end to the constrained presidency. Once again, personal, non-legal authority was combined with the rational-legal authority of the Presidency. Putin's return also brought an end to Russia's system of managed democracy. The first step in this process was a set of new laws, passed to systemically dismantle the opposition movement that had taken to the streets in 2011 in reaction to Putin's decision to return to the presidency. Putin used the lawmaking authority of the presidency in Article 84 to prosecute and intimidate key protestors much as he had with the regional governors and business elite in his first two terms.[5] But, this time, law was also used to associate any opposition with foreign attempts to undermine Russian constitutional sovereignty.

An early example of this strategy was a law requiring independent organisations and influential members of the political opposition to register as 'foreign agents'.[6] The amendment claimed to be about 'organizing proper public control over the work of non-profit organizations that

---

[5] 'Russia's Growing Number of Political Prisoners' *Meduza* (4 March 2015).
[6] Federal Law No 121-FZ of 20 July 2012, 'On Amendments to Legislative Acts of the Russian Federation regarding the Regulation of the Activities of Non-Profit Organisations Performing the Functions of a Foreign Agent' (in Russian) (*Konsultant Plus*) www.consultant.ru/document/cons_doc_LAW_132900/.

carry out political activities on the territory of the Russian Federation and are financed from foreign sources'.[7] In reality, the law effectively targeted key organisations in Russian civil society, many of which had international links and financing. This law labelled these organisations and their activities as inherently suspect, posing a danger to Russian unity and sovereignty. To that end, the new law imposed onerous reporting requirements on NGOs that sought to hold the state (and President) to account, 'tarnishing their reputation and seriously hampering their activities'.[8]

Three years later, the Russian legislature adopted another law allowing the prosecutor-general (without a court judgment) to declare foreign and international organisations that 'threaten the constitutional order of the Russian Federation, its defence capabilities or state security' as 'undesirable'.[9] This law was another step in associating any form of opposition with the external, hostile forces. It also shows the extent to which Russia's constitutional order was no longer a document opening Russia to international law but a shield against threats from the outside.

This closing of the system culminated in 2020 when the Russian presidential administration moved aggressively to destroy Russia's leading opposition movement headed by Alexei Navalny. This was a significant departure from the managed politics of the previous decades. During these years, critical voices in the political opposition were given room to participate in politics but the playing field was tilted heavily in favour of the Kremlin. In this system, opposition activists were generally given room to criticise the government (at least on the internet). Legal prosecution was selective and limited as a way to ensure elite loyalty.[10] Navalny, a lawyer turned blogger and then politician, had built his political movement in this environment. This included not just his well-publicised and slickly produced exposes of corruption that generated millions of views on YouTube. It also included legal aid work and building a large network of offices and supporters around the country.

In 2020, however, this all changed. The office of the President moved decisively against Navalny and his supporters. Navalny himself was poisoned in what was likely an assassination attempt orchestrated

---

[7] Quoted from Venice Commission 'Opinion on Federal Law N 121-FZ on Non-Commercial Organisations ("Law on Foreign Agents")' (Council of Europe 27 June 2014) 13.
[8] ibid 27.
[9] Federal Law No 129-FZ of 23 May 2015, 'On Amendments to Certain Legislative Acts of the Russian Federation' (in Russian) (*Konsultant Plus*) www.consultant.ru/document/cons_doc_LAW_179979/.
[10] W Partlett, 'Putin's Artful Jurisprudence' (2013) 123 *The National Interest* 35.

by the office of the Russian President. Although the Russian state has denied all involvement, the European Union has concluded that this assassination was impossible without the participation of the Russian President. In particular, they argued that a 'dedicated task force' within the Presidential Administration focused specifically on neutralising Navalny's influence must have been involved.[11] Moreover, other investigating agencies have found strong evidence suggesting that the Federal Security Service (FSB) was directly involved in the poisoning.[12] Vladimir Putin had placed the FSB under the direct control of the President in a 2000 presidential decree.[13]

After recovering and returning to Russia, Navalny was immediately arrested and accused of a series of crimes. Putin openly used his rational-legal authority to issue a decree promoting the judge in one of Navalny's cases to a higher position.[14] Meanwhile, most of Navalny's team faced prosecution and many fled the country. A Russian court declared his network of organisations and regional headquarters to be 'extremist', closing them down and barring thousands of employees and supports from running for office for three years. Finally, after Navalny's suspicious death in prison in February 2024, Putin issued another decree promoting a key official in the Russian prisons service.[15] This systematic dismantling of the Navalny movement sent a clear message: real opposition would no longer be tolerated.

II. CONFRONTATION WITH THE WEST

The closing of the Russian political system and the association of opposition with foreign interference also led to an increasingly adversarial relationship with the outside world and particularly the West.

---

[11] 'Accessible only to State authorities' *Meduza* (16 October 2020) https://amp.meduza.io/en/feature/2020/10/15/accessible-only-to-state-authorities.

[12] Bellingcat Investigation Team, 'FSB Team of Chemical Weapon Experts Implicated in Alexey Navalny Novichok Poisoning' (*Bellingcat*, 14 December 2020) www.bellingcat.com/news/uk-and-europe/2020/12/14/fsb-team-of-chemical-weapon-experts-implicated-in-alexey-navalny-novichok-poisoning/.

[13] Presidential Decree No 867 of 17 May 2000 'On the Structure of Federal Executive Bodies' (in Russian) (*Konsultant Plus*) www.consultant.ru/document/cons_doc_LAW_27233/.

[14] RI Novosti, 'The Judge in Navalny's New Case has been Promoted' (*RI Novosti*, 18 March 2022) https://ria.ru/20220318/sudya-1778915432.html.

[15] RFE/RL, Putin Promotes Deputy Chief of Russia's Prisons Days After Navalny's Death *RFE/RL* (20 February 2024) www.rferl.org/a/putin-promotes-deputy-chief-russia-prisons-navalny-death/32827360.html.

142 The Imperial President (2012–the Present)

This direction was clear even before Putin returned to the Presidency. In a February 2012 article, Putin criticised the United States for its desire for 'absolute invulnerability'.[16] He also signalled that Medvedev's cooperative approach to Libya was a mistake: 'No one should be allowed to implement a "Libyan scenario" in Syria'.[17] He continued, showing his distrust for the West by highlighting that 'we are against passing resolutions at the UN Security Council which could be taken as a signal for military intervention in the processes inside Syria'.[18] Furthermore, he argued that the mass protests in the streets in 2011 and 2012 were the product of United States interference.

This rhetoric reflected a neo-imperial understanding of the former Soviet republics on Russia's borders. After the Maidan revolution in Kiev, Putin ordered the Russian military to annex sovereign Ukrainian territory (Crimea) in 2014. The formal annexation of another country's sovereign territory posed a fundamental challenge to a key norm in the international legal system that prohibits annexation of sovereign land. It triggered a reaction in the West, including economic sanctions on Russia and a decision to suspend Russia from its involvement in key international institutions such as the G7 (which had previously been expanded to the G8 to include Russia).

This annexation signalled a clear break with Russia's past policy. For many years, Russia had sought to use economic and political tools to exert its influence over its neighbours like Ukraine. In fact, as we saw in the previous chapter, President Medvedev had worked hard to build cooperative relations with Europe and the United States. Putin's more confrontational approach placed the 'imperial President' as defender of Russian sovereignty. The media described this quick and decisive foreign policy victory as evidence of Putin's strong leadership. This strategy was successful as it led to skyrocketing popularity rankings for Putin.

III. 2020 CONSTITUTIONAL REFORMS

In early 2020, President Putin introduced a stage-managed constitutional reform to cement these changes by projecting the image of a strengthened Russian constitutional system built around an 'imperial

---

[16] V Putin, 'Rossiia i meniaiushchiisia mir' (in Russian) (*Moskovskie Novosti*, 27 February 2012) www.mn.ru/politics/78738.
[17] ibid.
[18] ibid.

President' who could strengthen the Russia social state and protect its identity against both internal and external enemies. President Putin announced this major constitutional reform in his annual speech to the legislature on 15 January 2020. Following this, President Putin used his institution-making power to direct a presidentially appointed Working Group to draft amendments that would be introduced to the Russian legislature.[19]

The amendments made hundreds of changes to the Constitution. None made any serious functional changes to the overall constitutional system. For instance, they inserted provisions that transformed the Constitution into a shield *against* decisions made by international tribunals.[20] This legal process was not new. It had existed since 2015 when an amendment to the law on the Constitutional Court of Russia gave the Constitutional Court the power to declare 'impossible to implement' judgements of international bodies for being inconsistent with the Constitution of the Russian Federation.[21] The amendments constitutionally entrenched this process and therefore ensured that the Constitution itself was viewed as a shield against hostile outside attempts to undermine Russian sovereignty.

The amendments also made the Russian Constitution the key document securing a neo-imperial version of Russian identity.[22] New constitutional provisions – awkwardly inserted into a chapter of the Constitution describing Russia's Federal Structure – reinforced growing imperial nostalgia in official Russian discourse. They therefore declare Russia to be the 'successor state' to the Soviet Union, protector of historical truth about the defenders of the Fatherland, and responsible for ensuring patriotism in children's education.[23] Another provision defines marriage as a union between a man and a woman.[24] Finally, additional

---

[19] Presidential Decree No 5-rp 15 of January 2020 'On the Working Group on the Preparation of Proposals for Amendments to the Constitution of the Russian Federation' (in Russian) (*Garant*) https://base.garant.ru/73409717/.
[20] Art 79 Constitution of the Russian Federation (*Council of Europe*) https://rm.coe.int/constitution-of-the-russian-federation-en/1680a1a237.
[21] Federal Constitutional Law N 7-FKZ of December 14, 2015 'On Amendments to the Federal Constitutional Law "On the Constitutional Court of the Russian Federation"' (in Russian) (*Konsultant Plus*) www.consultant.ru/document/cons_doc_LAW_190427/.
[22] This use of the Constitution in Russian exceptionalism has echoes of American exceptionalism where the Constitution emerges as a symbol of sovereign power that stand against malign international influence. See, eg S Gardbaum, 'The Myth and the Reality of American Constitutional Exceptionalism' (2008) 107 *Michigan Law Review* 391.
[23] Russian Constitution (n 20) Art 67^1.
[24] ibid Art $72(g^1)$.

provisions declare Russians to be the 'state-forming' people and emphasise the need for Russia to provide support to its 'compatriots' overseas in the protection of Russian cultural identity.[25]

A centralised state was described as necessary for preserving this unique identity. Explaining why the President should continue to dominate the Russian constitutional system, Vladimir Putin argued that 'In our country, if any institution appears over the President, this will mean nothing more than dual power. This would be an absolutely disastrous situation for a country like Russia'.[26] The President therefore remained the sovereign institution that would guarantee the preservation of Russia's imperial sovereignty and strength.

To that end, key amendments increased the general guardian powers of the presidency, adding an additional mediator role in supporting 'civil peace and conciliation in the country'.[27] Moreover, the President was given the authority to *remove* judges from office (including Constitutional Court judges) by introducing a proposal to the upper house.[28] The President also has enhanced power to appoint regional prosecutors.[29] Putin justified this change on the basis of legal unity, arguing that the current system allowed prosecutors to form 'informal, obligations towards local authorities' and therefore created the 'risk of losing objectivity and impartiality'.[30]

Finally, the reforms give the President increased presidential power over the legislature. This includes the authority to appoint 30 members of the upper house of Parliament (Federation Council) of which seven can be lifetime appointments.[31] In addition, in the (unlikely) event that the legislature overrides the veto of the President (unlikely given presidential control over the upper house of the legislature), the amendments provide the President with the authority to ask the Constitutional Court to review this law for constitutionality.[32] Given the deference the Constitutional Court has paid to the President since 1995, this power will operate as a kind of 'super-veto'.

The amendments also alter the management powers of the President. Some of the amendments appear to weaken the President's

---

[25] ibid Arts 68–69.
[26] 'Putin: Dual Power is Disastrous for the Country' *Kommersant* (22 January 2020) www.kommersant.ru/doc/4227277.
[27] Russian Constitution (n 20) Art 80.2.
[28] ibid Art 83(f³).
[29] ibid Art 83(f¹).
[30] Putin, 'Presidential Address' (n 1).
[31] Russian Constitution (n 20) Art 95.2.
[32] ibid Art 107.3.

management powers over the executive-branch government by determining the makeup of the government. For instance, an amendment now *requires* the President to appoint certain deputy ministers that have been appointed by the Prime Minister and confirmed by the lower house of the legislature (Duma).[33] But a closer analysis shows that the President actually has more management power. The amendments exempt from this process of Prime Ministerial appointment the most important executive-branch ministers such as the Minister of Justice, Foreign Affairs, Defence, Internal Affairs and Emergency Situations. These ministers are now to be appointed by the President after 'consultation' with the upper house of the Russian legislature (which is already controlled by the President).[34] In addition, other textual changes emphasise the President's control over the executive-branch government, most notably stating the 'personal responsibility' of the Prime Minister to the President and the President's general authority 'to exercise general power over the government'.[35] These constitutional powers therefore constitutionalise the growing presidential domination over the executive-branch government and the bureaucracy.

Finally, the amendments ensure more centralised power in the Presidency in the short term by permitting Vladimir Putin to run for two more terms. They do so by including a new provision that reset the number of terms to zero for any current or former Russian President.[36] This zeroing provision therefore allows Putin to combine his vast non-legal, personal authority with the rational-legal authority of the President until 2036.

In addition to placing more authority in the President, the reforms also formally expand federal dominance in a number of areas, including education, culture and health.[37] Moreover, the amendments now include local government in an overall system of 'public power' (*publichnaya vlast*). This change provides an additional constitutional basis for presidential control of local government as the President is now charged with

---

[33] ibid Art 112.2 and 112.3.

[34] ibid Art 83(e¹).

[35] ibid Art 113 and Art 83(b) (respectively). It is important to note that the English translation provided to the Council of Europe (by the Russian Constitutional Court) here is not complete and fails to fully translate the second sentence Art 113. It should read: 'The Chairman of the Government of the Russian Federation is personally responsible to the President of the Russian Federation for the implementation of the powers assigned to the Government of the Russian Federation.'

[36] ibid Art 81.3¹.

[37] See, eg ibid Art 71(g), (m), (t).

guaranteeing the harmonised functioning of all 'organs in the unified system of public power'.[38] Finally, a new provision no longer allows local government to *'establish'* local taxes and levies but only to *'introduce'* them, signifying further fiscal centralisation.[39]

Taken together, these amendments did not make significant functional changes to the way that the Russian system operated in practice. Why amend the Constitution? The answer is that the amendment process was theatrical, a process intended to justify Russia's increasingly centralised system as necessary for protecting Russia's imperial identity and power in the world.[40] These constitutional changes were therefore an extended normative argument for why the Russian President (and Vladimir Putin) should have additional rational-legal authority.

To ensure that this normative message was internalised broadly amongst the Russian population, the amendments were presented to the Russian people in a national plebiscite. This popular vote was legally unnecessary. Because the 2020 amendments did not alter Chapters 1, 2 or 9 of the Constitution, Russia's amendments only need to be ratified by Russia's existing legislative institutions. This legislative process would, however, have been easily ignored by the Russian people. In fact, from the beginning, the whole amendment process had been top-down. There was little public participation in the drafting of the constitutional amendments. Instead, the amendments were the product of the presidential administration and a presidentially appointed Working Group.[41]

The stage-managed nature of these theatrical amendments was clear from the legal rules governing the vote. The vote was called an 'all-Russian plebiscite' (*vserossiskoe golosovanie*) and not a 'referendum' (*vsenaradnoe golosovanie*). This was a deliberate decision to avoid the more stringent rules surrounding formal referendums contained in federal law. The referendum law includes strict requirements on campaigning as well as 50 per cent of the overall population to participate for an affirmative answer.[42] The turnout requirement itself is important as it tends to judge general enthusiasm for the reforms as well as the simple mathematic outcome.

---

[38] ibid Art 80.2.
[39] ibid Art 132.1.
[40] W Partlett, 'Russia's 2020 Constitutional Amendments: A Comparative Analysis' (2021) 23 *Cambridge Yearbook of European Legal Studies* 311.
[41] Presidential Decree (n 19).
[42] Federal Law No 5-FKZ of 28 June 2004 'About Referendums in the Russian Federation' (*Konsultant Plus*) www.consultant.ru/document/cons_doc_LAW_48221/.

The 'all-Russian plebiscite', by contrast, could proceed with no turnout requirement and no requirement for a 'yes' and a 'no' campaign. Further, the procedures for the 'plebiscite' were described in Article 2 of the law that included the constitutional amendments.[43] This special regime gave unilateral control over the plebiscite to the Central Election Commission (CEC).[44] The CEC had the power to determine the financing rules for the vote as well as deciding the accreditation of media representatives for the vote.[45] The decree also mandated that all state media outlets provide a certain amount of coverage of the vote per week.[46]

Finally, the vote was repeatedly described by Putin and his team as a demonstration of popular support for the President and the Russian constitutional system overall. For instance, President Putin's formal request to the Russian Constitutional Court to review the constitutionality of the amendments argued that the special plebiscite reflected the principle of 'popular sovereignty' in Article 3 of the Russian Constitution.[47] Further, Putin addressed the nation twice during the voting. One speech drew heavily on the deceptive logic of the constitutional dark arts by stressing that a yes vote was a 'vote for the country where we want to live, with cutting-edge education and healthcare, a reliable system of social protection and an effective government accountable to the people'.[48] Finally, the campaign strongly focused on the popular parts of the amendments. This included stressing provisions protecting historical truth about World War II and protecting national sovereignty.[49] It also included a strong campaign to highlight the social guarantees in

---

[43] Federal Law N 1-FKZ of March 14, 2020 "On improving the regulation of certain issues of the organization and functioning of public power" (in Russian) (*Konsultant Plus*) www.consultant.ru/document/cons_doc_LAW_346019/.

[44] ibid Arts 2.11–16.

[45] ibid Art 2.15.

[46] ibid Art 2.20.

[47] Presidential Request of 14 March 2020 'On the compliance with Chapters 1, 2 and 9 of the Constitution of the Russian Federation of the provisions of the Law of the Russian Federation on an amendment to the Constitution of the Russian Federation "On improving the regulation of certain issues of the organization and functioning of public power" and on the compliance of the Constitution of the Russian Federation, the procedure for the entry into force of Article 1 of the said Law' (in Russian) (*President of Russia*) http://kremlin.ru/events/president/news/62989.

[48] V Putin, 'Address to the Nation' (*President of Russia*, 30 June 2020) http://en.kremlin.ru/events/president/transcripts/statements/63584.

[49] A Roth, 'It Looks Like a Gameshow: Russia's Pseudo-Vote on Putin's Term Limits' *The Guardian* (Moscow, 26 June 2020) www.theguardian.com/world/2020/jun/26/it-looks-like-a-gameshow-russias-pseudo-vote-on-putins-term-limits.

the Constitution, including provisions ensuring a high minimum wage and adequate pensions.[50]

Moreover, official reaction to the positive results of the vote were later described as a vote of public support for a newly invigorated Russian constitutional system. In one of his first public speeches after the yes vote, President Putin addressed his appointed working group.[51] He noted the positive result of the vote and asked them to work hard on implementing the important changes that would stem from these changes. The 2020 constitutional reform was therefore an attempt to renew the authoritarian normativity of the Russian Constitution. By involving the people in these constitutional changes, the process aimed to reinforce the belief that more powers for the President would help improve Russian governance and secure its sovereignty.[52] The constitutional dark arts and its misleading logic remained a central part of Russian authoritarianism.

IV. FULL-SCALE INVASION OF UKRAINE

The broad rational-legal power of the imperial President contributed to a decision that would fundamentally reshape Russia and the world: The full-scale invasion of Ukraine on 24 February 2022. This decision to invade – described as a 'special military operation' – dramatically showed how opaque and closed the imperial presidency had become. In fact, it led to a situation where the Russian Prime Minister was only informed of the invasion the day before it commenced and therefore had less than a day to plan for the consequences of the invasion.

President Putin described his decision to invade in the anti-politics of the constitutional dark arts. This decision did not need broader societal debate, he argued, because it was an inescapable conclusion from the historical 'fact' that Russia and Ukraine are one people.[53] Putin based

---

[50] Matthew Luxmoore, 'Why So Few Protests Against Putin's Constitutional Shake-Up?' *RFE/RL* (28 January 2020) www.rferl.org/a/why-so-few-protests-against-putin-s-constitutional-shake-up-/30402490.html.

[51] V Putin, 'Meeting with the Working Group on Drafting Proposals for Amendments to the Constitution' (*President of Russia*, 3 July 2020) http://en.kremlin.ru/events/president/transcripts/statements/63599.

[52] Y Gorokhovskaia, 'Why Putin Needs a "Nationwide Vote"' (*Institute of Modern Russia*, 16 June 2020) https://imrussia.org/en/analysis/3123-why-putin-needs-a-.

[53] W Partlett, 'Putin's Past: The Return of Ideological History and the Strongman' (*American Historical Association, Perspectives on History*, 7 December 2022) www.historians.org/research-and-publications/perspectives-on-history/january-2023/putins-past-the-return-of-ideological-history-and-the-strongman.

this on an imperial reading of history in which any separate Ukrainian identity from Russia must be an 'unnatural' project of external manipulation that poses an existential threat to Russia's civilisational identity. The decision to invade and annex Ukraine, he argued, was not a political decision driven by contestable political values or beliefs. It was instead an objective decision that was unavoidable. In Putin's understanding of politics as the search for a single truth, anyone who opposes the invasion is wrong or is a traitor.

With this understanding of the war, the legal powers of the President have also been used to outlaw any form of opposition. Opposition to the regime or its decision to invade is therefore not political criticism but a denial of truth. This has fostered a new set of laws that broadly criminalise on any opposition to the war. For instance, this includes an amendment to the Criminal Code imposing a jail term of up to 15 years for spreading intentionally 'fake' news about the military, stepping up the information war over the conflict in Ukraine.[54] In addition, the Russian legislature has passed new laws that impose punishment for discrediting the armed forces of Russia. These administrative cases have been frequently used to further silence any opposition to the war.[55]

President Putin also made wide use of his decree powers to manage Russia's response to the escalating economic sanctions placed on the Russia after the full-scale invasion of Ukraine. These decrees have helped to sanction-proof the Russian economy. For instance, decrees have been directed at protecting Russian businesses from the impact of the sanctions.[56] A presidential decree has also established temporary control over certain assets owned by persons from 'unfriendly countries'.[57] These decrees also shape how courts will respond to the commercial claims deriving from the sanctions and their consequences.

---

[54] 'Russia fights back in information war with jail warning' *Reuters* (5 March 2022) www.reuters.com/world/europe/russia-introduce-jail-terms-spreading-fake-information-about-army-2022-03-04/.
[55] L McCarthy, D Rice and A Lokhmutov, 'Four Months of "Discrediting the Military": Repressive Law in Wartime Russia' (2023) 31 *Demokratizatsiya: The Journal of Post-Soviet Democratization* 125.
[56] Presidential Decree No 95 of 5 March 2022 'On the temporary procedure for fulfilling obligations to certain foreign creditors'(in Russian) (*Konsultant Plus*) www.consultant.ru/document/cons_doc_LAW_410994/.
[57] Presidential Decree No 302 of April 25, 2023 'On the temporary management of certain property' (in Russian) (*Garant*) www.garant.ru/products/ipo/prime/doc/406691329/.

V. EFFECTIVENESS

As the imperial President exploited its vast rational-legal authority to close off opposition and break with the West, it was also seeking to promote a more positive image of reform. These changes sought to project the image of a modern Russian social state that could improve the lives of everyday Russians. A key part of this effort was the provision of social guarantees. The 2020 constitutional reforms, for instance, included much-publicised social promises such as a guarantee that the minimum wage would not fall below the subsistence minimum.[58]

The imperial President also continued to use its decree powers to this end. Most notably, in 2012, 2018 and 2024, Putin issued decrees signalling his goals for these new presidential terms. These decrees covered a wide range of social goals, including increasing the birth rate, providing affordable housing, ensuring better quality education and science, health care, social policy and long-term economic policy. A key initiative in President Putin's 2018 and 2024 decrees has been additional economic support to families in order to overcome Russia's demographic crisis.[59] Driving this is broad and robust majoritarian support for a generous social welfare state, particularly after the economic deprivations of the immediate post-Soviet period.[60]

The President was not able to implement these guarantees himself. In many cases, these decrees rely heavily on implementation by regional government.[61] Implementing these socio-economic responsibilities requires significant resources, however, and the centralisation of the Russian system has left regional governments without the necessary resources to fulfil these objectives. This problem of unfunded mandates is widespread.[62] In fact, the problems of implementing these decrees

---

[58] Russian Constitution (n 20) Art 75.6.

[59] F Deprez, 'Putin's May Decrees and the 12 "National Projects" Take Shape, But Lacunae Remain' (*Intellinews*, 24 January 2019) www.intellinews.com/putin-s-may-decrees-and-the-12-national-projects-take-shape-but-lacunae-remain-155297/.

[60] SW Sokhey, 'Buying Support? Putin's Popularity and the Russian Welfare State' (*Foreign Policy Institute*, February 2018) www.fpri.org/wp-content/uploads/2018/02/SokheyRPE2.pdf, 4-5 (describing the popularity of social welfare reforms among key parts of the electorate for the Putin administration).

[61] G Di Bella, O Dynnikova and F Grigoli, 'Fiscal Federalism and Regional Performance in Russia' (2018) 4 *Russian Journal of Economics* 108, 114. In 2016, regional spending represented 95 per cent of general government expenditure for housing and utilities, 80 per cent for education and cultural activities and around 85 per cent for health including spending by territorial extra-budgetary medical funds.

[62] World Bank, 'Russian Federation: Reducing Poverty through Growth and Social Policy Reform' (Report No 28923-RU, Poverty Reduction and Economic Management Unit, Europe and Central Asia Region, World Bank, 2005) 114.

reflect deeply entrenched principal-agent problems that cannot be solved by the further centralisation of power.[63]

A well-known example occurred after Vladimir Putin's return to the Presidency in 2012. Upon assuming office, Putin signed an ambitious set of presidential decrees seeking to achieve certain socio-economic goals.[64] As one scholar explained, these decrees were broken down into 218 specific assignments (*poruchenia*), which 'specified ambitious goals for the government, including concrete target dates for the accomplishment of particular tasks'.[65] These decrees were left to the regions to implement but were not adequately funded by the centre; this has led to serious problems of non-compliance due to a lack of funding.[66] By one account, the regions 'still lack 15 percent of the revenues needed to implement the decrees'.[67] This kind of problem was not an isolated one: less than 30 per cent of the targets placed in a later set of centrally formulated goals (Strategy-2020) were implemented.[68]

Another clear example of the weaknesses of this presidentially dominated system in securing social guarantees was the disjointed and weak response of the Russian state to the coronavirus pandemic.[69] Rather than mounting a strong and decisive response as the centralised state tradition might suggest, the Presidency and federal government retreated from policy-making.[70] President Putin instead delegated vast responsibility to the regions to solve this problem. These regions did not have the resources to cope with the crisis and regional leaders often gave false information (such as low infection numbers) to their superiors in order to avoid dismissal, leading to an inability to understand where scarce

---

[63] V Gel'man, *The Politics of Bad Governance in Contemporary Russia* (Ann Arbor, University of Michigan Press, 2022) 73–75.

[64] W Pomeranz and K Smith, 'Commentary: Putin's Domestic Strategy: Counting the Trees, Missing the Forest' *Reuters* (3 June 2016) www.reuters.com/article/us-russia-putin-domestic-commentary-idUSKCN0YM08V.

[65] T Remington, *Presidential Decrees in Russia: A Comparative Perspective* (New York, Cambridge University Press, 2014) 2.

[66] ibid (describing how the regions lack the funding and resources to implement presidential decrees).

[67] ibid. See also F Burkhardt, 'Institutionalising Authoritarian Presidencies: Polymorphous Power and Russia's Presidential Administration' (2021) 73 *Europe-Asia Studies* 472.

[68] F Burkhardt, 'Institutionalizing Personalism: The Russian Presidency after Constitutional Changes' (2021) 6 *Russian Politics* 50, 67.

[69] T Khramova, 'Russia: Legal Response to Covid-19' in J King and OLM Ferraz et al (eds), *The Oxford Compendium of National Legal Responses to Covid-19* (online, Oxford University Press, 2021).

[70] ibid.

resources should be sent.[71] Overall, this response showed the continued weakness of the Russian state system, particularly in its ability to build a social state.

VI. POPULAR ACCOUNTABILITY

In this system where the ability to criticise the Russian President and government has been criminalised, even the appearance of popular accountability has been largely closed off. Under this system, elections have become more about demonstrating central power and authority rather than a forum for managed opposition. The managed electoral democracy of the previous decades was largely over, even at the regional level.[72]

The 2024 presidential election showed this clearly. The presidential administration so narrowed the competitive scope of politics that there were no candidates that opposed the war in Ukraine. Attempts by two candidates, Yekaterina Duntsova and Boris Nadezhdin, to run for President on an anti-war position were blocked by the Central Election Commission.[73] The main goal of the presidential administration was to ensure extremely high popular support for Vladimir Putin. In the end, Putin was reported to have won 87.8 per cent of the vote.[74] Independent election analysts described unprecedented levels of ballot rigging to reach this number. One expert estimated that electoral fraud gave Vladimir Putin an additional 22 million fraudulent votes.[75] The process and result of the 2024 elections therefore showed Russia's move from a managed form of anti-politics to a completely closed form of anti-politics.

---

[71] Gel'man (n 63) 156.

[72] A Pertsev, 'Russia's September Elections Mark a Return to Soviet-Style Regional Management' (*Riddle*, 8 September 2023) https://ridl.io/russia-s-september-elections-mark-a-return-to-soviet-style-regional-management/.

[73] 'Anti-War Candidate Barred from Russia's Presidential Election' *The Guardian* (24 December 2023) www.theguardian.com/world/2023/dec/23/anti-war-candidate-barred-russia-presidential-election-yekaterina-duntsova.

[74] Guy Faulconbridge and Andrew Osborn, 'Putin Wins Russia Election in a Landslide With No Serious Competition' *Reuters* (18 March 2024) www.reuters.com/world/europe/russias-presidential-vote-starts-final-day-with-accusations-kyiv-sabotage-2024-03-17/.

[75] Meduza, 'Putin 2024: Meduza breaks down the evidence pointing to the most fraudulent elections in modern Russian history' *Meduza* (21 March 2024) https://meduza.io/en/feature/2024/03/21/putin-2024.

VII. DOMESTIC LEGAL ACCOUNTABILITY

The new imperial President has also presided over further reductions in the independence of the Constitutional Court. Article 125.1 of the amended Constitution reduces the size of the Court from 19 to 11 judges, reducing its capacity to process claims from Russians and issue judgments. Moreover, an amended Article 83 gives the President entrenched constitutional authority to remove judges from the Court. Furthermore, in November 2020, the law governing the Court was amended to forbid dissents from majority opinions. As traced in the previous chapter, the issuing of dissenting opinions had flourished during the 1990s and 2000s, showing that some judges were committed to a different approach to interpretation grounded on the balanced state tradition.[76]

This intensifying top-down control has reduced the scope for the Court to regulate and protect individual Russians from the problems of the system. It also has placed the Court in a new role. The President has increasingly called on the Court to legitimise controversial policy decisions. The first example was a presidential request for the Court to review the constitutionality of the Treaty formalising Russia's annexation of the Crimean peninsula in Ukraine.[77]

In considering the request, the Court did not entertain any submissions arguing why the Treaty might be unconstitutional. Instead, the Court reasoned that the Treaty was adopted in a manner that was consistent with the division of power in Russia relating to treaty implementation.[78] The Court also agreed that the terms of the treaty – such as its transitional period – were constitutional.

The Court's decision, however, failed to address a central issue. In particular, the Court did not review the Treaty's compliance with Article 15 of the Constitution, which states that 'the generally recognized principles and norms of international law and international treaties of the Russian Federation are an integral part of its legal system'. The Constitutional Court itself has repeatedly confirmed that it relies on the 'generally

---

[76] Y Khalikova, 'Russia's Censored Judges' (*Riddle*, 4 December 2020) https://ridl.io/russia-s-censored-judges/.

[77] Decision of the Russian Constitutional Court N 6-P of 19 March 2014, 'In the Case of Verifying the Constitutionality of an International Treaty between the Russian Federation and the Republic of Crimea that has Not Entered into Force on the Admission of the Republic of Crimea to the Russian Federation and the Formation of New Entities within the Russian Federation' (in Russian) (*Konsultant Plus*) www.consultant.ru/document/cons_doc_LAW_160456/.

[78] ibid.

recognized principles and norms of international law' in reaching its conclusions.[79]

But in considering the Treaty, the Russian Constitutional Court did not determine whether the Treaty validly established Crimea's independence from Ukraine under international law and therefore complied with Article 15. Crimea's Declaration of Independence in large part justifies its independence on a non-binding, advisory opinion of the International Court of Justice involving the independence of Kosovo.[80] This opinion was officially condemned by Russia. In a letter to the ICJ about the Kosovo advisory opinion, the Russian government took the position that secession without the consent of the sovereign state was unlawful under international law except in 'extreme' circumstances when the people are 'subjected to severe oppression'.[81] Those extreme circumstances were not present in Kosovo and therefore, the letter concluded, the unilateral declaration of independence was unlawful.

The Court also did not consider whether the Treaty accorded with the importance that territorial integrity occupies in the current Russian Constitutional order. This position was made clear in the Russian Constitutional Court's Chechnya case of 1995 (discussed in chapter four), where the Court described state integrity as 'one of the foundations of the constitutional system of the Russian Federation'.[82] The Court also described in this case the centrality of territorial integrity to the international legal system and the United Nations Charter.[83] Elena Lukyanova, a prominent law professor, argued that given the centrality of state integrity to both the Russian Constitutional order and Russia's actions in the international legal system, it is difficult to see how Russia could constitutionally enter into a Treaty that violates Ukraine's own territorial integrity.[84]

---

[79] ibid.
[80] Advisory Opinion 'Accordance with International Law of the Unilateral Declaration of Independence in Respect of Kosovo' *International Court of Justice* (22 July 2010) www.icj-cij.org/sites/default/files/case-related/141/141-20100722-ADV-01-00-EN.pdf.
[81] 'Written Statement by the Russian Federation on the Accordance with International Law of the Unilateral Declaration of Independence by the Provisional Institutions of Self-Government of Kosovo' (Submission to the International Court of Justice, 16 April 2009) 39–40, www.icj-cij.org/sites/default/files/case-related/141/15628.pdf.
[82] Decision of the Russian Constitutional Court No 10-P of 31 July 1995 N 10-P, 'In the Case of Verifying the Constitutionality of Decree of the President of the Russian Federation of November 30, 1994 N 2137 "On Measures to Restore Constitutional Legality and Order on the Territory of the Chechen Republic"' (in Russian) (*Konsultant Plus*) www.consultant.ru/document/cons_doc_LAW_7552/.
[83] ibid.
[84] E Lukyanova, 'Sinister Law' *Novaya Gazeta* (Moscow, 20 March 2015) https://novayagazeta.ru/articles/2015/03/19/63473-o-prave-nalevo.

Another example of the Court's new role in legitimating presidential action involved a presidential request to consider the constitutionality of the 2020 amendments. The request asked the extent to which these changes to Chapters 3–7 were consistent with the democratic rights and guarantees in the early Chapters of the Constitution. In a 16 March 2020 judgment, the Court upheld the amendments.[85]

The Court explained that the amendments centralising more power in the hands of the President did not contradict the foundational principles of the Constitution such as the separation of powers in Article 10. In supporting this finding, the Court argued that the detailed structural provisions in the later chapters themselves give content to the abstract principles such as separation of powers in the earlier chapters. It reasoned that:

> The development and specification of the constitutional and legal foundations of the organization, competence and activities of individual federal bodies of state power are carried out not by Chapters 1 and 2 of the Constitution of the Russian Federation, but by the provisions of its Chapters 4 'President of the Russian Federation', 5 'Federal Assembly', 6 'Government of the Russian Federation' and 7 'Judicial power and prosecutor's office', which can be changed by the constitutional legislator.[86]

Applying this principle, the Court went on to argue that the 'principle of separation of powers and other foundations of the constitutional system relating to the status of federal bodies of state power' allow 'a high degree of discretion of the constitutional legislator in regulating the organization, powers and activities of the President of the Russian Federation, the State Duma, the Federation Council, Government of the Russian Federation and courts'.[87] This reasoning shows clearly how detailed structural rules shape the interpretation of the less determinate provisions in the early chapters of the Constitution.

Despite this new legitimating role, the Court continued to protect individual rights in less high profile cases. For instance, in a 2019 judgment, the Court struck down a federal law banning the ownership of

---

[85] Decision of the Russian Constitutional Court N 1-Z of March 16, 2020 'On the Compliance with the Provisions of Chapters 1, 2 and 9 of the Constitution of the Russian Federation of the Provisions of the Law of the Russian Federation on the Amendment to the Constitution of the Russian Federation "On Improving the Regulation of Certain Issues of the Organization and Functioning of Public Power", as well as on the Compliance with the Constitution of the Russian Federation of the Procedure for the Entry into Force of Article 1 of this Law in Connection with the Request of the President of the Russian Federation' (in Russian) (*Konsultant Plus*) www.consultant.ru/document/cons_doc_LAW_347691/.
[86] ibid.
[87] ibid.

media corporations for individuals with dual citizenship.[88] It based this on the fact that that the law was 'uncertain' and therefore potentially implicated key socio-economic guarantees about participation in a market economy. This judgment therefore drew on the same line of constitutional economics as previous cases had.

The full-scale invasion of Ukraine in February 2022, however, has reduced the ability of the Court to engage in this kind of action. For instance, the Court has refused to strike down or even question the legal certainty of any of the new draconian, censorship laws that have been passed since the beginning of the full-scale invasion. For instance, a challenge to a law making it an administrative offence to 'discredit' the armed forces was rejected without any discussion of whether the definition of 'discrediting' was sufficiently 'certain' in the legislation.[89]

The Russian Constitution's normative grounding in the centralised state tradition has increasingly been inserted into broader Russian political discourse. In 2023, a special course on the 'Foundations of the Russian State' was developed for university students. The textbook for this course described how the centralisation in the Constitution and the 2020 amendments were critical for the stability of Russian statehood (*gosudarstvennnost*).[90] It focuses heavily on new 2020 provisions that are aimed at protecting the sovereignty of Russia.[91] For instance, it points to new article 67.1 of the Constitution which states that Russia is the successor state to the Soviet Union, is 'united by a thousand-year history', and 'honours the memory of the defenders of the fatherland'.[92]

The textbook also argues that these constitutional changes are themselves critical in 'strengthening the sovereign foundations of statehood'.[93] To that end, it describes how the President from 1993 has operated outside of the principle of separation of powers.[94] This approach is described as

---

[88] Decision of the Russian Constitutional Court N 4-P of 17 January 2019, 'In the Case of Verifying the Constitutionality of Article 19.1 of the Law of the Russian Federation "On the Mass Media" in Connection with the Complaint of Citizen EG Finkelshtein' (in Russian) (*Konsultant Plus*) www.consultant.ru/document/cons_doc_LAW_316142/.

[89] Determination of the Constitutional Court of the Russian Federation dated 30 May 2023 N 1398-O, 'On the Refusal to Accept for Consideration the Complaint of Citizen Ilya Valerievich Yashin about the Violation of His Constitutional Rights by Part 1 of Article 20.3.3 of the Code of the Russian Federation on Administrative Offences' (in Russian) (*Garant*, 30 May 2023) www.garant.ru/products/ipo/prime/doc/406971202/.

[90] A Larionov, *Fundamentals of Russian Statehood: A Textbook for Students of Natural Sciences and Engineering Specialties* (in Russian) (Moscow, Delo Publishing House, 2023).

[91] ibid 321.
[92] ibid 326.
[93] ibid 329.
[94] ibid 331.

grounded on the Russian national tradition that 'strong leadership power in the head of state is a necessary condition for the independent and progressive development of the country'.[95]

VIII. INTERNATIONAL LEGAL ACCOUNTABILITY

The rise of the imperial President also led to Russia's final withdrawal from the European transnational human rights system. Most notably, in the aftermath of the full-scale invasion of Ukraine, the Council of Europe expelled Russia from the organisation on 16 March 2022. The Council explained that the expulsion was the product of the 'unjustified and unprovoked military attack against Ukraine, which is a blatant violation of international law, including the Statute of the Council of Europe'.[96] Pending the backlog of cases, Russia was now no longer subject to the jurisdiction of the European Court of Human Rights.

Russia's decoupling from international human rights law also led to the final closing of non-governmental, Russian organisations linked to the international human rights movement. Perhaps the best example was the liquidation of Memorial for its alleged failure to comply with the requirement of the foreign agent legislation.[97] Founded in the perestroika era, Andrei Sakharov was the first chairman of Memorial. It then became one of the foundational institutions of the international human rights movement in Russia and elsewhere in the former Soviet republics. It engaged in both rights protection and the preservation of historical memory about the victims of political repression in the past. The shuttering of this organisation puts the misleading logic of the constitutional dark arts in clear focus: over time, a centralised state is not likely to be a rights-protecting one.

IX. CONCLUSION

This chapter helps to better understand the trajectory of Russian politics as Putin enters his third decade in power. Since returning to the

---

[95] ibid 335.
[96] 'Statement by Committee of Ministers President on the Anniversary of the Expulsion of the Russian Federation from the Council of Europe' *Council of Europe Newsroom* (Strasbourg, 16 March 2023) www.coe.int/en/web/portal/-/statement-by-committee-of-ministers-president-on-the-anniversary-of-the-expulsion-of-the-russian-federation-from-the-council-of-europe.
[97] Andrew Osborn and Mikhail Antonov, 'Russia shuts Memorial Human Rights Centre in 'one-two punch'' Reuters (30 December 2021) www.reuters.com/world/europe/moscow-court-shuts-down-russias-memorial-human-rights-centre-2021-12-29/.

Presidency in 2012, Vladimir Putin has used his increasing power to further concentrate power in the Presidency and close Russian politics to both the opposition and the world. The 2020 constitutional reforms were made to justify this new imperial President to the Russian people. Since then, he has used this imperial presidency to launch a full-scale war in Ukraine and manage its consequences.

The imperial presidency appears stable for the time being. But it faces serious questions over the long term. The personalisation of power in Russia is acute: The election of Putin in March 2024 means that he now has been elected to a fifth consecutive presidential term and is entering his third decade in power. This personalisation threatens to further weaken lower-level institutions such as regional governments that fund important social services such as schools, health care and roads.

This raises a series of questions. As the personalisation of power intensifies, how will technocrats respond? This question has taken on new resonance since Putin's decision to launch a full-scale invasion of Ukraine. The war has stimulated economic growth in the short-term but long-term problems remain. Furthermore, the war has generated little enthusiasm among those technocrats, who have been forced to manage the difficult economic and political consequences of this invasion. For instance, Russia's central banker, Elvira Nabiullina, tried to resign after the decision to invade but was refused.[98] This raises the question if we will see a tension between the remaining managerial aspects of the system and its increasingly personalised approach to governance.

Second, the closing of the system to even managed political competition raises questions of how long this closed system can continue to generate legitimacy. As we have seen in the previous chapters, the ability to maintain at least the appearance of democracy and popular legitimacy has provided normative reasons for the exercise of top-down power.[99] If the basis for this authoritarian normativity continues to disappear, can coercion and intimidation become the central strategy of regime survival over the long term?

These potential questions and the problems they pose can possibly be managed by Vladimir Putin. As we have seen, Putin not only commands the rational-legal authority of the President, he also has deep reserves

---

[98] 'Russia Central Banker Tried to Quit over Ukraine; Putin said No' *Al Jazeera* (23 March 2022) www.aljazeera.com/economy/2022/3/23/russia-central-banker-tried-to-quit-over-ukraine-putin-said-no.

[99] G Yudin, 'Governing Through Polls: Politics of Representation and Presidential Support in Putin's Russia' (2020) 27 *Javnost – The Public* 2.

of non-legal authority. It is even possible he could lead another large-scale constitutional change at some point to renew popular support for the system. But he cannot remain President forever. At some stage, he will leave office. The rational-legal authority of the President in the Constitution will become central to power politics in a post-Putin Russia. In this post-Putin politics, capturing the Office of the President will be extremely important to wielding power. But will this rational-legal authority be enough for the system to continue to operate on the same basis as it does now? The next chapter will consider the role of constitutional law in this post-Putin Russia.

8

Constitutional Law in a Post-Putin Russia

On 1 February 2019, Vladislav Surkov – a key political spin doctor in the Kremlin – published an article entitled 'Putin's Long State'.[1] He argued that the political system that Putin had built would outlast him. The article opened with an anti-political attack on Western democracy. Democratic competition between political parties in the West, he argued, was an illusion, a cover for a 'deep state' which ultimately 'determines everything'.[2] Constitutional systems of checks and balances and political pluralism, therefore, are just a way of preserving 'a dynamic balance of baseness, a balance of greed, a harmony of cheating'.[3] If any individual or movement tries to change the system, he argued, the 'vigilant deep state rushes to the rescue and with an invisible hand drags the apostate to the bottom'.[4]

The deep Russian people (*gliubinyi narod*) and their political system, he argued, transcend this competitive politics. They do not recognise labels such as 'conservatism, socialism, liberalism'.[5] They instead rely on a connection with the President who can then provide for the stable, long-term management of problems. The leader performs this role through his special 'ability to hear and understand the people' and 'to see them through and through, to the full depth and to act in accordance with their views'.[6] Surkov further explained that:

> all institutions are subordinated to the main task – confidential communication and interaction of the supreme ruler with citizens. Various branches of

---

[1] V Surkov, 'Putin's Long State' *Nezavisimaya Gazeta* (11 February 2019) www.ng.ru/ideas/2019-02-11/5_7503_surkov.html.
[2] ibid.
[3] ibid.
[4] ibid.
[5] ibid.
[6] ibid.

government converge on the personality of the leader, being considered a value not in themselves, but only to the extent that they provide a connection with him. In addition to them, informal communication methods work through bypassing formal structures and elite groups.[7]

Although it falsely attributed Russian authoritarianism to the personal agency of Vladimir Putin, this article nicely captures the complementary logic of centralisation, populism and anti-politics in the constitutional dark arts. It also raises an important question: Is Russia's current system of political governance likely to remain after Putin is no longer President? Is it really a deeply entrenched 'long state'? The answer will be determined in part by the extent to which Russia's post-Putin leadership are willing to break with Russia's long adherence to centralisation.

In the short-term at least, Russia's crown-presidential constitutional system and its anti-political, centralising logic will support authoritarianism in a post-Putin Russia. Those hoping to keep Russia's authoritarian system in place will rely on its centralising constitutional provisions to maintain their concentrated power. They will justify this concentrated presidential power on the basis that it ensures political unity and harmony. This view of politics as unmediated representation and centralised management, they will likely argue, avoids the dangers of partisanship or political competition and is better able to adapt and respond to changing and dangerous domestic and international conditions.

These arguments will have a strong emotional appeal. But if one lesson emerges from Russian constitutional experience from 1993 until the present, the post-Putin political system will change. Without the vast informal authority of Putin, the new President will undoubtedly wield less power. Space will likely open up in the system for different voices and arguments. This could present an opportunity for those wanting a new democratic Russia. To seize this moment, they must seek a new constitutional foundation that finally breaks with centralisation.

I. STATUS QUO SUCCESSOR: CONTINUING THE
CONSTITUTIONAL DARK ARTS

The departure of Vladimir Putin from Russian politics will destabilise Russia's system of authoritarian politics. If Putin leaves office suddenly (through death or unexpected resignation) and without a clear successor,

[7] ibid.

there is likely to be a struggle between different factions to capture the vast rational-legal authority of the presidency. In this struggle, the office of the Prime Minister will emerge as a critical player in the politics of succession. When the office of the President is vacant, the Constitution mandates that the existing Prime Minister will automatically assume the Presidency and new presidential elections must be held within three months.[8] This could give a technocratic Prime Minister (such as Mikhail Mishustin) significant power to influence this struggle.

In a more controlled succession scenario, by contrast, Putin could designate a status quo successor by appointing him or her to the office of Prime Minister. This would follow the model set by Boris Yeltsin when he appointed Putin to Prime Minister six months before resigning and making Putin acting President. In this scenario, this status quo candidate can use the power of the prime ministerial office to build a public profile before becoming President.

In either scenario, the true test of the ultimate successor's ability to continue Russian authoritarianism will be the capacity to effectively use the vast powers of the presidency to stabilise the system, create a loyal team of officials, and win elections. Popular legitimacy will remain the foundational source of authority in the system. The status quo successor will therefore aim to draw heavily on the vast rational-legal powers that are available to the office of the President to establish high polling numbers and win elections.

These tasks will include the use of the management power of the presidential administration. It will also include large-scale use of the appointment power of the presidency to co-opt any emerging competitors and to place loyal people in positions of power. Early on, key appointments will include the head of the Central Election Commission to ensure that any real opponents are blocked from competing in the election. It will also include the use of the media (both traditional and online). Although it will take time, a successor will also need to use constitutional authority to buttress his or her non-legal authority.

This status quo successor could pursue different messaging strategies to win the first post-Putin election. One strategy would be to continue or even intensify the imperial rhetoric of late Putinism. This messaging would therefore seek to show how the status quo candidate is continuing the project that Vladimir Putin began. In this approach, no further

---

[8] Art 92 Constitution of the Russian Federation (*Council of Europe*) https://rm.coe.int/constitution-of-the-russian-federation-en/1680a1a237.

constitutional change would be pursued and Russia would remain a closed form of highly personalised presidentialism. This would be most likely in a scenario in which Putin left office very popular and the war in Ukraine and the economy were viewed as a success.

If the domestic political situation were less favourable, however, another strategy for a status quo successor would be to make some minor changes in order to build legitimacy. In this scenario, the successor might attempt to ground his candidacy on appeals to managerial and technocratic competence in the face of the economic and political challenges of a post-Putin Russia. In this scenario, the leader could appeal to the technocratic managerialism of the early 2000s when a newly elected Vladimir Putin was consolidating his power.

This strategy might be accompanied by attempts to 'liberalise' Russia's system of presidential absolutism by releasing political prisoners or allowing some of the opposition to once again compete for power. The reopening could also include promises of constitutional reform. These changes would likely draw on the logic of the constitutional dark arts. They could, for instance, involve inserting new rights or guarantees or more abstract guarantees of judicial independence. But these reforms are unlikely to represent a genuine attempt at building a balanced Constitution that breaks with Russia's traditional centralised tradition. This kind of constitutional reform would therefore be another example of 'theatrical' constitution-making as in 2020. Taken together, these changes would be an attempt to stabilise the post-Putin regime on the basis of popular legitimacy.

In either of these strategies, the status quo candidate will likely argue that centralised presidential authority remains necessary to effectively manage the threats of state disintegration and civil war in a post-Putin Russia. These types of arguments will therefore once again draw heavily on the justifications of the centralised state tradition. Fears of a state breakdown or a new 'time of troubles' (*smuta*) could be important in this set of reasons.[9] This would draw on long held Russian fears that limiting central authority can make things worse. A fear of a return to the problems of the 1990s could be part of this case.

These arguments have a strong emotional appeal in Russia. In fact, as we have seen in previous chapters, one of the key similarities between

---

[9] D Jenkins, 'How Russian History and the Concept of "Smuta" (Turmoil) Sheds Light on Putin and Prigozhin – And the Dangers of Dissent' (*The Conversation*, 29 August 2023) www.theconversation.com/how-russian-history-and-the-concept-of-smuta-turmoil-sheds-light-on-putin-and-prigozhin-and-the-dangers-of-dissent-210289.

Tsarist Russia, Soviet Russia and today's Russia is the persistence of the centralised state tradition and its fear of disunity and anarchy. As the next section will show, if there is an opening for Russian democratic reformers, they will need to break with this centralising tradition. This will not be easy. It will require rehabilitating the concept of a balanced Constitution by explaining that Russian weakness in the 1990s (and in other periods) was the direct result of constitutional centralisation and the personalised system that came with it. More importantly, this democratic movement will need to make the case for why a balanced constitutional system is more likely to create a system of effective and accountable power that better serves its citizens.

II. REAL DEMOCRATIC REFORM: THE NEED FOR A NEW CONSTITUTIONAL FOUNDATION

The centuries-long dominance of the centralised state tradition in Russia does not mean this tradition will remain in place indefinitely. Although Russia's centralised history might help to understand its ongoing authoritarian resilience, it does not determine it.[10] Societies and their political leadership are always free to choose a path that breaks with an authoritarian past. Much as the Germans did after World War II, Russians have agency to change their trajectory. The remainder of this chapter will suggest some possible ways to do this.

If there is a democratic opening in a post-Putin Russia, the leaders shaping a new Russia must be careful not to repeat the mistakes of the past. The search for answers from the past is already underway amongst Russian politicians, lawyers and economists. For instance, Alexei Navalny published an article that describes how the mistakes of the 1990s were a critical factor in leading to the current Russian system.[11] A critical lesson from this book is that real democratic reform must break with the anti-political form of centralised politics that underpins the 1993 constitutional order. Only the creation of a balanced state that encourages real pluralistic politics will help to build a more accountable and

---

[10] W Partlett, 'Historiography and Comparative Constitutional Scholarship' (2023) 1 *Comparative Constitutional Studies* 267, 281–83 (explaining why Russia's authoritarian history does not determine its future).

[11] A Navalny, 'I Can't Stand the Goat, But I Hate Those Who Let It Get The Cabbage' (*Meduza*, 11 August 2023) www.meduza.io/en/feature/2023/08/11/i-can-t-stand-the-goat-but-i-hate-those-who-let-it-get-the-cabbage.

democratic state that is able to deliver good governance to its citizens. This constitutional project will ultimately require the Russian democratic movement to rethink some of its methods.

A. More than the International

First, democratic reform will require seeing democratic change as more than just reopening Russia to international engagement and human rights law. Thirty years of Russian constitutional experience show that the international community lacks the legitimacy to make the necessary structural changes to the organisation of the state that are needed for real democracy and rights protection. A desire to avoid impinging on sovereignty is likely to continue to impair the ability of the international community to make difficult systemic changes to the organisation of power. This was the case even in the 1990s when Russia had a strong commitment to international engagement.

Moreover, international advocacy itself can distract from domestic reform by shaping the discourse of democratic struggle in problematic ways. A recent example that demonstrates the way in which international rights advocacy distorts democratic constitutional discourse can be found in criticism of the 2020 amendments made to the Russian Constitution. As argued in chapter seven, these amendments cemented a new, more powerful imperial President. In criticising these amendments, advocates of the project of democratic constitutionalism within Russia did not focus on the structural changes of these reforms. Instead, they worried more about the consequences of the reform for Russia's international law commitments. This has led to two problems.

First, the international framing of the opposition to the amendments narrowed attention to particular parts of the amendments that affect the constitutional relationship between Russia and international law. For instance, a report on the changes by the International Commission of Jurists focuses almost exclusively on the amendments that ultimately alter the status of international law in Russian domestic law.[12] This approach therefore ignored the effect of the reforms on the organisation of the Russian state and the further centralisation of power in the office of the President.

---

[12] International Commission of Jurists, 'Analysis of the Amendments to the Russian Constitution' (in Russian) (2020) www.icj.org/wp-content/uploads/2020/03/Russia-constitution-changes-Advocacy-Analysis-Brief-2020-RUS.pdf.

Second, this approach views Russian democracy as a project of catching up with or copying Western (or European) democracy. This can be seen in a petition on Change.org opposing the 2020 amendments. In this petition, a group of 120 leading Russian human lawyers, activists and rights defenders 'prepared and signed an open appeal from Russian citizens to the Council of Europe calling for an urgent legal review of amendments to the Russian Constitution and the procedure for their adoption'.[13] This appeal to the international was driven by the fact that many Russian constitutional advocates (who initiated the petition) are part of internationally affiliated, non-governmental organisations or are academics outside of the country. For instance, one of the key initiators is the Coordinator of the Advocacy Group EU-Russia Civil Society Forum. Other key initiators are overseas academics in Europe and the United States as well as members of the Moscow Helsinki Group, Amnesty International and Memorial.

The petition, in part, argues that these changes fundamentally undermine 'European constitutional values and democratic norms' as well as 'Russia's Council of Europe obligations'. One of the initiators of the change argued that opinion was important because the Venice Commission was 'one of the most authoritative international bodies on issues of constitutional law' and 'so that Russian citizens could formulate their opinion on the amendments taking into account European norms and obligations of Russia as a member of the Council of Europe'.[14] This appeal therefore hints that Russian democracy is a 'Europeanising' project.

The influence of the international sphere in Russian democratic movement has only been intensified by Russia's invasion of Ukraine and the closing of Russian politics. After the suspicious death of Alexei Navalny in prison, much of the democratic opposition now live and work outside of Russia. Democratic lobbying efforts now closely focus on foreign governments. This kind of activity might be necessary because of the exigencies of the war. But it must be downplayed in a post-Putin democratic reform movement seeking a historically rooted version of Russian democracy.

The idea that the Russian democratic project is an international one risks repeating the mistakes of Sakharov and the rights defenders.

---

[13] 'Council of Europe, Conduct an Urgent Legal Examination of Changes to the Russian Constitution!' (in Russian) (*Change.org*, 11 March 2020) www.change.org/popravki_konstitutsia.

[14] Golos (Voice), 'Human Rights Defenders Appeal to the Council of Europe' (in Russian) (Press Release, 14 April 2020) https://echo.msk.ru/blog/golosinfo/2624966-echo/.

This approach has strong legitimacy problems and can help to feed a nationalist backlash that argues that the project of democratic constitutionalism is ill-suited to or does not take sufficient account of Russian national context. Advocates of this approach can argue that the Russian Constitution should not reflect supra-national constitutional norms but instead, should reflect essential, historically grounded principles and values.[15]

To avoid these dangers, Russian democratic reformers should be careful to avoid describing Russian democracy as a convergence project with Western democracies. They therefore should seek to ground democratic principles and values in Russian history. As this chapter will describe in more detail later, Russia has its own democratic constitutional tradition. This tradition was particularly vibrant in the late Tsarist period, as the Constitutional Democrat argued that a balanced constitutional document could build a more stable and effective Russian state. This process of 'redeeming' Russian history is critical to ensure that democracy is not viewed as an external imposition.[16]

B. Away from Anti-Politics

Second, real democratic reform will also require Russia's democratic movement to fundamentally reject an anti-political form of democracy. This also could prove difficult. Anti-politics has strong appeal among the Russian public, which has low levels of trust in public power. The appeal of anti-politics could be particularly strong if a post-Putin Russia was itself facing serious threats of collapse or disintegration. In that context, many Russians would likely support a status quo successor promising a centralised state.

To respond, the Russian democratic movement could propose a temporary legal arrangement or Constitution that would allow centralised leadership to overcome the crisis. This solution would stress that a centralised system was a short-term solution to a crisis. It would also make clear that once the crisis recedes, a new balanced Constitution would be built that would encourage pluralistic and competitive politics. One of Russia's leading constitutional thinkers, Mikhail Krasnov, has argued that this kind of 'temporary constitution' would have been

---

[15] W Partlett and D Samararatne, 'Redeeming the National in Constitutional Argument' (2021) 54 *World Constitutional Law* 461.
[16] ibid.

the correct approach in the early 1990s.[17] It would have allowed Yeltsin to overcome the crisis but would not have revitalised Russia's centralised state tradition and enabled a leader like Putin to rebuild Russian authoritarianism.

In the long term, however, the opposition will need to make the case for a balanced Constitution that breaks with Russia's long history of centralised and anti-political leadership. This argument will require abandoning some of the most successful opposition tactics. Anti-politics has been important in driving the success of Russia's most successful democratic opposition movement built by Alexei Navalny.

First, the Navalny movement speaks directly with 'the people' through social media sites such as YouTube and Instagram.[18] These platforms allow the Navalny team to make broad, non-ideological criticisms of the current Russian leadership. Before his death, Navalny himself took a number of different political positions, from supporting Russian nationalism to traditional liberal positions. This set of positions has led to confusion. For instance, Amnesty International initially labelled Navalny a 'prisoner of conscience', rescinded this status when his nationalist statements came to light, but then reinstated it.[19] Today, the Navalny team's main message remains a non-ideological about the corruption of the current Russian elite; this message remains central to the movement now led by his widow, Yulia Navalnaya. This critique continues to appeal to all voters and focuses on personalities rather than issues.

Second, the Navalny team is itself highly technocratic. From the beginning, lawyers have been a critical part of the Navalny movement. Navalny was a commercial lawyer and he began his movement by recruiting lawyers to 'do the dull, methodical work of writing complaints, filing complaints, and attending hearings in the courts and anti-monopoly committees'.[20] His team also relies heavily on polling for its policy direction. For instance, the Navalny movement used polling to help craft a strategy for the 2024 presidential race. To do this, it sent out a questionnaire to thousands of Russian politicians, journalists and public figures

---

[17] T Boiko, 'Imaginary Separation of Powers' (in Russian) *Daily Journal* (Moscow, 27 September 2018) www.ej.ru/?a=note&id=32958.
[18] S Glazunova, '"Four Populisms" of Alexey Navalny: An Analysis of Russian Non-Systemic Opposition Discourse on YouTube' (2020) 8 *Media and Communication* 121.
[19] 'Amnesty International Restores Alexei Navalny's Prisoner of Conscience Status' *The Guardian* (Ottawa, 8 May 2021) www.theguardian.com/world/2021/may/07/alexei-navalny-amnesty-international-prisoner-of-conscience-restored.
[20] M Gessen, 'Lyubov Sobol's Hope for Russia' *The New Yorker* (19 July 2021) www.newyorker.com/magazine/2021/07/26/lyubov-sobols-hope-for-russia.

to determine their strategy for the 2024 presidential race.[21] After receiving more than 50,000 responses, the Navalny team opted for a strategy that would encourage Russians to vote for any candidate that was not Putin.[22]

A critical question that emerges therefore is how the Navalny movement – or others seeking to replicate this movement's success – would govern Russia. A recent book on Alexei Navalny and his movement's vision for a future Russia has argued that they are determined to break with anti-politics.[23] The authors describe how broad appeals to many different viewpoints is necessary to defeat the current regime. This first stage, however, is only temporary. The book describes how the Navalny movement envisions 'a second stage' where a 'crude opposition between elites and people would dissolve and "normal" politics would be possible'.[24] In this vision, the book concludes, the Navalny movement would be one of 'several' parties who would compete for power in a system of competitive politics.[25]

The transition from a system of anti-politics to one grounded on real competitive politics, however, will not be easy. Not all members of the opposition share a desire to build a pluralistic and competitive form of democratic politics. In fact, it will be very appealing to all political players competing for power in Russia to appeal to represent the whole people and solve their problems effectively. Constitutional change could, however, help to ensure this transition. A new balanced Constitution with checks on the concentration of power could signal a break with this anti-politics and a commitment to a different kind of democratic politics. In the process of debating and drafting this new constitutional text, it can be stressed that the Russian state must – for the first time – be organised in a way that balances power and therefore recognises the plurality of interests and views of the Russian people. Furthermore, a balanced organisation of power is the only way to build better quality governance that is truly accountable to the people. If successful, it would truly represent a revolutionary change to the long Russian constitutional tradition.

---

[21] D Litvinova, 'With Putin's Reelection All But Assured, Russia's Opposition Still Vows to Undermine His Image' *AP News* (9 December 2023) www.apnews.com/article/putin-russia-opposition-presidential-election-ed74cfa0fb957317188de39fe9ae7d15.

[22] 'So Here's the Russian Opposition's Strategy to Confront Putin in the March 2024 Presidential Election' (*Meduza*, 8 December 2023) www.meduza.io/en/feature/2023/12/07/so-here-s-the-russian-opposition-s-strategy-to-confront-putin-in-the-march-2024-presidential-election.

[23] JM Dollbaum, M Lallouet, and B Noble, *Navalny: Putin's Nemesis, Russia's Future?* (Oxford, Oxford University Press, 2021).

[24] ibid 184.

[25] ibid.

III. A NEW CONSTITUTIONAL STRUCTURE

In creating this new democratic Constitution, drafters need not rewrite the entire Constitution. Assuming the foundational, early chapters of the 1993 Constitution remain unamended, these democratic principles and individual rights could be retained. Only small changes would therefore be needed to ensure that these provisions signal a clear commitment to a balanced state. For instance, one change would ensure that the separation of powers in Article 10 makes clear that there are checks on the power of the President. Another change should include a clear statement that federalism is not grounded on the principle of state unity and a top-down vertical of power.

Most of the focus, however, must be placed on ending the centralisation of power in the office of the President. This requires more than just redrafting the provisions on the judiciary. Independent courts will undoubtedly be an important institution in a democratic Russia; they will play a critical role in building a rule of law system in Russia. But guarantees of judicial reform and independent courts are unlikely to work without a balanced constitutional system that is committed to pluralism and political competition. Real change requires rewriting key provisions in Chapters 4, 5 and 6 of the Constitution that organise power. These provisions must be redrafted in order to disperse power between the public institutions of the Russian state. This requires attention to the detailed relationship between the President, executive-branch ministry (headed by the Prime Minister) and the legislature. In a system that balances power between these institutions, courts are less likely to be captured by one institution and politicised.

Russian constitutional experts themselves have recognised the importance of this kind of broad structural reform. In 2012, a team of constitutional lawyers from the law faculty at the Higher School of Economics led by Mikhail Krasnov drafted a new Constitution that sought to balance power between key political institutions.[26] The explanatory note accompanying the draft described 'the need to change the existing structure of political institutions of public power in Russia'.[27] In particular, the new draft seeks to 'limit the prerogatives of the president as a political player', by clearly defining its role as a custodian and not political manager of the entire system.[28] Furthermore, the President,

---

[26] N Korchenko, 'The President Serves One Term' (in Russian) *Kommersant* (14 March 2012) www.kommersant.ru/doc/1892250.
[27] ibid.
[28] ibid.

according to the draft, is elected for a term of seven years, but only once in a lifetime. Finally, the draft proposes to return a number of powers to the legislature, including control over the executive-branch ministry.

This draft Constitution offers important lessons if Russia is to retain an elected head of state President alongside an elected parliament. In particular, a democratic system must limit the management power of the President, giving the elected legislature real authority to control and remove members of the executive-branch government, including the Prime Minister. This kind of system would also include the ability of the legislature to force the resignation of the executive-branch government (or individual ministers) through a no confidence vote. Moreover, a democratic system of power must limit the vast decree powers of the President, notably the ability to unilaterally create public institutions as well as make decrees with the force of law. In this system, the head-of-state President could become a unifying figure that leaves the everyday, management role over Russian politics to ministers responsible to Parliament.

Russia's democratic opposition has argued, however, that Russia should go further in reforming its constitutional structure. In particular, some members of the opposition have called for limiting the power of the Russian President by turning to a parliamentary system. For instance, Mikhail Khordokovsky has called for the transition to a parliamentary republic that would be balanced by decentralisation.[29] He has written:

> I firmly believe that a parliamentary republic in Russia cannot be based exclusively on a partisan system of governance ... If power in the partisan system is not balanced [between different parties] then the balance of power should be decided by [Russia's] regions themselves. This means Russia should be a de facto state of regions.[30]

Before his death, Alexei Navalny argued that 'Russia needs a parliamentary republic. That is the only way to stop the endless cycle of imperial authoritarianism'.[31] Although admitting that this system alone is 'no panacea', he argued that this new constitutional system is critical to 'a radical reduction of power in the hands of one person, the formation

---

[29] 'Mikhail Khodorkovsky: Our Future Russia Needs a Powerful Parliament, Regionalism and Free Press' (*Khodorkovsky*, 28 November 2018) www.khodorkovsky.com/mikhail-khodorkovsky-future-russia-needs-powerful-parliament-regionalism-free-press/.
[30] ibid.
[31] A Navalny, 'This is What a Post-Putin Russia Should Look Like' *The Washington Post* (30 September 2022) www.washingtonpost.com/opinions/2022/09/30/alexei-navalny-parliamentary-republic-russia-ukraine/.

of a government by a parliamentary majority, an independent judiciary system, and a significant increase in the powers of local authorities'.[32]

There is little question that the office of the President will continue to pose a threat to a balanced constitutional system. But parliamentary systems can also be highly centralised under the office of the Prime Minister. This is particularly true with majoritarian parliamentary systems that allow the Party with the most seats to form the government. As we will see in chapter nine, the constitutional dark arts operate in this parliamentary context by giving the party leader vast power without any serious political checks and balances.

On the other hand, if the voting rules are changed to be less majoritarian (by, for instance, adopting a proportional representation system), this can lead to unstable coalition governments that themselves are unable to solve pressing problems. This could lead to ineffective governance. Finally, federal reforms that overly decentralise power can also pose problems. Most notably, too much decentralisation can allow subnational entities themselves to undermine the democratic guarantees in the Constitution. As Stephen Holmes has written, the paralysis of power poses as many threats to democratic governance as the concentration of power.[33]

Avoiding these problems requires striking a delicate balance. To get this balance right, any introduction of parliamentarism will require close attention to the details. This will require scrutinising how institutions relate to one another. Most importantly, it will involve creating a system that places real political checks on the concentration of power but that also allows ensures an effective system of governance.

One option is to consider a balanced parliamentary system that Steffen Ganghof calls 'semi-parliamentarism'.[34] This system is grounded on a bicameral parliament in which 'voters, as the ultimate principal, select two separate but equally legitimate legislative agents, only one of which then becomes the principal of the prime minister and his or her cabinet'.[35] One house (normally the lower house) has the power to form and dismiss the government in addition to the power to originate legislation and monetary bills. It should be elected according to majoritarian

---

[32] ibid.
[33] S Holmes, 'What Russia Teaches Us Now: How Weak States Threaten Freedom' (1997) 33 *The American Prospect* 30.
[34] S Ganghof, 'A New Political System Model: Semi-Parliamentary Government' (2018) 57 *European Journal of Political Research* 261.
[35] ibid 265.

principles to ensure stable and efficient government. The other house (normally the upper house) is required to agree to legislation and carries out general non-binding oversight of government affairs. It should be elected according to proportional voting rules in order to ensure more representative and inclusive forms of lawmaking. In Russia, this proportional voting system could be organised in a way that reflects Russian federalism.

This system places a key political check on majoritarian domination by forcing the majoritarian party to negotiate with a proportionally elected upper house. It also avoids a key danger of presidential systems that is particularly pressing in the Russian context: the dangers of excessive personalisation of power in one individual.[36] In addition, it also allows for a key strength of parliamentarism – the link between the leader and a party – while also allowing for the stability of government by including majoritarian rules for its selection. This is also very important in the Russian context: an important critique of parliamentarism in the Russian context has long been the idea that parliamentarism is not stable enough to ensure control of Russia's broad landmass. Overall, this system balances the 'advantages of "majoritarian" and "proportional" democracies'.[37]

Whether Russia reforms its system of presidentialism or creates a parliamentary system, this process will have important consequences for Russian politics. These provisions will draw on the justifications of the balanced state tradition. They will therefore provide important support to attempts to build a more impartial Constitutional Court that will help to deepen Russian democracy. As we have seen in the previous chapters, the Russian Constitutional Court has emerged as a key centralising force since 1995 by applying the reasoning of the centralised state tradition to important disputes. A newly formed Constitutional Court under a balanced democratic Russian Constitution would change course. With a new set of Justices, it should develop an interpretative approach which ensures that balances authority between different public institutions. Furthermore, on rights protection, the Court will adopt a version of the proportionality test that more closely scrutinises whether a law limiting a right is actually *necessary* for achieving a legitimate state purpose. This closer review will ensure that the rights of individuals will be seriously enforced.

[36] ibid 262.
[37] ibid 276.

IV. BUILDING A MORE EFFECTIVE AND ACCOUNTABLE RUSSIAN STATE

Real democratic constitutional reform in Russia requires more than just textual constitutional reform. It also involves breaking with the centralised state discourse and embracing the balanced state tradition. Justifying this new constitutional discourse will require arguing that a balanced Russian Constitution will do more than limit the Russian authoritarianism. This new normative system of constitutional governance can also be justified as providing better quality governance.

This transformation of Russian constitutional discourse involves challenging a number of entrenched justifications linking state centralisation with Russia's security and safety as well as the social state. A critical one is that the failure to centralise power will weaken Russia and threaten the integrity of the country. For instance, William Pomeranz describes how the concept of unified state power has long been viewed in Russia as 'essential in holding an empire and (post-1991) a multinational country together'.[38]

In justifying this new Constitution, the democratic movement must make a positive case for the benefits of democracy and rights-protection. The Navalny movement was particularly effective at this type of messaging. It built a series of projects that exposed how centralisation and personalisation lead to poor quality governance.[39] It then showed how democratic accountability would lead to better governance outcomes. Some of this work relied on enabling the long tradition of legal petitioning that has existed in Russia for centuries and is currently reflected in the constitutional right of every citizen to send individual and collective petitions to state bodies. This system of petitioning, however, has worked poorly in Russia's centralised system. The Navalny movement's online platforms made this petitioning easy, providing a place for Russians to quickly enter information about everyday problems and then linking them with local lawyers from the Navalny team who know exactly how to effectively petition the authorities to follow the law.

For example, the Navalny movement used this strategy to allow people to lodge complaints about the condition of 'communal' property in

---

[38] W.E. Pomeranz, *Law and the Russian State: Russia's Legal Evolution from Peter the Great to Vladimir Putin* (London, Bloomsbury Publishing, 2018) 168.
[39] I Fomin, 'What Can Navalny Teach Us About Fighting Putin's Regime?' *Moscow Times* (Moscow, 19 February 2024) www.themoscowtimes.com/2024/02/19/what-can-navalny-teach-us-about-fighting-putins-regime-a84145.

apartment buildings, from ensuring cleanliness to repairing the heating systems.[40] This platform showed clearly the benefits of bottom-up accountable governance. Its success also challenged the dysfunctional centralised system. In 2012, the chief state housing inspector of the Russian Federation, Nikolai Vasyutin, attempted to deflect criticism by arguing that the complaints were not a sign of dysfunctionality, but instead the political machinations of 'opposition circles'.[41] This kind of work was therefore important in not just exposing the weakness of the Russian state but also showing the possibilities of a more democratic Russia in securing the Russian state's social obligations.

This link between constitutional democracy and a social state is not new to Russia democratic politics. It was an important part of Russia's late Tsarist tradition of liberal constitutional thought. This movement explicitly linked constitutional limitations on Tsarist power and a more balanced Russian Constitution with a more effective Russian state. In particular, this 'statist liberalism' viewed constitutional reforms limiting the centralised power of the Tsar as a way of strengthening the state and making it better able to provide for its citizens.

This statist Russian constitutional tradition can be traced from the early nineteenth century and culminated in the Russian provisional government. Its ideas involved a Tsar restrained by the Constitution as well as an elected Duma and a state council. Mikhail Speransky was a key early thinker in this tradition. A 'disciple of Montesquieu', he attempted to apply the lessons of the balanced Constitution of England to the Russian context.[42] Although Speransky was ultimately unsuccessful, his ideas were influential amongst a group of Russian nobles called the Decembrists. They called for a constitutionally limited monarchy, a representative assembly and the liberation of the serfs. A leading Decembrist, Nikita Muraviev, introduced his draft Constitution with the argument that 'the arbitrary rule of one man' cannot become a principle of government 'because the experience of all nations and all epochs has shown that autocratic power is equally ruinous for both rulers and society'.[43]

---

[40] 'How Navalny Discredited All Levels of Government with His "RosZhKH"' (in Russian) *Fontanka.ru* (14 November 2012) www.fontanka.ru/2012/11/14/227/.
[41] ibid.
[42] J Gooding, 'The Liberalism of Michael Speransky' (1986) 64 *Slavonic and East European Review* 401, 403.
[43] N Muraviev, 'Project for a Constitution' in WJ Leatherbarrow and DC Offord (eds), *A Documentary History of Russian Thought: From the Enlightenment to Marxism* (Ann Arbor, Ardis, 1987) 42–43.

The Decembrists located this balanced constitutional tradition in Russian history. In particular, they pointed to the city-republic of Novgorod as example of an older Russian constitutional system that did not centralise power in one individual.[44]

In the mid-nineteenth century, after Russia's military defeat in the Crimean War and concerns about the weakness of the Russian state, these ideas shaped policy. Tsar Alexander II drew on this liberal statism when he introduced what would be called the 'Great Reforms'. These constitutional changes devolved powers to local governments (*zemstvos*), created more independent courts, lessened censorship and abolished serfdom.[45] These reforms enacted many of the constitutional reforms that the Decembrists had been asking for years earlier. They therefore were an important step toward realising a balanced Constitution in a way that was adapted to Russian conditions.

These reforms were also supported by an increasingly powerful intellectual movement. A leading thinker in this movement was Boris Chicherin. Chicherin was an academic who argued that the efficacy of Russian law required limitations on the personal power of the Tsar. He stressed that 'law and order will never be able to establish itself where everything depends on one personal will and where each person can have the power to put himself above the law'.[46] Chicherin also criticised the Russian government for its over-reliance on executive regulations (*rasporiazheniia*) and not laws (*zakony*). This kind of executive governance, Chicherin argued, leads to inefficiencies and inequalities. Chicherin instead argued that laws should be used to ensure the uniformity of legal application. Chicherin stressed that this reform must be adapted to Russian historical conditions and therefore be targeted at building and strengthening the state. In Chicherin's thesis defence, he stated that 'All [epochs] have one goal, one task – the building of state'.[47]

Chicherin's statist liberalism therefore pursued the same goal that the Russian centralised state tradition did: the development of an effective Russian state.[48] In fact, Chicherin's political thinking was heavily

---

[44] S Rabow-Edling, 'The Decembrists and the Concept of a Civic Nation' (2007) 35 *Nationalities Papers* 369, 371.

[45] B Eklof, J Bushnell and L Zakharova (eds), *Russia's Great Reforms, 1855–1881* (Bloomington, Indiana University Press, 1994).

[46] Quoted from Paul Miliukov, *Russia and Its Crisis* (Chicago, University of Chicago Press, 1905) 329–30.

[47] Quoted from GM Hamburg, 'Peasant Emancipation and Russian Social Thought: The Case of Boris N Chicherin' (1991) 50 *Slavic Review* 890, 894.

[48] JL Black, 'The "State School" Interpretation of Russian History: A Re-Appraisal of its Genetic Origins' (1973) 21 *Jahrbücher für Geschichte Osteuropas* 509.

influenced by German statist ideas – traceable in part to Hegel – which saw each nation as having distinctive requirements in developing a state that could organically unite the government and the people.[49] But there was a key difference: Chicherin's contribution was to argue that this statist tradition was best pursued through a system of constitutionally limited and balanced state power.

This statist liberalism was then critical in motivating the Constitutional Democrats (Kadet) party.[50] A leading thinker in this movement, Pavel Miliukov, himself described how the liberal tradition in Russia 'connoted the idea of state intervention'.[51] This Russian statist liberalism was also grounded in an active welfare state that provided for its citizens. Miliukov viewed liberal change as linking 'constitutional democracy and social reformism'.[52] Another leading Kadet member, Maxim Vinaver, argued that the Kadets carried with them an 'image of a state with noble features'.[53]

The Kadet party played a key role in late Tsarist Russia. In 1905, under immense pressure after Tsarist Russia's defeat in war to the Japanese, another breakthrough for this constitutional movement was made. After a number of uprisings, the Tsar yielded to the demands of the Kadets and agreed to the Fundamental Laws which ultimately began to implement key constitutional principles, including the long-called for law-based state.[54] In particular, this reform introduced a legislative assembly (Duma) that would make law. The Tsar, however, remained the guarantor of a system still committed to a unified state.[55] For instance, Article 1 stated that the Russian state was 'one and indivisible'.[56]

The Fundamental Laws ultimately failed because of this continued centralisation, shown most clearly when the Tsar dissolved the Duma. In response, the liberal statists led by the Kadets called on citizens to 'stop paying taxes and sending recruits to the army'.[57] When the Tsarist regime finally collapsed in 1917, the liberal statists came to power in

---

[49] A Kelly, '"What Is Real Is Rational": The Political Philosophy of B. N. Chicherin' (1977) 18 *Cahiers du Monde russe et soviétique* 195, 202.
[50] DW Treadgold, 'The Constitutional Democrats and the Russian Liberal Tradition' (1951) 10 *The American Slavic and East European Review* 85, 87.
[51] Miliukov (n 46) 224.
[52] MK Stockdale, *Paul Miliukov and the Quest for a Liberal Russia, 1880-1918* (Ithaca NY, Cornell University Press, 1997).
[53] Quoted from Treadgold, 'The Constitutional Democrats' (n 50) 85.
[54] Pomeranz, *Law and the Russian State* (n 38) 64–67.
[55] ibid 64.
[56] ibid.
[57] ibid 68.

the provisional government. In power, they called for the election of a Constituent Assembly to create a permanent constitutional republic in Russia.[58] This Assembly would then build a Russian constitutional state that would be energetic and accountable to the people. In addition, the provisional government called for the decentralisation of power into democratic local governments.[59] These reforms were aimed at increasing the authority of the state by bringing in 'active creative forces' that had not previously taken direct part in the government.[60]

Although they ultimately failed, the late Tsarist liberal statist movement was united by a powerful argument. It argued that a balanced state that contains checks on the personal power of the Tsar was not just a way to limit the state. On the contrary, they described a balanced state as ensuring a more effective and stable form of governance. This explains why these constitutional ideas were most influential at times of crisis for the Russian state. For instance, the Great Reforms of the 1860s were adopted in response to the problems of the Russian military in the Crimean War. Moreover, the Fundamental Laws were a response to military defeat at the hands of the Japanese.

This historical example carries important lessons for today. In particular, it can be used to counter arguments that Russia's great power status is best secured through centralisation. It shows that a decentralised, balanced system is not a weak one. Instead, Russia's power in the world can better be ensured by creating a balanced state structure that unleashes the potential of its people. Moreover, it also demonstrates that a balanced Constitution is not any more of a foreign, Western project than the centralised state tradition. Instead, it is one that has a deep history in Russian national thought and that has long competed with centralised state tradition.

V. CONCLUSION

Russia is not historically fated to remain a centralised, authoritarian country. On the contrary, Russian authoritarianism today is grounded on a man-made constitutional system that is committed to a centralised state. This system can be changed: Constitutions themselves are

---

[58] L Schapiro, 'The Political Thought of the First Provisional Government' in R Pipes (ed), *Revolutionary Russia* (Cambridge MA, Harvard University Press, 1968) 97, 98.
[59] ibid 98.
[60] ibid.

intentional products of human agency and therefore are always themselves subject to change and reform. The text of a new Constitution can reshape the underlying constitutional culture. Although this constitutional change will not be sufficient on its own to build a democratic Russia, it is a necessary and significant step along that path.

A post-Putin Russia could offer opportunities for this kind of change. But real democratic constitutional reform will not be easy. It will require explaining why a fundamental break with Russia's long normative attachment to centralisation is the right approach. In describing the importance of this break and the value of balance, the Russian democratic movement must link the weakness and dysfunctionality of the current state with centralisation. In so doing, they can argue that a balanced Constitution is a more effective way to enable the state to be responsive to the Russian people. In making this positive claim for a balanced Constitution, Russians can learn from the reasoning and arguments of the Tsarist-era liberal statist movement.

This has implications for the international community as well. Those hoping to support Russian democratic reform will need to look beyond personal guarantees from a new Russian leader or the promise of more constitutional rights. Instead, they must seek to encourage deeper structural and normative constitutional changes that can allow Russia to finally break with its deeply held commitment to a centralised state. If this kind of real change is made, it is likely to benefit not just Russian democracy and individual rights protection but also the world.

9

Countering Constitutional Authoritarianism

ON 21 JULY 2016, Donald Trump addressed the Republican National Convention to accept his nomination for President. Attacking corrupt special interests for rigging the system and failing to put the interests of the American people first, Trump argued that only he could truly represent the American people.[1] His personal leadership, he argued, would overcome 'the chaos in our communities' and restore law and order by 'ensuring the laws of the United States are enforced'.[2] Appealing to the idea of a unified people, he concluded the speech with the declaration that 'I am your voice'.[3] The message was clear: Trump would personally ensure that the popular will would be implemented.

Donald Trump's call for an unmediated relationship between himself and the American people is just one reminder that the dangerous anti-political claims of the constitutional dark arts are not limited to Russia. Democracy and centralisation are now increasingly being combined in political rhetoric and Constitution-making around the world. In these contexts, centralised leadership is increasingly being justified as a providing a better, more direct and less messy form of democracy.

Globally, the deceptive claims of the constitutional dark arts can be found in two distinct contexts. First, they have provided a powerful basis for renewing authoritarian rule in contexts that have long had dictatorial rule and a commitment to the centralised state tradition. In this populist authoritarianism, they have allowed authoritarian leaders to renew centralised and personalised power on popular and legal legitimacy.

---

[1] 'Full Text: Donald Trump 2016 RNC Draft Speech Transcript' (*Politico*, 21 July 2016) www.politico.com/story/2016/07/full-transcript-donald-trump-nomination-acceptance-speech-at-rnc-225974.
[2] ibid.
[3] ibid.

Second, the justifications of the constitutional dark arts are increasingly being used to undermine the balanced state tradition in established democracies. In this populist threat to democracy, elected leaders claim that the centralisation of power in one office is better able to achieve democracy and rights protection.

Although the misleading claims of the constitutional dark arts have helped to build a new version of authoritarianism, they can be countered. The Russian experience shows that centralisation has not achieved any of its goals. As the previous chapters have shown, this kind of centralised system weakens popular accountability and rights protection. It also contributes to poor quality governance. Over time, the constitutional dark arts are better at creating the *image* of stable and effective democratic governance than its reality.

I. AUTHORITARIAN POPULISM

Amidst the 'third wave' of democracy, many communist or one-party systems collapsed or faced serious legitimacy problems.[4] In these contexts, many dictators renewed their political legitimacy by relying on the techniques and justifications of the constitutional dark arts. In particular, they have argued that only the centralisation of authority in an elected leader can provide the needed stability and unity to achieve democracy and rights protection. This populist authoritarianism can be found in the former Soviet republics, Africa and Latin America.

The collapse of the Soviet Union at the end of 1992 led to 15 newly independent countries. In all of these countries, the collapse of the Soviet Union left a vacuum of power; new Constitutions were needed to rebuild legitimate public authority and power. Leaders in many of these states followed Russia's lead in re-establishing legitimacy on the basis of the hybrid Constitutions of the constitutional dark arts and their justifications.[5]

As in Russia, referendums and appeals to popular sovereignty were central to this strategy. For instance, in Belarus, after a protracted struggle with the legislature, newly elected President Aleksandr Lukashenko used a referendum to introduce a series of constitutional amendments

---

[4] SP Huntington, 'Democracy's Third Wave' (1991) 2(2) *Journal of Democracy* 12.
[5] W Partlett and H Kupper, *The Post-Soviet as Post-Colonial: A New Paradigm for Understanding Constitutional Dynamics in the Former Soviet Empire* (Cheltenham, Edward Elgar, 2022).

that preserved the long list of rights in the Constitution but that amended the later chapters of the Belarus Constitution. These changes transformed Belarus into a crown-presidential system.[6] In making these changes, Lukashenko argued that centralised presidential power was necessary to strengthen the state and end what he called the senseless battles of a checks and balances system.[7] He stated that 'the leading role of the president' is 'critical and indisputable' in carrying out the necessary changes required by the transition away from communism.[8] Echoing Russian ideas of power, Lukashenko stated later in a speech that his ideal Constitution had 'three branches of power; legislative, executive, and judicial. And all these branches grow on the tree of the presidency'.[9] These amendments have allowed Lukashenko to dominate Belarusian politics for 30 years.[10]

Kazakhstan followed a similar path. In 1995, President Nazarbaev called a referendum to create a new crown-presidential Constitution. Leaving the long list of individual rights guarantees in the Constitution unchanged, he instead weakened the authority of the legislature and strengthened presidential power. He argued that presidential centralisation was needed to resolve differences between the branches of government and allow the people to truly exercise power in Kazakhstan.[11] Crown-presidentialism therefore became a central part of Kazakhstan's authoritarian modernism discourse.

Other central Asian republics have followed this model. In Uzbekistan, President Islam Karimov pushed through a new Constitution to break with communism and build what he called a democratic Uzbekistan. This constitutional order includes a long list of individual rights and democracy guarantees together with provisions centralising power in the office of the President. President Karimov then used this authority

[6] W Partlett, 'Crown-Presidentialism' (2022) 20 *International Journal of Constitutional Law* 204, 221–22.
[7] W Partlett, 'The Dangers of Popular Constitution-Making' (2012) 38 *Brooklyn Journal of International Law* 193, 227.
[8] Quoted from ibid.
[9] Quoted from A Lukashuk, 'Constitutionalism in Belarus: A False Start' in J Zielonka (ed), *Democratic Consolidation in Eastern Europe: Institutional Engineering*, vol 1 (Oxford, Oxford University Press, 2001) 309.
[10] W Partlett, 'The Importance of Constitutional Law for Belarusian Democracy: An Analysis of the Amended 1994 Constitution and Considerations for Democratic Reform' (*International IDEA Interim Analysis*, December 2020) www.constitutionnet.org/sites/default/files/2020-12/the-importance-of-constitutional-law-for-belarusian-democracy.pdf.
[11] R Zhakupov, 'Kazakhstan's Constitution: From Soviets to Democratic Values' *The Astana Times* (Astana, 18 August 2017) www.astanatimes.com/2017/08/kazakhstans-constitution-from-soviets-to-democratic-values/.

to consolidate his control over competing Uzbek clans in the name of economic and democratic reform.[12]

The techniques of the constitutional dark arts remain in use today. In 2023, Uzbekistan amended its Constitution to include new individual rights and social guarantees. These new additions, the President argued, create a 'people's constitution' that guarantees a 'social state' and 'prosperity'.[13] In addition to these changes, however, the reforms also changed the term limits provision to allow the current President to serve two additional seven-year terms as well as further centralise power in the office of the President. These changes therefore seek to justify the further centralised power of the President in the language of social democracy and individual rights guarantees.

These constitutional systems have operated much as Russia's constitutional system does. The centralisation of power in the office of the President has led to rights abuses and poor-quality governance. For instance, a key member of the Belarusian opposition, Sergei Tikhanovsky, built his opposition movement on the basis of a YouTube station that exposed the everyday problems and dysfunctionality of Belarusian governance.[14] Furthermore, neither elections nor judicial review has been able to effectively hold the President to account. Again a clear example is Belarus. After a rigged presidential election in 2020, the Belarusian President relied on his rational-legal authority to deploy law enforcement against the protestors.[15]

Crown-presidentialism has also been used to re-legitimise authoritarian governance on the African continent. A good example is Zimbabwe's 2013 Constitution. Operating for decades under a temporary constitutional arrangement, Zimbabwe's system of authoritarianism was given a permanent constitutional basis in 2013. This Constitution was in part an attempt to legitimise the dominance of Robert Mugabe's Zimbabwe African National Union – Patriotic Front (ZANU-PF) in the face of a

[12] E. Frantz, *Authoritarianism: What Everyone Needs to Know* (New York, Oxford University Press, 2018).
[13] MS Erol, 'In the "My Constitution" Referendum, the Uzbek People Said "YES": "Reforms Take Time; But There Is No Time to Lose"' (*Ankara Center for Crisis and Policy Studies*, 5 May 2023) www.ankasam.org/in-the-my-constitution-referendum-the-uzbek-people-said-yes-reforms-take-time-but-there-is-no-time-to-lose/?lang=en.
[14] R Dixon, 'Belarus Court Jails Leading Opposition Figure Sergei Tikhanovsky for 18 Years' *The Washington Post* (14 December 2021) www.washingtonpost.com/world/europe/belarus-opposition-blogger-jailed/2021/12/14/6ecc6f16-5cd6-11ec-b1ef-cb78be717f0e_story.html.
[15] Human Rights Watch, 'Belarus: Events of 2021' www.hrw.org/world-report/2022/country-chapters/belarus.

powerful challenge from the Movement for Democratic Change. The foundational chapters of the new Constitution included a broad range of individual rights, including the right to life, liberty, and freedom of conscience.[16] The Constitution also states that courts must take into account 'international law and all treaties and conventions to which Zimbabwe is a party' when they are interpreting a constitutional right.[17]

But it simultaneously centralises vast power in the hands of the President. The President assumes a pseudo-monarchical position, with the 'Legislature of Zimbabwe' described as 'Parliament and the President acting in accordance with this Chapter'.[18] In this position, the President has the authority to dissolve the legislature if it rejects an appropriation bill[19] or declares no confidence in the government.[20] The President also has full management authority, with all the ministers (including Prime Minister) appointed by and accountable to the President.[21] These provisions drew on a deeply held commitment in Mugabe's ZANU-PF party to centralisation stemming from its background as a liberation movement.[22]

Another example from Africa is South Sudan's 2011 Constitution, which sought to build legitimate authority after a bloody civil war.[23] This document includes a large list of individual rights as well as democratic guarantees. These had been included in the Constitution with little debate and reflected suggestions by international groups such as the Max Planck Institute and the National Democratic Institute. They were placed in the Constitution to signal to the international community and the South Sudanese population that the Constitution was a modern, democratic one.

But, alongside these guarantees, detailed structural provisions create a crown-presidential system that centralises vast power in the office of the President.[24] Most importantly, the President possesses unilateral management power to appoint and remove executive branch ministers.[25]

---

[16] Chapter 4 of Zimbabwe Constitution of 2013 (*Constitute: The World's Constitutions to Read, Search, and Compare*) www.constituteproject.org/constitution/Zimbabwe_2013.
[17] ibid Art 46(1)(c).
[18] ibid Art 116.
[19] ibid Art 143.3.
[20] ibid Art 109.5.
[21] ibid Arts 104 and 107.
[22] R Southall, 'Democracy in Southern Africa: Moving beyond a Difficult Legacy' (2003) 30 *Review of African Political Economy* 255, 259.
[23] Constitution of South Sudan (*Constitute: The World's Constitutions to Read, Search, and Compare*) www.constituteproject.org/constitution/South_Sudan_2011.
[24] ibid.
[25] ibid Art 112.

The President also exercises vast guardian powers. This includes the power to appoint members of the upper house of the legislature.[26] It also includes the authority to 'remove a state Governor and/or dissolve a state Legislative Assembly in the event of a crisis in the state that threatens national security and territorial integrity' and then the power to 'appoint a state care-taker Governor who shall prepare for election within sixty days'.[27] Kevin Cope refers to this exercise of the constitutional dark arts as the combination of 'transnational rights' and a 'local' desire for centralised power.[28]

These centralising provisions were justified as necessary to overcome division and ensure effective government.[29] But these provisions have done the opposite. This centralised power meant that the courts were fundamentally unable to seriously implement the broad rights guarantees in the constitutional text. In fact, the Chief Justice of the Supreme Court has been charged with corruption and collaboration with the President in violation of standards of judicial independence and impartiality.[30] Mark Deng describes how the provisions allowing the President to replace regional governors have not stabilised the country but have instead fostered 'political instability' because at least one removed governor has taken up arms against the central government.[31]

Similar trends can be found in Latin America. Roberto Gargarella describes how rights have increasingly been inserted into Latin American Constitutions since then 1980s. In many cases, these rights were an attempt to overcome past legacies of authoritarian rights abuses by opening these systems to international human rights law. But these changes have been placed within a 'distinctively presidentialist organization of power based on the concentration of functions in the hands of the president'.[32] For instance, the Venezuelan Constitution created

---

[26] ibid Art 58(b)(2).
[27] ibid 101(r) and (s).
[28] KL Cope, 'Intermestic Constitution: Lessons from the World's Newest Nation' (2013) 53 *Virginia Journal of International Law* 309.
[29] M Deng, 'South Sudan's Transitional Constitution: The Making, Failure and Lessons' (2024) 16 *African Journal of Legal Studies* 5.
[30] M Deng, 'South Sudan's Chief Justice is Overstepping his Bounds: Why it Matters for the Rule of Law' (*The Conversation*, 11 May 2021) www.theconversation.com/south-sudans-chief-justice-is-overstepping-his-bounds-why-it-matters-for-the-rule-of-law-160406.
[31] Deng (n 29).
[32] R Gargarella, *Latin American Constitutionalism, 1810–2010: The Engine Room of the Constitution* (Oxford, Oxford University Press, 2013) 156–57.

new rights and opportunities for public participation. But these changes came along with 'significant expansion' in presidential powers, including broader decree powers and less authority for parliament to oversee the President.[33]

The 1988 Brazilian Constitution is another example. It sought to overcome Brazil's previous dictatorship by introducing a number of new rights and democratic institutions. It therefore 'prohibited the use of torture, reestablished direct and secret suffrage'.[34] At the same time, however, it also continued a strong presidential system that 'was very much in line with the reforms introduced in the executive branch by the same dictatorship'.[35] These Constitutions reflected a general trend in Latin America which embraced 'rights-based' remedies to dictatorship and rejected anti-presidential ones.[36]

Roberto Gargarella describes how this continued presidential centralisation in the 'engine room of the constitution' has ultimately undermined the ability of these systems to effectively implement rights and liberal democracy. In particular, it has led to a pattern of instability that has undermined the protection of rights and weakened democracy.[37] Two hundred years of Latin American history, Roberto Gargarella concludes, shows that 'in order to achieve certain basic objectives in terms of constitutional rights … it [is] crucial to introduce fundamental changes related to the organization of power'.[38]

Comparative scholars have also noted this phenomenon more broadly. Rosalind Dixon describes a common technique where constitutional rights are used as 'bribes' to rights and democracy activists to support structural change that concentrate power in one public office.[39] In this practice, she argues, 'constitutionalizing rights may be linked to broader forms of structural constitutional change, which are distinctly antidemocratic in character'.[40] She describes how democratic reformers must be careful to avoid this trap and advises how 'unbundling' these reforms can help to ensure better and more democratic forms of constitutional amendment.

---

[33] ibid 175.
[34] ibid 150.
[35] ibid 150.
[36] ibid 151.
[37] ibid 150.
[38] ibid 204–05.
[39] R Dixon, 'Constitutional Rights as Bribes' (2018) 50 *Connecticut Law Review* 767, 771.
[40] ibid.

II. THE POPULIST THREAT TO DEMOCRACY

The constitutional dark arts have also played a central role in populist attacks on established democracy.[41] Elected leaders have claimed that centralisation is a better way to achieve a form of democracy in which one elected leader represents the people. Where successful, these movements have undermined pluralism and the balanced state tradition. This centralised governance has damaged effective and accountable democratic governance.

Turkey is a good example. For many years, Turkey was a pluralistic multi-party democracy underpinned by the balanced state tradition. In 2017, President Erdogan proposed a series of formal constitutional amendments in a referendum. He and his supporters justified these as creating a stronger and more democratic Turkish state. The amendments produced the classic hybrid Constitution of the constitutional dark arts.[42] The changes did not amend the provisions guaranteeing Turkey's status as a republic and a 'democratic, secular and social state governed by rule of law'.[43] They also did not change the long list of rights protections in the Turkish Constitution and the existence of a formally strong Constitutional Court.

Erdogan's key constitutional reforms instead altered detailed structural provisions in the chapters describing the organisation of the Turkish state. These changes transformed Turkey from a parliamentary system to a crown-presidential one. It gave the President vast management powers, abolishing the Prime Minister completely and allowing the President to appoint 'vice-presidents' and 'ministers' to oversee the implementation of policy.[44] These ministers are no longer subject to parliamentary oversight or removal through no-confidence votes. The amendments also give the President strong 'guardian' authority, making the office of the President the head of state and affording it the power to dissolve the parliament.[45] Furthermore, the President is charged with 'safeguard[ing] the existence and independence of the state, the indivisible integrity of the country and the nation, and the absolute sovereignty of the nation'.[46]

---

[41] T Daly, 'Democratic Decay: Conceptualising an Emerging Research Field' (2019) 11 *Hague Journal on the Rule of Law* 9.
[42] 'Turkey 1982 (rev 2017)' (*Constitute: The World's Constitutions to Read, Search, and Compare*) www.constituteproject.org/constitution/Turkey_2017.
[43] ibid Arts 1 and 2.
[44] ibid Art 106.
[45] ibid Art 116.
[46] ibid Art 103.

188 Countering Constitutional Authoritarianism

Finally, the President is given vast power to issue decrees and call referenda. These changes were justified in the language of centralised state discourse, with the Turkish Prime Minister arguing that 'This change will make Turkey stronger in the region, and it will act faster against threats from inside and outside'.[47]

This crown-presidentialism has given President Erdogan vast formal power to dominate formerly independent institutions such as courts, the election commission and the national bank. Control of these institutions has also helped Erdogan consolidate his power over informal political ordering by weakening and co-opting opposition groups. Erdogan has used these powers to maintain authoritarian control amidst growing discontent and opposition among his former political allies. For instance, the crown-presidential powers recently played a critical role in allowing Erdogan to win re-election in 2023. During the campaign, he unilaterally increased the salaries of public employees and exercised his control over the Central Bank to lower interest rates to stimulate short-term economic growth.[48] He and his team described his leadership as representing the entire Turkish people. One of Erdogan's political allies referred to attempts to unseat President Erdogan to be a 'political coup attempt' by hostile external forces.[49] In his acceptance speech, President Erdogan described how the people had spoken and '85 million have won as a whole'.[50]

Hungary is another good example. Viktor Orban has called for suspending politics and creating a 'central political forcefield' that would govern the country for decades.[51] As part of this project, Orban has sought constitutional change. A new 2011 Constitution was introduced and justified as a necessary democratic replacement to Hungary's

---

[47] K Fahim and A Faiola, 'Turkish Battle over "Executive Presidency" Prompts Tensions with the Netherlands and Divisions at Home' *The Washington Post* (Istanbul, 12 March 2017) www.washingtonpost.com/world/middle_east/turkeys-testy-campaign-overexecutive-presidency-sows-divisions-at-home-and-abroad/2017/03/12/6f329df0-fe98-11e6-9b78-824ccab94435_story.html.

[48] MH Yavuz, 'A Torn Country: Erdogan's Turkey and the Elections of 2023' (2023) 30(3) *Middle East Policy* 81.

[49] 'Interior Minister Soylu refers to Upcoming Elections as "West's Coup Attempt"' *Duvar.English* (28 April 2023) www.duvarenglish.com/interior-minister-soylu-refers-to-upcoming-elections-as-wests-coup-attempt-news-62297.

[50] 'Erdogan Victory Speech: "Today Nobody has Lost"' *BBC News* (29 May 2023) www.bbc.com/news/av/world-europe-65743197.

[51] D Hutt, 'Hungary Election: Who is Viktor Orban and How Has He Stayed in Power for So Long?' *Euronews* (30 March 2022) www.euronews.com/2022/03/30/hungary-election-who-is-viktor-orban-and-how-has-he-stayed-in-power-for-so-long.

communist-era Constitution.⁵² The preamble to this Constitution declares that it does not recognise 'foreign occupations' and instead is grounded on Hungary's 'historical constitution'.⁵³
Consistent with the constitutional dark arts, this Constitution remains committed to liberal democratic principles and rights. Its early provisions declare an adherence to the 'separation of powers' and 'the inviolable and inalienable fundamental rights of man'.⁵⁴ But key details in the later chapters centralise power in the hands of the government. The new Constitution expands the size of the Constitutional Court, allowing the Fidesz Party the power to pack the new seats with Fidesz loyalists. It also creates a new National Judicial Office, controlled by the party, and one with broad powers over both judicial selection and the assignment of cases within the ordinary judiciary. David Landau describes how 'the new Constitution both undermines horizontal checks on the majority' and can therefore play a role in helping the party 'to perpetuate itself in power indefinitely'.⁵⁵

The constitutional dark arts do not always involve explicit constitutional change in established democracies. They can also target long-standing norms or conventions that disperse power between different institutions or groups. This is particularly the case in the exercise of executive power, which over time has developed internal checks on the concentration of power in the head of the executive. For instance, after being elected in 2016, President Donald Trump proceeded to move to centralise executive power, trampling on traditions of independence and declaring that he had 'the absolute right to do whatever he wanted to with Department of Justice'.⁵⁶ Furthermore, in Westminster systems, victorious Party leaders are ignoring or eroding centuries-old conventions – such as an independent civil service or the principle of responsible government – on the basis of the illusory claims of the constitutional dark arts. One report suggests these techniques are not just undemocratic; they also carry the 'potential for inferior decisions or outcomes'.⁵⁷

---

⁵² 'Hungary 2011' (*Constitute: The World's Constitutions to Read, Search, and Compare*) www.constituteproject.org/constitution/Hungary_2011.
⁵³ ibid.
⁵⁴ ibid.
⁵⁵ D Landau, 'Abusive Constitutionalism' (2013) 47 *UC Davis Law Review* 189, 209.
⁵⁶ 'Trump: I Can Do Whatever I Want with The Justice Department' *CBS News* (29 December 2017) www.cbsnews.com/news/trump-i-can-do-whatever-i-want-with-justice-department/.
⁵⁷ Victorian Ombudsman, 'Alleged Politicisation of the Public Sector: Investigation of a Matter Referred from the Legislative Council on 9 February 2022' (6 December 2023) 70, www.ombudsman.vic.gov.au/our-impact/investigation-reports/alleged-politicisation-of-the-public-sector/.

We have seen this more subtle form of the constitutional dark arts in India. The current Prime Minister, Narendra Modi, has adopted a populist form of anti-politics. Described as 'India's first Prime Minister-President',[58] Modi's monthly 'Mann Ki Baat' radio show allows him to speak directly to the people. His speeches have declared the necessity of unified leadership in advancing the public good. In a speech to senior public servants in 2023, Modi argued that political parties 'are self-serving instruments of self-serving leaders, and that these organisations are intrinsically pitted against the collective good and cannot be trusted to guard and advance common welfare, public interest and national well-being'.[59]

Modi's anti-political agenda of executive centralisation has relied on the incremental erosion of key constitutional conventions that ensure balance in the Indian Constitution. This includes breach of conventions about non-interference in regional matters, respect for the opposition, and consensus in the Cabinet room.[60] It has also included the breakdown of conventions seeking to ensure judicial independence.[61] Tarun Khaitan describes this strategy as 'killing' a Constitution 'by a thousand cuts'.[62] Gautham Bhatia has described the role of the Supreme Court in this trend, as judges over time have increasingly decided constitutional cases in ways that promote the centralisation of authority.[63]

III. STRENGTHS OF THE CONSTITUTIONAL DARK ARTS

The centralised sovereign authority of the constitutional dark arts enables authoritarianism in two ways. First, it is a critical *functional* tool for top-down, authoritarian state building, giving one leader vast legal authority to issue legal commands and concentrate power (including non-legal forms of authority). Second, it is a powerful *normative* tool that bolsters the overall influence of the centralised state tradition in national constitutional discourse and allows one institution to justify its dictatorial powers.

---

[58] A Kumar, 'The Presidential Prime Minister Narendra Modi' *The Print* (18 September 2017) www.theprint.in/opinion/presidential-prime-minister-narendra-modi/9535/.
[59] H Khare, 'Modi's Anti-Politics Tirade is Preparing the Ground for an Authoritarian Switch-Over' *The Wire* (24 April 2023) www.thewire.in/politics/narendra-modi-anti-politics-bureaucracy.
[60] T Khaitan, 'Killing a Constitution with a Thousand Cuts: Executive Aggrandizement and Party-State Fusion in India' (2020) 14 *Law and Ethics of Human Rights* 49, 70–72.
[61] ibid 73–75.
[62] ibid 49–50.
[63] G Bhatia, *The Indian Constitution: Conversations with Power* (unpublished manuscript).

A. The Legal Tools of Authoritarianism

Authoritarianism is not a spontaneous form of social ordering. It requires resolving elite competition by ensuring that one leader or faction dominates politics. Centralising structural rules provide important tools for leaders to build and maintain centralised, personalised rule. Henry Hale describes how the formal constitutional centralisation of power in the office of the President allows one individual to 'signal' to competing groups that they are the 'patron' to serve.[64] Geddes, Wright and Frantz describe how the centralisation of power in the hands of one leader 'limits the ability of other officers to overthrow him' and allows him or her to 'Reward his supporters and punish those who oppose him'.[65]

We have seen this in the Russian context. Russian crown-presidentialism allows the President to unilaterally create and shape an array of offices such as the Presidential Administration, the Security Council, the Prime Minister and the executive branch ministry. These institutions help the Russian President to control state media, co-opt competitors and eliminate any opposition.

The centralised sovereign authority of the constitutional dark arts also allows the sovereign leader to co-opt or control democratic institutions such as courts and legislatures. This manipulation provides the appearance of democracy and has proven difficult to classify. Political scientists have began to develop the idea of 'autocracy with adjectives' or 'hybrid' authoritarianism.[66] For instance, Steven Levitsky and Lucan Way have introduced the influential concept of 'competitive authoritarianism' which encompasses 'civilian regimes in which formal democratic institutions exist and are widely viewed as the primary means of gaining power, but in which incumbents' abuse of the state places them at a significant advantage vis-a-vis their opponents'.[67] In this system, they argue, 'competition is real but not fair'.[68] Constitutional rules and authority play an important role in this process.

---

[64] HE Hale, 'The Informal Politics of Formal Constitutions: Rethinking the Effects of "Presidentialism" and "Parliamentarism" in the Cases of Kyrgyzstan, Moldova, and Ukraine in Constitutions' in T Ginsburg and A Simpser (eds), *Constitutions in Authoritarian Regimes* (New York, Cambridge University Press, 2014) 239.
[65] B Geddes, J Wright and E Frantz, *How Dictatorships Work: Power, Personalization, and Collapse* (Cambridge, Cambridge University Press, 2018) 215.
[66] S Levitsky and LA Way, *Competitive Authoritarianism: Hybrid Regimes after the Cold War* (Cambridge, Cambridge University Press, 2010).
[67] ibid 5.
[68] ibid.

Structural constitutional rules can also allow populist leaders to undermine established democracy.[69] David Landau has described how would-be-dictators no longer erode democratic accountability through violent military coups or revolutions. Instead, he describes how technical but 'abusive' constitutional reform has become a critical way 'to undermine democracy'.[70] This is done in a way that ensures that these documents appear 'democratic from a distance'. But when looked at closely 'they have been substantially reworked to undermine the democratic order'.[71]

Finally, structural rules can also help to bolster the sovereign leader's non-legal forms of authority. For instance, control of the media can help the formation of charismatic authority by projecting the image of a strongman leader. Centralised authority can also allow modern-day dictators to draw on traditional forms of monarchical institution building. For instance, monarchs have long created 'royal councils' that aid in centralised rule.[72] This institution-building has also often allied the leader with religious organisations. In Russia, this power has allowed the President to coordinate activity with the Russian Orthodox Church and build the presidency's traditional authority.[73]

B. Authoritarian Normativity

Political players, even authoritarian ones, must justify their actions.[74] In particular, they seek to describe the exercise of power and the contingent political arrangements around them as inevitable, necessary or natural. The centralising rules of the constitutional dark arts help to justify dictatorship. These rules come with a set of justifications and reasons for why a centralised state is natural for that jurisdiction and better able to achieve particular outcomes. This authoritarian normativity provides an additional set of reasons and justifications for encouraging obedience to

---

[69] KL Scheppele, 'Autocratic Legalism' (2018) 85 *Chicago Law Review* 545.
[70] Landau (n 55) 191.
[71] ibid.
[72] EM Bandeira, 'The 22 Frimaire of Yuan Shikai: Privy Councils in the Constitutional Architectures of Japan and China, 1887–1917' in I Sablin and EM Bandeira (eds), *Planting Parliaments in Eurasia, 1850–1950: Concepts, Practices, and Mythologies* (New York, Routledge, 2021).
[73] J Anderson, 'Putin and the Russian Orthodox Church: Asymmetric Symphonia?' (2007) 61(1) *Journal of International Affairs* 185.
[74] David Beetham, *The Legitimation of Power* (Basingstoke, Palgrave, 1991) 11.

a centralised or dictatorial system.[75] It is then critical in ensuring 'organized activity directed to the application and enforcement of the order'.[76] It therefore helps to form a normative community in which key elites such as judges, legislators and academics cooperate to enable the centralisation of power.

Three main justifications underpin the internal normativity of constitutional dark arts. First, and most fundamentally, centralisation is justified on the basis that it provides decisive leadership, stability and unity. Previous chapters have shown how Vladimir Putin has consistently and frequently justified vast presidential power on this basis. Initially, Putin used this rhetoric to attack domestic threats to unity; more recently, however, he has focused on the importance of centralised presidential power to combat external threats to Russia's identity and sovereignty.[77] These justifications have also appeared in the reasoning of the Constitutional Court and the extra-curial writings of Valery Zorkin, the Chairman of the Russian Constitutional Court.

Second, centralisation is justified on the ground that it provides for a more direct and better form of democratic representation. We can again see this in the Russian context. Putin and his team frequently point to his popularity in responding to those accusing him of undemocratic actions.[78] This rhetoric was used in the Russian legislature in debates about the new constitutional amendments. Similarly, in Turkey, Erdogan's victory in a close presidential election was described by one of Erdogan's presidential aides as reflecting the 'trust' and 'support' that the Turkish people have 'for President Erdogan's policies and vision for the country'.[79]

Third, centralisation is justified by arguing that it is necessary to secure the system of law and legality. In this idea, centralised power is necessary to guarantee the unity and authority of law.[80] As chapter

---

[75] T Frye, *Weak Strongman: The Limits of Power in Putin's Russia* (Princeton, Princeton University Press, 2021) 13.
[76] ibid 389.
[77] V Surkov, 'Putin's Long State (*Dolgoe Gosudarstvo Putina*)' (in Russian) *Nezavisimaya Gazeta* (11 February 2019) www.ng.ru/ideas/2019-02-11/5_7503_surkov.html (describing democratic pluralism as an illusion and arguing that a better and more 'honest' approach is a close connection between the leader and the people).
[78] G Yudin, 'Governing Through Polls: Politics of Representation and Presidential Support in Putin's Russia' (2020) 27 *Javnost – The Public* 1, 2.
[79] F Altun, 'Erdogan's Re-Election is Good News for Turkiye – And the World' *Al Jazeera* (31 May 2023) www.aljazeera.com/opinions/2023/5/31/erdogans-re-election-is-good-news-for-turkiye-and-the-world.
[80] Gargarella (n 32) 160.

five described, in 2000, Putin repeatedly argued that the restoration of legal and constitutional unity required centralised presidential power. The Russian Constitutional Court has also made similar arguments, famously justifying broad presidential decree power in the First Chechen War as necessary for protecting Russian territorial integrity and rights.[81]

The hybrid Constitution of the constitutional dark arts therefore allows the sovereign office not just a number of tools to assert power, but also a wide range of justifications and reasons for obeying those legal commands. Whether they appeal to emotion or reason, these arguments are an important source of cohesion in authoritarian governance. In the Russian context, researchers have described how Russia has developed a 'statist' ideology that signals deference to a 'strong stable state' that is grounded on Russian exceptionalism and nationalism.[82] This book shows how the Constitution helps to underpin this statist ideology by providing a set of reasons for why a centralised state built around one sovereign officeholder is better. The centralised Constitution helps to form the basis of a 'belief' in the rightness of the sovereign's exercise of power, which Weber places at the base of 'every kind of willingness to obey' and therefore all legitimate authority.[83]

IV. WEAKNESSES OF THE CONSTITUTIONAL DARK ARTS

An important reason to identify and understand the justifications and reasons underpinning the constitutional dark arts is that it helps to counter these normative systems. Harold Laski explains that 'it is only by seeking to understand' the goals and justifications of our opponents can we 'be able worthily to meet' that challenge.[84] As we have seen, the centralisation of the constitutional dark arts is often justified on the ability of concentrated constitutional authority to provide stable governance, unmediated popular accountability and unified legality.

Experience shows, however, that centralised regimes undermine these very goals over time. Russia shows how and why. Its centralised sovereign

---

[81] See ch 4 of this book.
[82] WE Pomeranz, *Law and the Russian State: Russia's Legal Evolution from Peter the Great to Vladimir Putin* (London, Bloomsbury Publishing, 2018); M Snegovaya, 'The Ideology of Putinism: Is It Sustainable?' (*CSIS*, 27 September 2023) www.csis.org/analysis/ideology-putinism-it-sustainable.
[83] Max Weber, *Theory of Social and Economic Organization* (T Parsons (ed), AM Henderson and T Parsons (trans)) (New York, Free Press, 1947) 388.
[84] H Laski, 'The Pluralistic State' (1919) 28 *The Philosophical Review* 562, 575.

authority has enabled one office to entrench its power and fostered personalised governance. The greater the power in the centre, however, the less power and capacity that has been given to other institutions. This dynamic has contributed to poor quality governance, weak popular accountability and poor rule of law. Thus, in sum, the authoritarian normativity of the constitutional dark arts is empty, a cover for a system of arbitrary and dysfunctional governance that benefits a small ruling class.

A. A Weak and Poorly Governed State

A critical justification for centralisation is that it overcomes division and creates a strong state. This 'strong' state is then described as better able to engage in effective policymaking by avoiding political considerations or partisan ideology and instead grounding policy on technocratic decisions. Often underlying this claim is the idea that technocratic bureaucracies wielding the tools of modern managerialism are highly effective in ensuring targeted policymaking. Another common claim is that centralisation is better at rapid modernisation. This claim is often supported by the ability of the centre to rationally distribute goods and resources according to long-term, centralised plans.

Centralised sovereign authority can yield important short-term stability in times of crisis or emergency. Moreover, it can help one leader to consolidate and hold on to power. But, over time, constitutional centralisation is likely to have corrosive effects on the ability of other state institutions to effectively implement centralised policy. When all power is centralised in one institution, we frequently see the excessive personalisation of power. This personalisation of power undermines accountability from other institutions and allows the use of public power for private ends.

The personalisation of power encourages the use of public power for personal gain. Turkey presents a good example of this problem. In the year before the election, President Erdogan drew heavily on his power over the Central Bank to ensure a victory in the election. Despite spiralling inflation and deep economic problems, Erdogan removed two members of the Central Bank and directed the Bank to cut interest rates. These cuts gave the economy a short-term boost and therefore aided Erdogan's re-election campaign.[85] In the long-term, however, these lower

---

[85] M Young, 'Why is Turkey's President Cutting Interest Rates, Spurring Inflation and Lowering the Value of the Lira?' (*Malcolm H Kerr Carnegie Middle East Center*, 2 December 2021) www.carnegie-mec.org/diwan/85896.

rates would have damaging economic consequences. Erdogan acknowledged as much when he appointed a new central bank President who raised rates after the election.[86]

Another example is 1990s Russia. As chapter four demonstrated, President Boris Yeltsin frequently circumvented the elected legislature and drew on his access to public goods to secure its own self-interest. This personalised approach to economic reform lacked any of the key legal guarantees that are at the centre of an efficient market economy.[87] For this reason, this reform benefited only a small group of individuals, including the oligarchs who gained these shares and President Yeltsin.

The personalisation of power also encourages informal arrangements where powerful leaders allow officials to engage in corrupt activities in return for personal loyalty. As recent research has discovered, 'Dictators who allow rampant corruption often use their security police to collect information about it so that officials who displease them for any reason can be humiliated, deprived of office, and jailed when their corruption is "discovered"'.[88] We have seen this technique in Russia. Even after Putin's recentralisation of power, corruption has flourished in Russia. This corruption has continued in order to enable Vladimir Putin to enforce the loyalty of powerful regional executives and businessmen. Although this has consolidated centralised authority, it has not improved the rule of law or the quality of state governance. Instead, it has damaged the ability of the state to provide important social goods, particularly outside of Moscow.

There is also strong evidence that centralisation undermines effective policy-making. In centralised systems, sovereign leaders often value 'loyalty more than competence when promoting officers or making administrative appointments'.[89] Moreover, public officials face little accountability from below; instead, accountability comes from above as they must please their superiors to advance their careers. This can lead to central policy decisions that are grounded on poor or deliberately misrepresented information.[90]

A good example of this is Vladimir Putin's decision to invade Ukraine in February 2022. This decision was made in part on the basis of the

---

[86] P Kirby, 'Turkey Hikes Interest Rates as Erdogan Stages Economic U-Turn' *BBC News* (22 June 2023) www.bbc.com/news/world-europe-65971791.

[87] K Pistor, *The Code of Capital: How the Law Creates Wealth and Inequality* (Princeton, Princeton University Press, 2019).

[88] Geddes, Wright and Frantz (n 65) 191.

[89] ibid.

[90] V Gel'man, *The Politics of Bad Governance in Contemporary Russia* (Ann Arbor, University of Michigan Press, 2022) 95–96.

(false) belief that Ukraine would collapse very quickly and that most Ukrainians themselves would welcome a Russian invasion. This (incorrect) view of how the war would play out was itself the product of faulty information about public opinion in Ukraine. A leading Russian expert on the FSB noted that 'After two weeks of war, it now appears that Putin has finally realized that he was misled: afraid of angering the Russian leader, the Fifth Service simply told him what he wanted to hear'.[91]

Finally, centralised systems of power grounded on popular legitimacy also foster special problems of long-term political instability. Most notably, this kind of system often leads to a problematic and dangerous process of leadership succession. Monarchies solve the problem of succession through family ties; ideological one-party states from the hierarchy in the ruling party. But populist leaders have fewer mechanisms to mediate these transitions. In fact, in these systems, there are often strong reasons to avoid naming a successor as this will undermine the personal political power of the sovereign leader and expose him or her to the power of the state. This kind of personalism means that you are more likely to see major conflict or even regime collapse when the sovereign dictator leaves office.[92] Moreover, it is generally more difficult for new elites in personalised regimes to reconsolidate power.[93]

These are just a few examples demonstrating why a centralised state is better at projecting the image of an effective state than actually delivering it. They show that, particularly over the long term, centralisation is likely to undermine the authority of the state and its ability to effectively respond to serious policy difficulties.

B. Managed Popular Accountability

Another critical justification for the constitutional dark arts is that centralisation enables unmediated popular representation and accountability. This direct democracy rationale is open to criticism that it mistakenly views the people as a unified group. But, even if we put that objection aside and agree that the people speak with one voice, this kind of rationale cannot be defended over the long term. Populist leaders are often highly popular in the beginning and represent the wishes of the

---

[91] Quoted from Frye (n 75) xi.
[92] Geddes, Wright and Frantz (n 65) 192.
[93] ibid 201–02.

people. Over time, however, this popularity often wanes and these leaders use their vast power to 'manage' public opinion to remain in power. These entrenchment techniques then insulate the leader from real popular accountability. This leads to a situation that has been described as 'one person, one vote, one time' where the people can have one meaningful opportunity to vote for a leader but cannot do so after that initial election.

Russia's experience of 'managed democracy' shows the techniques for manipulating popular opinion and therefore avoiding real accountability. These methods include control of the media as well as fourth branch institutions such as election commissions. It also includes the creation of fake parties to siphon off opposition votes or the use of administrative resources to pressure people to vote in a particular way.[94] These management techniques create a kind of 'political technology' that deprives the people of any ability to really control the sovereign leader over time.[95] In this way, centralisation does not create a direct accountability relationship between the people and the sovereign leader. Instead, it severs this relationship and allows the leader to exercise public power in his or her private interest rather than the broader public interest.

C. Poor Legality and Rights Protection

The centralising provisions of the constitutional dark arts claim to provide for a powerful leader who can ensure effective sovereignty and therefore guarantee legal unity and rights protection. But this centralised domination often fails to secure strong legal institutions. The concentration of power in one leader inevitably undermines the institutional independence and authority of legal institutions. In fact, the sovereign leader is likely to use its vast authority and powers of appointment to ensure loyalty from courts and other legal institutions. It therefore creates a legal system where certain important interests or individuals are able to transcend or avoid legal obligation and law becomes an instrument of political power.[96]

---

[94] A Wilson, *Political Technology: The Globalisation of Political Manipulation* (Cambridge, Cambridge University Press, 2023).
[95] ibid.
[96] E Fraenkel, *The Dual State: A Contribution to The Theory of Dictatorship* (E Shills trans) (Oxford, Oxford University Press, 2018).

This personalism and institutional decay undermines legality as conflicts are resolved not by impartial, trusted courts applying the law but instead by biased courts or the personal intervention of the sovereign dictator. When the office of the President is unable or unwilling to solve such a dispute, violence can emerge as a way of settling the disagreement. During the personalised Russian presidency of the 1990s, business disputes were frequently settled outside of court through violence. This system also damages economic growth because it weakens the secure legal mechanisms that are critical to economic growth.[97]

Centralisation can also undermine the protection of rights. In a system committed to the benefits of centralised power, the interests of the individual are undervalued. In this kind of system, courts are likely to defer to broad legislative limitations on rights. In Russia, this can be found in the deferential form of 'reverse proportionality' that the courts have taken to individual rights claims. In this approach, courts are willing to allow broad limitations of a right on the basis of a claim that these limitations are linked with a legitimate state goal.

Centralisation can also create more practical problems for social rights protection. In Russia, central government often orders regional governments to protect socio-economic rights, such as affordable housing and health care.[98] Weak local institutions often lack the resources or competence to effectively deploy state resources to effectively implement these rights obligations. These regional governments have long been starved of resources and staffed with incompetent but loyal administrators by the central government.[99] A well-known example occurred after Vladimir Putin's return to the presidency in 2012. Upon assuming office, Putin signed an ambitious set of presidential decrees seeking to achieve some of the socio-economic goals.[100] These decrees were left to the regions to implement but were not adequately funded by the centre; this led to serious problems of non-compliance due to a lack of funding.[101]

---

[97] Pistor (n 87).
[98] G Di Bella, O Dynnikova and F Grigoli, 'Fiscal Federalism and Regional Performance in Russia' (2018) 4 *Russian Journal of Economics* 108, 114. In 2016, regional spending represented 95 per cent of general government expenditure for housing and utilities, 80 per cent for education and cultural activities and around 85 per cent for health including spending by territorial extra-budgetary medical funds.
[99] World Bank, 'Russian Federation: Reducing Poverty through Growth and Social Policy Reform' (Report No 28923-RU, Poverty Reduction and Economic Management Unit, Europe and Central Asia Region, World Bank, 2005) 114.
[100] W Pomeranz and K Smith, 'Commentary: Putin's domestic strategy: Counting the trees, missing the forest' *Reuters* (3 June 2016) www.reuters.com/article/idUSKCN0YM087/.
[101] ibid.

V. CONCLUSION

The constitutional dark arts therefore provide important tools for a centralised sovereign to consolidate power and dominate politics. But this centralisation comes at a high cost. In particular, it undermines the institutional authority of other institutions. This weakness can lead to serious regime instability and weak rule of law. It also fosters what Vladimir Gelman calls 'the politics of bad governance'.[102]

This conclusion provides a powerful lesson for combating this new form of constitutional authoritarianism. These systems contain the seeds of their own destruction. In fact, the Russian example shows how these weaknesses can be exploited. As described in chapter eight, the Navalny movement has repeatedly highlighted the weakness of Russia's current constitutional system, threatening one of its key justifications.

The next chapter will describe the broader philosophical roots of this kind of anti-centralist critique. For centuries, political philosophers have argued that centralisation is counter-productive and unable to achieve its stated purposes. These philosophers have instead extolled the virtues of a constitutional balance. This kind of balanced Constitution, this tradition argues, is more likely to recognise and utilise the authority of a broader range of institutions. This recognition builds more effective authority and more effective governance. This tradition of political philosophy carries important lessons for democratic constitutional theory.

---

[102] Gel'man (n 90) 1–25.

10

Renewing Democratic Constitutionalism

ON 19 OCTOBER 1993, a key American diplomat stationed in Moscow sent United States Secretary of State Warren Christopher a cable. The cable warned Secretary Christopher about the constitutional draft that Yeltsin was preparing for a referendum in December 1993. In particular, it described the 'preponderance of authority' in the office of the Russian President in Yeltsin's constitutional draft.[1] In later discussions between Warren and his counterpart, these concerns were ignored. In fact, a subsequent conversation between United States President Bill Clinton and Boris Yeltsin did not mention the presidential centralisation in the Constitution at all.[2]

In the heat of the moment in 1993, the failure to recognise the authoritarian potential of the Russian Constitution could be partially excused by personal trust in the leadership of Russian President Boris Yeltsin. Yeltsin was commonly viewed by the West as the only leader interested in reforming the Soviet system and opening Russia to the world. Boris Yeltsin had close personal ties with many Western leaders, most notably United States President Bill Clinton. But, even today, the role of the Russian Constitution in Russian authoritarianism is misunderstood. In fact, the Russian Constitution is often incorrectly described as a French-style semi-presidential system that has become little more than a sham.[3]

---

[1] 'Cable from American Embassy Moscow to Secretary of State: Secretary's Visit to Moscow: Domestic Political Dynamics' (*George Washington University National Security Archive*, 19 October 1993) https://nsarchive.gwu.edu/document/30734-document-10-cable-american-embassy-moscow-secretary-state-secretarys-visit-moscow.

[2] 'Memorandum of Telephone Conversation: Telcon with President Boris Yeltsin of the Russian Federation' (*George Washington University National Security Archive*, 22 December 1993) www.nsarchive.gwu.edu/document/16853-document-11-memorandum-telephone-conversation.

[3] See, e.g. T Colton and C Skach, 'A Fresh Look at Semipresidentialism: The Russian Predicament' (2005) 16 Journal of Democracy 113.

As chapters four to seven of this book have described, however, key parts of the Russian Constitution have not failed. Instead, the centralising structural provisions in its later chapters have contributed to a system of presidential dictatorship. In particular, the vast authority lodged in the Russian President has allowed this office to dominate politics and undermine the guarantees of democracy and rights protection. Moreover, these centralising structural provisions have allowed the President to justify this presidential dictatorship as consistent with stable, democratic governance. These justifications have helped to transform the central institutions meant to protect democracy and individual rights – courts and elections – into ones that now legitimise centralised, authoritarian power. In addition, international law norms and institutions were similarly incapable of arresting Russia's growing authoritarianism.

The persistent failure to see these structural constitutional provisions and understand their political and normative consequences for Russian politics exposes a key blind spot in our understanding of democratic Constitutions. It shows that democratic Constitutions are far more than documents that contain rights provisions and democratic guarantees. Instead, democratic Constitutions more fundamentally are made up of structural constitutional rules which come with a *normative* commitment to competitive and pluralistic politics.

This structural-normative understanding can then help us renew and deepen our understanding of democratic constitutionalism. In particular, it shows the importance of linking the study of democratic constitutional design with normative political philosophy. For thousands of years, anti-centralist political philosophers have argued that a democratic Constitution not only limits power but also builds more effective governance by preserving the authority of different institutions of the state to cooperate in solving collective political problems. This insight reveals that constitutional structural provisions in democracies must do more than disperse authority between different institutions; they must do so in a way that balances power so that these institutions can cooperate and compromise. This balanced system of democratic constitutional authority is about more than just limiting the state; it is about ensuring more effective governance.

I. THE DANGERS OF LEGAL CONSTITUTIONALISM

Our blindness to the impacts of the centralising structural provisions in the Russian Constitution can be attributed to a powerful paradigm for understanding Constitutions. This legal paradigm – which is particularly influential among lawyers and constitutional theorists – views democratic Constitutions through the lens of rights and courts. This approach encourages us to think of constitutional democracy as primarily a process of *limiting or constraining* the state through judicially-enforced rights or democratic provisions. In this vision, democratic constitutionalism is founded on an apolitical and reason-based form of legal accountability.

Seen through this legal lens, constitutional rights and democracy guarantees are more important in democratic Constitutions than the detailed structural provisions that apportion power between the institutions of state. These individual rights provisions and democracy guarantees operate independently of the centralisation of power in the hands of one sovereign office.[4] To the extent that the two are linked, the rights provisions 'compensate' or constrain the excesses of this the centralisation of power. A written commitment to rights, democratic principles and independent courts is therefore sufficient for ensuring democracy.

This rights and court-centred understanding of democratic constitutionalism is sometimes traced to United States Supreme Court's landmark *Marbury v Madison* case where Justice John Marshall wrote that 'it is emphatically the province and duty of the judicial department to say what the law is'.[5] But, even after this case, the decisive role of judges and lawyers in constitutional interpretation and implementation was contested in the United States. Although courts did apply the Constitution as a law in specific cases and controversies, the Constitution was also heavily debated by legislators and other non-judicial actors.[6] Constitutional law therefore involved a dialogue between courts and non-legal political actors.[7]

After World War II, however, democratic Constitutions increasingly became viewed as legal documents containing rights provisions that were primarily enforced by courts. This was most clear in the role of the United States Supreme Court in the civil rights movement in the United States. Martin Loughlin describes how the 'rights revolution' has

---

[4] R Gargarella, *Latin American Constitutionalism, 1810–2010: The Engine Room of the Constitution* (Oxford, Oxford University Press, 2013) 157–58.

[5] *Marbury v Madison* 5 US 137, 177 (1803).

[6] LD Kramer, *The People Themselves: Popular Constitutionalism and Judicial Review* (Oxford, Oxford University Press, 2004).

[7] MV Tushnet, 'Popular Constitutionalism as Political Law' (2006) 81 *Chicago Kent Law Review* 991, 997.

'dramatically strengthen[ed] the power of the judiciary'.[8] He argues that this rights revolution fostered the idea of the 'total constitution' in which the judiciary regulates all parts of political life.[9]

The combination of rights discourse and legal constitutionalism was not just an American story. Another critical player in this global spread of legal constitutionalism was the German Constitutional Court. Seeking to learn the lessons of Nazi Germany, the drafters of the German Basic Law inserted provisions into the Constitution that would be used to protect democracy. These included both rights provisions as well as provisions banning 'associations' whose purposes were directed against the 'constitutional order or the concept of international understanding'.[10] Alongside individual rights provisions, the democracy-protecting provisions became known as 'militant democracy' and have empowered the German Constitutional Court to defend democracy through litigation. A final key player in this paradigm has been the international human rights movement. As described in chapter two, this movement has placed reason-based, rights adjudication at the centre of democratic governance since 1975.

In this understanding, democracy increasingly became the domain of judges and lawyers. For instance, a leading proponent of this kind of judge-led, legal constitutionalism – Ronald Dworkin – discusses a fictitious judge called 'Hercules' who uses his 'superhuman' powers to resolve legal questions.[11] Hercules uses these powers to find the 'right answer' to virtually all judicial questions, even those we might term 'hard cases'.[12] A Justice of the United States Supreme Court used similar language to describe the judge's role as akin to a 'demi-god to whom objective truth has been revealed' and a kind of 'legal pharmacist, dispensing the correct rule prescribed for the legal problem presented'.[13]

The rise of the rights-protecting, judicially centred democratic Constitution clearly has undoubtedly had positive impacts on democracy. For instance, judges and courts played an important role in overcoming

---

[8] M Loughlin, *Against Constitutionalism* (Cambridge MA, Harvard University Press, 2022) 191.
[9] ibid 130.
[10] Constitution of the German Federal Republic, Art 9 *Constitute* www.constituteproject.org/constitution/German_Federal_Republic_2014.
[11] R Dworkin, *Taking Rights Seriously* (London, Bloomsbury Academic, 2013) 132–59.
[12] ibid 335–48.
[13] WJ Brennan Jr, 'Reason, Passion, and "The Progress of the Law"' (1988) 10 *Cardozo Law Review* 3, 4–5.

the Jim Crow system in the American south.[14] It also has played an important role in transforming German political governance. But an overly legal understanding of a democratic Constitution also has problems. First, it can foster an anti-political version of democracy grounded on a distrust for political competition and mobilisation. This can undermine the internal practice of democracy as well as attempts at protecting rights and democracy more broadly. Second, it can limit the ability of international institutions to effectively promote democracy. Third, it can feed into the problematic belief that constitutional democracy naturally requires a small libertarian state.

A. An Anti-Political Understanding of Democracy

Legal constitutionalism grounds democracy and rights protection on an anti-political process that aspires to solve problems of democratic disagreement through litigation and judicial decision-making. It views many political disputes as moral ones that can be resolved through reason, where 'lawyers and judges are working political philosophers of a democratic state'.[15] Taken as the basis of democracy, this approach to democracy risks undermining or devaluing political pluralism and compromise in political decision-making. It therefore can foster an anti-political form of democracy stripped of partisanship and contestation.

This legal understanding of a Constitution has fostered a view of democratic constitutionalism as a specialised practice, one best known to lawyers and judges. As Martin Loughlin describes it, 'the meaning of the Constitution is the preserve of legal artistry' and 'these jurists share an appreciation of the authoritative status of the text and a conviction that its meaning can be disclosed through skilful legal analysis'.[16] This legalism poses a risk of 'draining the lifeblood from democracy, not just as a system of collective decision-making but, perhaps more importantly, as a way of life'.[17] Loughlin also warns how this approach to democracy diverts important issues 'to a forum that is relatively remote,

---

[14] J Bass, *Unlikely Heroes: The Dramatic Story of the Southern Judges of the Fifth Circuit who Translated the Supreme Court's Brown Decision into a Revolution for Equality* (Tuscaloosa, AL, University of Alabama Press, 1990).
[15] R Dworkin, *Justice for Hedgehogs* (Cambridge, Belknap Press, 2011) 415.
[16] Loughlin (n 8) 140–41.
[17] ibid 168.

unaccountable, costly, and operates on the principle of individual complaint' and which is 'insulated from the cut and thrust of ordinary life'.[18]

In addition, others have voiced concern that an overly strong focus on *legal* democracy is likely to weaken political mobilisation and accountability. Tony Judt warns that the anti-politics of rights discourse has 'misled a generation of young activists into believing that, conventional avenues of change being hopelessly clogged, they should forsake political organization for single-issue, non-governmental groups unsullied by compromise'.[19] In particular, he describes how it has led an entire generation of smart young students to attend law school to change the world, rather than enter politics.

The anti-politics of legal constitutionalism can also reinforce a growing threat to traditional democratic politics in many established democracies. As levels of trust in democratic institutions (such as political parties) plummet, a 'void' has opened up between voters and their representatives.[20] In response, leaders are increasingly arguing that only a constitutional system that allows them to directly and personally represent the whole people is able to overcome this problem. At the same time, these leaders often argue that traditional partisan politics can and should be replaced by a technocratic politics of truth. This anti-politics envisions the use of depoliticised institutions to engage in policy-making.[21] Courts can be a critical institutional player in this kind of anti-politics because they resolve disputes through a reasoned and apolitical form of decision-making.

This alliance of technocratic institutions with a populist leader reflects a powerful new political logic that one recent book calls 'technopopulism'.[22] Populism and technocracy are often thought to be contradictory ideas. But they share a common anti-politics. They both rely on a view of popular will as unitary and governance as the search for truth. Moreover, both 'advance an unmediated conception of the common good' and reject the idea that political values and positions may not be reconcilable across all of society.[23]

---

[18] ibid.
[19] T Judt, *Ill Fares the Land: A Treatise on Our Present Discontents* (New York, Penguin, 2010) 162–64.
[20] P Mair, *Ruling the Void: The Hollowing of Western Democracy* (London, Verso, 2013) 1.
[21] D Matthews-Ferraro, 'Book Review: Technopopulism: The New Logic of Democratic Politics' (2022) 25 European Journal of Social Theory 189.
[22] CJ Bickerton and CI Accetti, *Technopopulism: The New Logic of Democratic Politics* (London, Oxford University Press, 2021).
[23] ibid 3.

This technopopulism has dangerous consequences for pluralistic democratic governance. First, appeals to represent the whole people inevitably limit room for dissenting views or debate. According to this logic, political opponents are 'perceived as "enemies" rather than "adversaries", and the outer texture of democratic politics becomes more sour and confrontational'.[24] This dynamic means that the traditional struggle between 'left and right ideological poles' is replaced by a 'struggle between the whole and the parts, in which one side of the conflict appears inherently superior'.[25] For this reason, politicians 'are much less likely to recognize and accept each other's political legitimacy'.[26] This can lead to attempts to entrench power in the name of the people through the increased use of the coercive power of the state (including the criminal justice system) against political opposition or critics. This punitive turn suppresses pluralism and silences debate and discussion.

A second consequence of this logic is that politics becomes less substantive and more ideologically empty. The anti-politics of technopopulism reject pluralistic democracy grounded on 'competing mass parties' that represent different parts of society and which 'recognize each other's political legitimacy'.[27] In the place of this traditional partisan competition and compromise are moral and universal appeals to a single truth. This tends toward a politics of identity and culture and a focus on 'personality, image, and competence'.[28] Taken together, this means the 'substantive content' of politics is being 'progressively marginalised', including distributional economic questions such as housing costs and inter-generational wealth.[29]

Legal constitutionalism can therefore help to reinforce this highly centralised, polarised, and punitive politics that is drained of real substantive content. This kind of system is not only more conflictual, it is also less likely to improve governance. There are numerous examples in established democracies. In France, for instance, Emmanuel Macron has used this logic to govern in a way that appeals to his own personality and competence in overseeing a post-ideological politics of solving problems.[30]

---

[24] ibid 147.
[25] ibid 34–35.
[26] ibid 20.
[27] ibid 34.
[28] ibid 149.
[29] ibid 148.
[30] C Bickerton, 'The Rise of the Technopopulists' *The New Statesman* (9 September 2021) www.newstatesman.com/international/2020/10/rise-technopopulists.

B. Ineffective International Democracy Promotion

The anti-politics of legal constitutionalism can also undermine international efforts at promoting democracy and rights protection. Organisations such as the United Nations or non-governmental organisations spend considerable resources promoting democracy and rights. For instance, Article 1 of the United Nations Charter states that a key purpose of the UN is to 'promot[e] and encourage[e] respect for human rights and for fundamental freedoms'.[31]

But these international organisations often take an anti-political approach to this goal. The United Nations, for instance, states that it aims to promote 'democracy' but does not advocate 'a specific model of government'.[32] Instead, it seeks to promote democracy as 'a set of values and principles that should be followed for greater participation, equality, security and human development'.[33] The United Nations Human Rights Council has stated that the 'separation of powers' is a critical component of rights protection.[34] But this focus remains highly legalistic with great stress in the separation of powers on the 'independence of the judiciary' rather than a balance of authority between powerful public institutions.

Transnational institutions like the European Commission on Democracy Through Law (commonly known as the Venice Commission) take a similar anti-political approach to democracy and rights promotion. Founded in 1990, this Commission was grounded on the idea that democracy can be secured through legal reform. It therefore seeks to provide non-political, technical advice in advancing democratic governance. A vivid example of the limitations of this legal approach can be seen in the Venice Commission's discussion of the 1993 Russian Constitution.[35] This report limits itself to 'technical/legal' questions.[36] In so doing, it focuses very little on the political consequences of the broad constitutional authority given to the President in the later chapters of the

---

[31] Charter of the United Nations (1945) www.un.org/en/about-us/un-charter.
[32] 'Democracy' (United Nations) www.un.org/en/global-issues/democracy.
[33] ibid.
[34] UN Human Rights Council, 'Human Rights, Democracy, and the Rule of Law' (19 April 2012) UN Doc A/HRC/RES/19/36.
[35] Venice Commission, Council of Europe, 'Opinion on the Constitution of the Russian Federation as Adopted by Popular Vote on 12 December 1993' (24 March 1994) www.venice.coe.int/webforms/documents/default.aspx?pdffile=CDL(1994)011-e.
[36] ibid.

Russian Constitution. Instead, the report places 'particular importance' on the provisions creating a Constitutional Court. These provisions, it argues, will play a 'decisive' role in shaping the political consequences of any other provisions.[37]

As 30 years of engagement by the international human rights law community shows, this anti-political strategy is unlikely to work. To really promote rights and good governance, the international community must adopt a more consciously structural approach that focuses on the domestic organisation of political power. This reflects the fact that neither rights protection nor democracy can be a technical, legal matter. They instead are grounded on a system of pluralistic politics that recognises different sites of authority.

If international organisations are not comfortable with explicit discussions of state construction because they prefer to remain apolitical, they are better off not seeking to promote rights or democracy at all. The current technical, anti-political approach can be more than just ineffective. It can also allow authoritarian regimes to build international democratic legitimacy without building a constitutional system that disperses power. Russia again is a good example. The rights provisions in the early chapters of the Russian Constitution were widely viewed as signalling its democratic transition. As the Venice Commission wrote, the foundational chapters contain guarantees that ensure that the Constitution 'does not give rise to any serious question as to its conformity with the principles of a democratic State governed by the rule of law and respectful of human rights'.[38] This allowed Russia to enjoy the status as a democracy in the international legal system without actually adopting a constitutional structure that promoted pluralistic, democratic governance.

C. A Libertarian View of a Democratic State

Legal constitutionalism can also falsely associate constitutional democracy with a libertarian or laissez-faire form of economics and a weak state.[39] The legal paradigm of democratic Constitutions is animated by

---

[37] ibid.
[38] ibid.
[39] S Moyn, *Not Enough: Human Rights in an Unequal World* (Cambridge MA, Harvard University Press, 2019).

the negative idea of state limitation rather than a positive conception of a more effective state. In this negative vision, the democratic Constitution is ill-suited to the creation of a social state or egalitarian measures, particularly those aimed at regulating or redistributing wealth and overcoming poverty. Instead, the democratic Constitution should direct state action toward preserving or promoting private market ordering. Hayek was one of the leading theorists of this anti-regulatory understanding of the state.[40] More recently, Cass Sunstein summed up this position in the 1990s when he counselled new democracies to avoid placing positive social and economic rights in their Constitutions because these would be 'dangerous' and undermine the norm that 'governments should not be compelled to interfere with free markets'.[41]

It was this understanding of a constitutional democracy that motivated Boris Yeltsin in the early 1990s. As described in chapter four, President Boris Yeltsin and his supporters prioritised economic liberalisation over political reform. They saw a drastic reduction of state control over the economy and the shrinking of the Russian state as necessary preconditions for democracy. This understanding also drove the thinking of many American officials during Russia's constitutional drafting period. As the Chief Political Analyst at the United States Embassy from 1990 to 1994 stated:

> The U.S. government chose the economic over the political. We chose the freeing of prices, privatization of industry, and the creation of a really unfettered, unregulated capitalism, and essentially hoped that rule of law, civil society, and representative democracy would develop somehow automatically as a result of that.[42]

Democratic constitutionalism need not, however, be associated with a small, limited state. As the following sections will describe, structural rules in a democracy do not only limit the concentration of authority in one public office. They also build more effective and durable public order over time. This more effective state can then exercise this authority by, for instance, intervening in the market or limiting the power of powerful private interests.

---

[40] F Hayek, *Law, Legislation, and Liberty: Rules and Order*, vol 1 (Chicago, Chicago University Press, 1973).
[41] CR Sunstein, 'Against Positive Rights' (1993) 2 *East European Constitutional Review* 35, 36.
[42] 'Transcript: Return of the Czar' (*Frontline*, 9 May 2000) www.pbs.org/wgbh/pages/frontline/shows/yeltsin/etc/script.html.

II. THE POLITICAL AND NORMATIVE FOUNDATIONS OF DEMOCRATIC CONSTITUTIONALISM

Given these dangers of an overly legal understanding of the Constitution, renewing our understanding of democratic constitutionalism requires turning our attention to the constitutional rules that allocate power between institutions and therefore organise political power. These structural rules are *foundational* in democratic political ordering. They serve as the 'ultimate – and sometimes the proximate – source for whatever protection we have for our fundamental rights'.[43] In other words, the ultimate success of constitutional democracy and rights guarantees relies on the *system* of politics constituted by structural provisions in the Constitution.

Political scientists frequently study these types of rules. This research, however, often fails to examine the *normative* dimensions of these structural rules. It instead analyses Constitutions (and constitutional institutions) empirically, reflecting a positivist preference for value-neutral inquiry.[44] This understanding can lead to a reductive understanding of Constitutions as simply the product of power politics.[45] This approach can also lead to an understanding of constitutional courts as purely strategic actors.[46]

Russia's post-Soviet constitutional experience shows, however, that structural constitutional provisions carry an important normative dimension that shape discussions of how politics should be structured. In Russia, this authoritarian normativity enables the President to wield vast authority not through extra-legal force or threats, but on the basis of constitutional arguments about the proper exercise of power. These arguments can then be made both inside and outside of court; this normative content both empowers and limits political actors in the system.

This insight helps to better understand not just authoritarian orders but also democratic ones. Democratic constitutional orders contain structural rules that both constitute and value a political system of dispersed institutional power and pluralistic politics. This system of

---

[43] M Tushnet, *Why the Constitution Matters* (New Haven, Yale University Press, 2010).
[44] Robert A Dahl, 'The Behavioral Approach in Political Science: Epitaph for a Monument to a Successful Protest' (1961) 55 *American Political Science Review* 763.
[45] T Ginsburg and A Simpser (eds), *Constitutions in Authoritarian Regimes* (New York, Cambridge University Press, 2014).
[46] See eg A Trochev and PH Solomon Jr, 'Authoritarian Constitutionalism in Putin's Russia: A Pragmatic Constitutional Court in a Dual State' (2018) 51 *Communist and Post-Communist Studies* 201.

democratic normativity helps to ensure the protection of rights and real democratic accountability both inside and outside of court. In particular, it gives institutions good reasons for preserving their authority and capacity to participate in politics. Renewing and deepening our understanding of democratic Constitutions requires better understanding how detailed structural rules can generate this democratic normativity.

This research can build on an older political science literature that has studied the normative consequences of Constitutions. This research includes Juan Linz's work on the 'perils' of presidentialism that seeks to understand how constitutional design concepts shape democratic governance.[47] It also can build on the work of scholars of 'political constitutionalism', who examine how constitutional rules shape politics and hold officials to account outside of court and through political processes. A leading example of this work is Richard Bellamy who places republican theory at the basis of his normative theory of political constitutionalism.[48]

This existing research remains limited, however, by the use of broad concepts such as parliamentarism, presidentialism and semi-presidentialism that gloss over significant differences.[49] For instance, parliamentarism can span a number of different forms. Some are likely to encourage democratic politics; others are not. Presidentialism is much the same. As we have seen in great detail in this book, a separation of powers system with an elected President can be arranged in non-democratic ways.

Deepening our understanding of democratic Constitutions must therefore seek to look beyond these broad concepts. This form of detailed research can take a number of different forms. For instance, Steffen Ganghof's work conceptualises a specific type of parliamentary governance that is normatively attractive from a democratic point of view.[50] In so doing, he qualifies some of the broader conceptual concepts in the field. Moreover, this work must also recognise that there are no 'one size fits all' solutions for renewing democratic constitutionalism. The answers will differ depending on the institutional and historical context.

---

[47] J Linz, 'The Perils of Presidentialism' (1990) 1 *Journal of Democracy* 51.
[48] R Bellamy, *Political Constitutionalism: A Republican Defence of the Constitutionality of Democracy* (Cambridge, Cambridge University Press, 2007).
[49] L Burton-Crawford and J Goldsworthy, 'Constitutionalism' in C Saunders and A Stone (eds), *The Oxford Handbook of the Australian Constitution* (Oxford, Oxford University Press, 2018) 357.
[50] S Ganghof, *Beyond Presidentialism and Parliamentarism: Democratic Design and the Separation of Powers* (Oxford, Oxford University Press, 2021).

For instance, political constitutionalism must break free from its dependence on the institutional practices taken from the British context so that it can be understood in other contexts.[51]

III. A BALANCED AND ENERGETIC CONSTITUTIONAL DEMOCRACY

This research must also be linked with a better understanding of the broader normative goals of democratic politics. Democratic politics is about more than judicial rights protections and periodic elections. It is more fundamentally a political system that disperses power between institutions that interact with one another and the people in a way that promotes accountability and cooperation. Recent democratic constitutional theory has argued that this dispersion of power does more than just limit the state by limiting the concentration of public power. It also ensures that the system of public power is able to operate effectively in responding to the people.

Nick Barber makes this point when he stresses that constitutionalism is not just a way of ensuring 'limited government';[52] it also ultimately helps to ensure that the state 'possesses a set of institutions that are able to act'.[53] Richard Ekins describes how a 'balanced' Constitution 'tempers' government in two senses: one in 'disciplining it, and thus avoiding unconstitutional abuses of power' and the other in 'strengthening it, such that it is a better means to secure the common good'.[54] This kind of empowered state can therefore respond to what Jeff King calls the 'social dimension' of the rule of law, where the state can regulate the 'arbitrary' use of private power.[55]

This structural perspective has lessons for established democracies. It demonstrates that the common focus on renewing and building more resilient constitutional democracy must go beyond discussions of judicial reform or appointment. It also must focus on the technical, structural

---

[51] W Partlett, 'Australian Popular Political Constitutionalism' (2024) *Federal Law Review* (forthcoming).

[52] NW Barber, *The Principles of Constitutionalism* (Oxford, Oxford University Press, 2018) 2 (this is what he calls the idea of 'negative constitutionalism').

[53] ibid 8.

[54] R Ekins, 'The Balance of the Constitution' (2022) 67 *The American Journal of Jurisprudence* 199.

[55] J King, 'The Rule of Law' in R Bellamy and J King (eds), *The Cambridge Handbook of Constitutional Theory* (Cambridge University Press, forthcoming) ch 18.

rules that ultimately apportion power to different political institutions. The system of power must balance power between institutions but not do so too broadly and therefore undermine the ability of the system to effectively exercise public power.

The importance of this kind of balanced but effective constitutional system for democratic politics is increasingly relevant to contemporary constitutional questions. For instance, in the United States of America, scholars are now increasingly looking beyond the United States Supreme Court to solve the pressing challenges facing the American constitutional system.[56] This research focuses on the structural provisions in the United States Constitution and constitutional discourse that values too many checks on the public power. This system ultimately weakens the state to such an extent that powerful private interests increasingly wield power in the American polity and the state is no longer able to effectively pursue the common good.

Lisa Miller's recent work is a good example. In a recent article, she argues that the American system of checks and balances is increasingly threatening the ability of the United States to operate as an accountable democratic state.[57] She ascribes this to a form of 'veto exceptionalism' in the United States which justifies too many structural limitations on the power of the majority. She argues that to solve this problem requires fundamental changes to American constitutional order, including changes that 'expand[] the authority of the federal government, broaden[] the scope and power of the electorate, and [are] aimed at dismantling the influence of powerful political minorities'.[58]

This kind of argument joins other research that sees too many constitutional checks and balances in the American constitutional system and calls for a new, more effective structure of constitutional governance in the United States. Mark Tushnet argues that Americans must seek to reform key structural flaws in their constitutional system to make the Constitution work better.[59] Sanford Levinson argues that there need to be important changes made to the structural rules in the United States Constitution.[60] Levitsky and Ziblatt argue that significant constitutional

---

[56] See, eg J Fishkin and WE Forbath, *The Anti-Oligarchy Constitution: Reconstructing the Economic Foundations of American Democracy* (Cambridge MA, Harvard University Press, 2022).

[57] LL Miller, 'Checks and Balances, Veto Exceptionalism, and Constitutional Folk Wisdom: Class and Race Power in American Politics' (2023) 76 *Political Research Quarterly* 1604.

[58] ibid 1616.

[59] Tushnet (n 43).

[60] S Levinson, *Framed: America's 51 Constitutions and the Crisis of Governance* (Oxford, Oxford University Press, 2012).

changes are necessary in order to avoid a constitutional system that allows the tyranny of the minority.[61] In these arguments, the central players in reforming the system are not lawyers or courts but instead politicians and the people.

In considering a better constitutional design for the United States (or any state), it is important to get the details of this balance right. Although removing some checks on power is important, it is important not to move too far toward centralisation in solving this problem. Finding this correct balance has been a central question in political philosophy for centuries. In fact, a long tradition of anti-centralist philosophers have explained that good Constitutions should aspire to create a balanced state that can advance the common good. This tradition has important lessons for democratic constitutionalism.

IV. ENGAGING WITH ANTI-CENTRALIST POLITICAL PHILOSOPHY

To better understand the ways in which a balanced constitutional order helps to create a more effective state, we can and should turn to the normative arguments advanced by political philosophers for centuries about the benefits of a balanced Constitution. This anti-centralist tradition spans thousands of years and encompasses a number of intellectual movements from republicanism to pluralism. These different movements have advanced a number of different arguments to counter those of the centralists.

A common theme across these different threads of anti-centralist thought is that a balanced constitutional state with checks and balances is better at providing effective authority than a centralised state. A balanced Constitution views the people as a plural concept, one that naturally embodies different communities and interests.[62] It therefore sees disagreement and division as inevitable because of the 'distinct perspectives' that different people have on particular issues.[63] Rather than eliminating or flattening out these differences through the decision of one sovereign individual, it instead views the public good as emerging from an interactive process of deliberation between different public

---

[61] S Levitsky and D Ziblatt, *Tyranny of the Minority: How to Reverse an Authoritarian Turn and Forge a Democracy for All* (New York, Penguin, 2023).

[62] N Aroney, G Duke and S Tierney, 'A Theory of Plural Constituent Power for Federal Systems' (2024) *Global Constitutionalism* 1.

[63] J Rawls, *Political Liberalism* (New York, Columbia University Press, 1993) 56.

institutions. A balanced state therefore creates the structure for a discussion about the public good, requiring persuasion and compromise rather than top-down domination. This anti-centralist thought is therefore underpinned by the idea that a balanced Constitution affords institutional authority to a broad range of public institutions.

This anti-centralist argument can be traced back to the Roman Republic (509–27 BCE). One of the earliest examples is Polybius, who drew on the Constitution of the Roman republic to develop a theory of checks and balances in which different public institutions provide an institutional check on one another in the governance structure.[64] Polybius did not view this system of balanced government as limiting the power of the Roman state; on the contrary, he closely associated it with the effective exercise of imperial power by the Roman republic.[65] He also argued that this system was more stable than one grounded on centralisation. A little more than a century later, the leading late Roman orator Marcus Tullius Cicero would draw on this theory in his explanation of why the Roman Constitution was superior to all others.[66]

A theory of the benefits of a balanced Constitution also remained influential in the medieval period. This was true in Christian thought and its normative case for a balanced Constitution in which different organisations cooperate in finding the common good together. In the City of God, for instance, St Augustine described the importance of a 'cooperative order', in which different associations are recognised as exercising authority.[67] Joel Harrison describes how this broader tradition of Christian constitutional thought has long sought to break with the idea of 'constitutionalism-as-constraint' and instead views proper constitutional order as directed toward 'the relative positioning of mutually implicated authorities and groups, each exercising their authority in order to pursue a shared orientation to the good'.[68]

This balanced Constitution tradition continued to influence thinkers after the medieval period. Many of these thinkers took republican Rome as a model for organising the polity, relying on Polybius's characterisation

---

[64] K von Fritz, *The Theory of the Mixed Constitution in Antiquity* (New York, Columbia University Press, 1954).

[65] R Balot, 'Polybius' Advice to the Imperial Republic' (2010) 38 *Political Theory* 483.

[66] E Asmis, 'A New Kind of Model: Cicero's Roman Constitution in *De Republica*' (2005) 126 *The American Journal of Philology* 377.

[67] St Augustine, *Concerning the City of God against the Pagans*, H Bettenson trans (New York, Penguin, 2003) book 19.13.

[68] J Harrison, 'Sovereignty: Dual, Plural, and One' in N Aroney and I Leigh (eds), *Christianity and Constitutionalism* (New York, Oxford University Press, 2022) 178.

of a regime where different public institutions interact in a cooperative order. For instance, James Harrington's theory of balanced sovereignty rejected Hobbes' arguments about the benefits of centralised political order. Instead, Harrington argued that the best way to secure authority and therefore sovereignty in the state is a mixed or balanced Constitution that combines monarchy, aristocracy and democracy.[69] This balanced Constitution, Harrington argued, was more likely to lead to legitimate authority because it would recognise different sources of authority and therefore create a broader interest in obedience. Thus, he concluded, 'that only a government with a division of functions can claim a balanced and absolute sovereignty'.[70]

Writing in reaction to the centralisation in his home country of France, Montesquieu argued in his now famous *The Spirit of the Laws* that a balanced Constitution would ensure order and tranquillity and would lead to good governance.[71] Centralisation, by contrast, was likely to devolve into what Montesquieu described as despotism.[72] This despotism would engender fear and 'tranquil servitude'.[73] In particular, he described how centralised despotism isolated people from one another, weakened individual initiative and creativity, and therefore led to corruption. A balanced or 'moderate' order like the English Constitution, he argued, would better foster an active citizenry that could better advance the interests of the state.

This anti-centralist republicanism also motivated the drafters of the state and federal Constitutions in late eighteenth-century United States. Their primary concern in Constitution-making was organising politics in a way that would guarantee not just individual rights and liberty but also establish effective public authority that could secure the common good. Thus, the foundational question in the American revolutionary period was not what rights to insert into the new written Constitutions but instead how to properly disperse constitutional authority.

Relying heavily on the work of Harrington and Montesquieu, James Madison argued that a state structure that separated powers in a way that placed checks and balances on the concentration of power would help to ensure that constitutional provisions were more than 'parchment

---

[69] A Fukuda, *Sovereignty and the Sword: Harrington, Hobbes, and Mixed Government in the English Civil Wars* (Oxford, Clarendon Press, 1997) 123.
[70] ibid 125.
[71] C Montesquieu, *The Spirit of Laws* (T Nugent trans) (London, Bell, 1896).
[72] R Boesche, 'Fearing Monarchs and Merchants: Montesquieu's Two Theories of Despotism' (1990) 43 *The Western Political Quarterly* 741.
[73] ibid.

barriers'.[74] Courts were not viewed as key enforcers of these written documents. On the contrary, rights were to be protected by political action structured by the constitutionally created institutions of the state. In fact, American constitutional drafters envisaged a Constitution as an arrangement of governing institutions that could create 'a machine that would go of itself'.[75]

Hannah Arendt described the link between a balanced Constitution and the construction of effective authority in the American revolutionary period.[76] The 'true objective' of the American Constitution, she argues, was:

> to create more power, actually to establish and duly constitute an entirely new power centre, destined to compensate the confederate republic, whose authority was to be exerted over a large, expanding territory, for the power lost through the separation of the colonies from the English crown.[77]

She explained that the American founders saw democratic Constitution-making as a bottom-up process of building authority that recognised pre-existing communities and their ability to enter into covenants. She therefore argued that the American drafters did not see the people 'in terms of a fiction and an absolute, the nation above all authority and absolved from all laws' but instead as 'a working reality, the organised multitude whose power was exerted in accordance with the laws and limited by them'.[78] She described how 'Binding and promising, combining and covenanting are the means by which power is kept in existence'. This process of agreement making, she continued, would then balance authority in the state in a way that would constitute a 'stable' structure that would be the result of the people's 'combined power of action'.[79]

She highlighted in particular the thinking of Thomas Jefferson and his interest in a plural state that would operate at the local level and enable small-scale participatory government.[80] For Jefferson, republican

---

[74] James Madison, 'Federalist 48' *The Avalon Project: Documents in Law, History and Diplomacy* https://avalon.law.yale.edu/18th_century/fed48.asp.
[75] *Elkinson v Deliesseline* 8 Fed Cas 593 (1823) (Justice William Johnson), cited in ES Corwin, 'The Constitution as Instrument and as Symbol' (1936) 30 *American Political Science Review* 1071, 1075.
[76] H Arendt, *On Revolution* (New York, Penguin, 1990).
[77] ibid 154.
[78] ibid 166.
[79] ibid 175.
[80] ibid 252–55.

government required a scheme 'to divide [government] among the many, distributing to every one exactly the function he [was] competent to'.[81] These smaller corporate units would then form a 'gradation of authorities' that would constitute 'a system of fundamental balances and checks for the government'.[82] This system of plural authority recognition would in turn, Arendt argued, provide 'a mechanism, built into the very heart of government, through which new power is constantly generated'.[83] Arendt also described how John Adams saw this dispersal of authority in a similar way, as a method 'to generate more power, more strength, more reason, and not to abolish them'.[84]

Arendt demonstrates that American constitutional thinkers drew on previous republican thinking in seeing the first and most fundamental goal of written democratic Constitutions as advancing the public good and protecting liberty by empowering different groups to participate in collective self-government. This balance does more than control other forms of authority (particularly charismatic and traditional). It was viewed as ensuring a stable form of authority grounded on the preservation of existing authority.

The anti-centralist ideas of a balanced but authoritative Constitution were also a powerful influence on the British pluralist movement of the late nineteenth and early twentieth century. These thinkers emphasised the importance of creating public space for intermediate institutions between the individual and the state. One of its early thinkers was Henry Maitland. A medieval historian, he recovered the idea of plural sovereignty and the idea that the state could be conceptualised as a group person comprising many other corporate groups, from colonies and local government to companies and charities. This drew on the work of the German theorist Otto von Gierke, who described the state as a community of communities.[85] In the British context, Maitland challenged the idea of centralised parliamentary sovereignty for 'sucking the life blood of all other institutions', particularly those of local government, with the result that the borough had descended into corruption and local government had become an 'appalling mess' of different

---

[81] ibid 254.
[82] ibid.
[83] ibid 151.
[84] ibid 152.
[85] G Heiman (ed), *Otto Gierke: Associations and the Law: The Classical and Early Christian Stages* (Toronto, University of Toronto Press, 1977) 7, 9 (pointing to an 'organic ordering of parts' that was ultimately directed toward a 'supra-individual unity of life').

boards and authorities.[86] He argued that the idea of sovereignty as 'a supralegal, suprajural plenitude of power concentrated in a single point at Westminster' should give way to an idea of sovereignty as the whole community.[87]

Harold Laski was another key thinker in the British pluralist tradition. Laski rejected the idea that centralised power must be placed in the hands of a sovereign leader in order to avoid anarchy or civil war. Laski insisted instead that the recognition of multiple sites of authority helps to preserve and build authority and order because it ultimately recognises and conserves traditional sources of authority that have existed in the past. It also ensures, he explained, that the duties of citizenship are not suppressed by an all-powerful sovereign institution. He described how the 'division of power' makes people 'more apt to responsibility than its accumulation'.[88] Pluralism, he further argued, therefore helps to unleash the 'creative energies of men'.[89] This position stands in stark contrast to top-down conceptions of authority as existing from one sovereign will.

Most recently, Philip Pettit has explicitly drawn on the republican tradition to argue against Hobbes and other centralists that before the state there is an anarchical state of nature.[90] He writes that 'there is little reason to think ... that the absence of a state would leave people ungoverned by conventions and norms'.[91] He also rejects the idea that a balanced Constitution is necessarily divided and unable to exercise real sovereignty. Instead, he argues, the balanced state should strive toward a sovereign power that is not 'a monarch, a legislature, or anything of that concrete kind'.[92] Instead, he explains that the sovereign 'may be a superordinate body that emerges from the interaction and cooperation of such individuals and agencies.[93]

He therefore also draws on the Gierkian idea that multiple sites of authority need not present conflicting claims that undermine unified governance. Instead, these different sites of authority can be encouraged

---

[86] FW Maitland, *Township and Borough: Being the Ford Lectures Delivered in the University of Oxford in the October Term of 1897* (Cambridge, Cambridge University Press, 1898) 94–95.
[87] FW Maitland (trans), 'Introduction' in O Gierke, *Political Theories of the Middle Ages* (Boston, Beacon Press, 1958) xliii.
[88] HJ Laski, 'The Pluralistic State' (1919) 28 *The Philosophical Review* 562, 569.
[89] ibid 574.
[90] P Pettit, *The State* (Princeton, Princeton University Press, 2003) 31–32.
[91] ibid 124.
[92] ibid 160.
[93] ibid.

to cooperate in a way that ultimately helps to achieve one common good.[94] He describes how this functional state should 'be organized as a corporate agent to pursue its role, but ought at the same time to be composed out of decentralized, mutually constraining units'.[95] This community of communities, he argues, therefore helps to create a more durable form of authority out of multiplicity.

This anti-centralist thought reveals a key common theme across the centuries: that balancing power in the Constitution is not just a project of limiting or constraining the state. Instead, it is one that enables a plurality of institutions and corporate bodies to cooperate in solving common problems. This plural state system is therefore more able to ensure obedience and build a more durable form of authority. This tradition of theorising about the advantages and benefits of a balanced Constitution has important implications for democratic constitutional theory. In particular, it shows that deepening and renewing our understanding of democratic constitutionalism requires further study of how structural provisions can adapt to contemporary changes and context to promote a pluralistic politics of cooperation and compromise.

V. CONCLUSION

This chapter outlines why the experience of the Russian Constitution helps us better understand democratic constitutionalism. Our failure to understand Russian constitutional law exposes a key deficiency in our understanding of democratic constitutionalism. It shows that an overly *legal* understanding of democratic Constitutions is dangerously incomplete. This legal understanding can encourage an anti-political understanding of democracy and associate constitutional democracy with a weak, libertarian state. Taken too far, both can threaten democratic governance more generally.

Moreover, it shows the central importance of understanding the normative effects of detailed structural rules in constitutional text. These provisions are more than just a technical rule book in democratic systems. Instead, they help to constitute a form of politics that is grounded on a plurality of existing institutions. These institutions shape the exercise of public power on the basis of persuasion and compromise

---

[94] Harrison (n 68) 187.
[95] Pettit (n 90) 3.

rather than domination and unity. Understanding these normative aims is critical in renewing and deepening our understanding of democratic constitutionalism. In pursuing this work, we are taking part in a long normative tradition of anti-centralist thought that has sought to adapt the broader normative goals of democratic governance to the everyday challenges of the present.

Conclusion
Constitutions at the End of History

In 1989, Francis Fukuyama published an article that would define an era.[1] He argued that the world had reached the 'the end of history', the final stage in 'mankind's ideological evolution'.[2] This endpoint signalled that 'Western liberal democracy' had emerged 'as the final form of human government'.[3] He described this period as a 'sad time' when 'daring, courage, and imagination' will be 'replaced by economic calculation, the endless solving of technical problems, environmental concerns, and the satisfaction of sophisticated consumer demands'.[4]

In at least one way, Fukuyama was right. The end of the Cold War has seen the rise of a powerful brand of anti-politics where political pluralism is being replaced by unmediated populist representation and technocratic policy-making. In this vision, democratic Constitutions are no longer primarily about creating an effective framework for pluralistic politics. Instead, they are about empowering a powerful elected sovereign office to oversee a constitutional system with judicially enforced rights and democracy guarantees. This system claims to be able to solve disagreement through reason and law rather than mobilisation and compromise.

Russia was an early adopter of this anti-political form of the constitutional dark arts. Its fate shows both how this system goes wrong and how to counter it. It demonstrates that suspending politics and trusting in a powerful elected President and a court system is unlikely to protect democracy and rights. Rather than allowing an electorally accountable President to overcome disorder and guarantee rights democracy, these constitutional systems have helped to foster dictatorship and poor-quality governance. Pointing out these problems is a powerful way to counter the deceptive claims underpinning the constitutional dark arts.

---

[1] F Fukuyama, 'The End of History?' (1989) 16 *The National Interest* 3.
[2] ibid 2.
[3] ibid 4.
[4] ibid 18.

I. BETTER UNDERSTANDING RUSSIA

This story therefore helps us better understand Russia today. Since 1993, Russia's political development has been shaped by its constitutional text and continued commitment to centralised authority. Operating above the political system in a position that the Communist Party and the Tsar once occupied, the Russian President has been the central player, ultimately able to transform courts and elections into institutions that bolster presidential power.

This finding therefore joins other recent research that seeks to understand Russia beyond a focus on Putin.[5] It shows the *constitutional system* that underpins Russian authoritarianism today. When Putin leaves office, this system will remain. It could trigger a destabilising struggle between different factions to capture the office of the Presidency. Whoever wins this struggle will attempt to use this centralised constitutional system to rebuild Russian authoritarianism without Putin.

Moreover, long-term democratic reform will require more than just Putin leaving office; it will require a new constitutional foundation. This new foundation must break Russia's centuries long commitment to centralised power by adopting a constitutional system committed to a balanced state that recognises plural sites of authority. This new balanced constitutional state need not be a libertarian one. Instead, it can be constructed in order to ensure a more effective state that is accountable to the people and therefore able to secure the common good. A balanced Constitution therefore need not be seen as undermining Russia's power in the world. On the contrary, as the Tsarist statist liberals argued in the nineteenth and early twentieth century, a balanced Russian Constitution can better unleash the economic and cultural potential of its people and preserve Russia's overall international influence.

II. AN OLD IDEOLOGICAL DEBATE CONTINUES

Russia's post-Soviet constitutional experience also has important implications beyond Russia. It shows where Fukuyama was wrong. We have not reached the end of history. In fact, an older debate about the proper

---

[5] T Frye, *Weak Strongman: The Limits of Power in Putin's Russia* (Princeton, Princeton University Press, 2021); Brian Taylor, *State Building in Putin's Russia: Policing and Coercion After Communism* (Cambridge, Cambridge University Press, 2011).

organisation of the state continues. Centralised political organisation has recently been gaining ground in this debate as deceptive claims about its *democratic* benefits have grown in influence.

This is true not just in places like Russia with long histories of adherence to centralised authority. It is now increasingly influential in established democracies, where the people are increasingly losing trust in the institutions of democratic governance. In these settings, elected leaders have argued that centralisation is necessary to democracy. In Turkey, for instance, President Recep Erdogan has successfully centralised vast power in the office of the Turkish President by claiming that centralised and personalised power is the only way to preserve the will of the people. Seeing the terms of this debate can help us to better understand both constitutional ordering as well as understand how best to defend democracy against its enemies.

These authoritarian populist projects often centre around constitutional law. The Constitution allows leaders to explicitly link centralisation with elections, rights and judicial review. The Constitution is therefore a critical tool in allowing one leader to base his or her power on both popular and legal legitimacy. Put simply, the leader becomes the personal guarantor of democracy.

Russia's post-Soviet experience demonstrates both why these claims are likely to fail and how to counter them. It shows that the centralisation of broad power in one office is not compatible with democracy or even stable, effective governance over time. Instead, it leads to personalised leadership, intensifying dilemmas around leadership succession and ineffective institutions. Finally, it fosters poor quality governance as the state is unable to understand or respond to the wishes of its populace.

These problems provide a critical opening for the supporters of a balanced Constitution. Pointing out its inability to deliver on its core claims can be a powerful method of undermining a key source of its legitimacy: popular support. In this context, the Russian experience is again instructive. By far the most successful opposition movement has been the one built by Alexei Navalny. This movement has placed the corruption and weakness of the current regime at the centre of its messaging. Despite being denied access to much of the media, this strategy proved so successful it triggered a massive crackdown against the movement, culminating in Navalny's death in prison in 2024. Democratic oppositions elsewhere should take note: These systems are weaker and more vulnerable than they appear.

III. DEMOCRATIC CONSTITUTIONALISM IN THE TWENTY-FIRST CENTURY

In countering this centralising logic, we must also understand the overall goals of democratic constitutionalism. Centuries of anti-centralist political philosophy have viewed a good form of politics as necessarily involving compromise between groups and interests who have different perspectives and values. This pluralism cannot and should not be stamped out or managed from the top-down; it instead should be channelled through a constitutional system that encourages compromise and cooperation. In this process, no one group or entity claims to have the whole truth; on the contrary, they respect the opinions and positions of those in opposition and cooperate toward advancing the general good.

This anti-centralist tradition has informed the balanced constitutional tradition and its approach to democratic constitutionalism. Most obviously, the balanced state tradition warns against the over-centralisation of power. Russia's experience is just one of many showing the dangers of overly centralised power. We have seen the problems of anti-political centralisation in other places like Turkey, Hungary and Kazakhstan. And we can see also see it in established parliamentary systems like India where elected party leaders have centralised vast power by undermining key unwritten constitutional rules that ensure pluralism and balance.

The balanced state tradition also warns against constitutional systems that are too divided and decentralised to provide effective public power. The United States is a good example, where a spiralling number of checks and balances threaten the ability of the state to operate effectively in actually responding to the will of the people. With weak public power, powerful private monopolies end up exercising power for private, self-interested ends rather than public ones.

The balanced state tradition therefore reminds us that *democratic* Constitutions are more than just documents that limit the centralisation of power. They are more fundamentally documents that bring order and balance to a process of pluralistic politics. To find this balance, scholars must look beyond individual rights provisions and democratic guarantees to the detailed structural rules that organise the system of politics. Moreover, in studying these structural constitutional rules, they must understand that these rules are not just the tools of powerful actors; they are themselves part of a normative system that values a particular form of ordered pluralistic politics.

Defenders of democratic Constitutions must then ask how constitutional rules can be drafted, reformed and interpreted to build this kind of balanced system. In exploring these questions, they can and should build on pre-existing work that links constitutional structure with normative theory. This includes work on 'political constitutionalism' that examines the consequences of Constitutions outside of court.[6] It also encompasses political science work that studies the normative consequences of detailed constitutional design choices.[7]

This work will help to form the basis of a better understanding of how to adapt democratic constitutionalism to its contemporary challenges. Although the precise answers will differ depending on the context, one thing remains the same. Democratic constitutionalism involves a normative commitment to a form of constitutional politics that recognises plural sites of authority in formulating public policy. This form of political ordering cannot and should not be managed from the top; the different participants must take part in a constitutionally ordered process of discussion, negotiation and compromise. The ordering of this process is not only more likely to promote democratically accountable governance and the protection of individual rights. It is also a better way of improving the quality of governance.

---

[6] See, eg R Bellamy, *Political Constitutionalism: A Republican Defence of the Constitutionality of Democracy* (Cambridge, Cambridge University Press, 2007).

[7] See, eg S Ganghof, *Beyond Presidentialism and Parliamentarism: Democratic Design and the Separation of Powers* (Oxford, Oxford University Press, 2021).

Bibliography

Ackerman, B, 'The Rise of World Constitutionalism' (1997) 83 *Virginia Law Review* 77.
Alm, J and Martinez-Vazquez, J, 'Russian Tax Morale in the 1990s' (2005) 98 *Proceedings of the Annual Conference on Taxation and Minutes of the Annual Meeting of the National Tax Association* 287.
Anderson, J, 'Putin and the Russian Orthodox Church: Asymmetric Symphonia?' (2007) 61(1) *Journal of International Affairs* 185.
Angelov, GG, 'Legal Framework of Privatization in Russia' (1993) 2 *Minnesota Journal of International Law* 207.
Appleby, G, 'Unwritten Rules' in C Saunders and A Stone (eds), *The Oxford Handbook of the Australian Constitution* (Oxford, Oxford University Press, 2018).
Aslund, A, 'Why Doesn't Russia Join the WTO?' (2010) 33(2) *The Washington Quarterly* 49.
Asmis, E, 'A New Kind of Model: Cicero's Roman Constitution in *De Republica*' (2005) 126 *The American Journal of Philology* 377.
Atchison, DD, 'Notes on Constitutionalism for a 21st-Century Russian President' (1998) 6 *Cardozo Journal of International and Comparative Law* 239.
Bailyn, B, *The Ideological Origins of the American Constitution*, enlarged edn (London, Harvard University Press, 1992).
Balme, S and Dowdle, M, 'Introduction: Searching for Constitutionalism in 21st Century China' in S Balme and M Dowdle (eds), *Building Constitutionalism in China* (New York, Palgrave Macmillan, 2009) 1–20.
Balot, R, 'Polybius' Advice to the Imperial Republic' (2010) 38 *Political Theory* 483.
Bandeira, EM, 'The 22 Frimaire of Yuan Shikai: Privy Councils in the Constitutional Architectures of Japan and China, 1887–1917' in I Sablin and EM Bandeira (eds), *Planting Parliaments in Eurasia, 1850–1950: Concepts, Practices, and Mythologies* (New York, Routledge, 2021) 150–87.
Barany, Z, 'The Tragedy of the Kursk: Crisis Management in Putin's Russia' (2004) 39 *Government and Opposition* 476.
Barber, NW, *The Principles of Constitutionalism* (Oxford, Oxford University Press, 2018).
Barenboim, P et al, *Constitutional Economics* (Moscow, YustitsInform, 2006).
Barr, MD, 'Lee Kuan Yew and the "Asian Values" Debate' (2000) 24 *Asian Studies Review* 309.
Bass, J, *Unlikely Heroes: The Dramatic Story of the Southern Judges of the Fifth Circuit who Translated the Supreme Court's Brown Decision into a Revolution for Equality* (Tuscaloosa, University of Alabama Press, 1990).
Baturo, A, '*Continuismo* in Comparison: Avoidance, Extension, and Removal of Presidential Term Limits' in A Baturo and R Elgie (eds), *The Politics of Presidential Term Limits* (Oxford, Oxford University Press, 2019) 75–100.
Baturo, A and Mikhaylov, S, 'Reading the Tea Leaves: Medvedev's Presidency through Political Rhetoric of Federal and Sub-National Actors' (2014) 66 *Europe-Asia Studies* 969.
Bellamy, R, *Political Constitutionalism: A Republican Defence of the Constitutionality of Democracy* (Cambridge, Cambridge University Press, 2007).

Belov, S, 'Values of the Russian Constitution in the Text and Practice of Constitutional Interpretation' (2019) 131(4) *Comparative Constitutional Law* 79.

Belton, C, *Putin's People: How the KGB Took Back Russia and Then Took on the West* (New York, Farrar, Straus and Giroux, 2020).

Bickerton, CJ and Accetti, CI, *Technopopulism: The New Logic of Democratic Politics* (Oxford, Oxford University Press, 2021).

Bivens, M and Bernstein, J, 'The Russia You Never Met' (1998) 6 *Demokratizatsiya: The Journal of Post-Soviet Democratization* 613.

Black, JL, *Nicholas Karamzin and Russian Society in the Nineteenth Century* (Toronto, University of Toronto Press, 1975).

—— *The Russian Presidency of Dmitry Medvedev, 2008–2012: The Next Step Forward or Merely a Time Out?* (Oxfordshire, Routledge, 2015).

—— 'The "State School" Interpretation of Russian History: A Re-Appraisal of its Genetic Origins' (1973) 21 *Jahrbücher für Geschichte Osteuropas* 509.

Boesche, R, 'Fearing Monarchs and Merchants: Montesquieu's Two Theories of Despotism' (1990) 43 *The Western Political Quarterly* 741.

Brennan Jr, WJ, 'Reason, Passion, and "The Progress of the Law"' (1988) 10 *Cardozo Law Review* 3.

Brudny, YM, 'In Pursuit of the Russian Presidency: Why and How Yeltsin Won the 1996 Presidential Election' (1997) 30 *Communist and Post-Communist Studies* 255.

Burkhardt, F, 'Institutionalising Authoritarian Presidencies: Polymorphous Power and Russia's Presidential Administration' (2021) 73 *Europe-Asia Studies* 472.

—— 'Institutionalizing Personalism: The Russian Presidency after Constitutional Changes' (2021) 6 *Russian Politics* 50.

Burton-Crawford, L and Goldsworthy, J, 'Constitutionalism' in C Saunders and A Stone (eds), *The Oxford Handbook of the Australian Constitution* (Oxford, Oxford University Press, 2018) 357–78.

Cassiday, JA and Johnson, ED, 'Putin, Putiniana and the Question of a Post-Soviet Cult of Personality' (2010) 88 *The Slavonic and East European Review* 681.

Cohen, HG, 'Can International Law Work? A Constructivist Expansion' (2009) 27 *Berkeley Journal of International Law* 636.

Colley, L, *The Gun, the Ship and the Pen: Warfare, Constitutions and the Making of the Modern World* (London, Profile Books, 2021).

Colton, TJ and Skach, C, 'A Fresh Look at Semi-Presidentialism: The Russian Predicament' (2005) 16 *Journal of Democracy* 113.

Cope, KL, 'Intermestic Constitution: Lessons from the World's Newest Nation' (2013) 53 *Virginia Journal of International Law* 309.

Corwin, ES, 'The Constitution as Instrument and as Symbol' (1936) 30 *American Political Science Review* 1071.

Cowling, K and Tomlinson, PR, 'Post the "Washington Consensus": Economic Governance and Industrial Strategies for the Twenty-First Century' (2011) 35 *Cambridge Journal of Economics* 831.

Robert A Dahl, 'The Behavioral Approach in Political Science: Epitaph for a Monument to a Successful Protest' (1961) 55 *American Political Science Review* 763.

Daly, T, 'Democratic Decay: Conceptualising an Emerging Research Field' (2019) 11 *Hague Journal on the Rule of Law* 9.

Danilenko, GM, 'The New Russian Constitution and International Law' (1994) 88 *The American Journal of International Law* 451.

Darden, K, 'The Integrity of Corrupt States: Graft as an Informal State Institution' (2008) 36 *Politics and Society* 35.

Deng, MAW, 'Defining the Nature and Limits of Presidential Powers in the Transitional Constitution of South Sudan: A Politically Contentious Matter for the New Nation' (2017) 61 *Journal of African Law* 23.

Deng, M, 'South Sudan's Transitional Constitution: The Making, Failure and Lessons' (2024) 16 *African Journal of Legal Studies* 5.

Di Bella, G, Dynnikova, O, and Grigoli, F, 'Fiscal Federalism and Regional Performance in Russia' (2018) 4 *Russian Journal of Economics* 108.

Dixon, R, 'Constitutional Rights as Bribes' (2018) 50 *Connecticut Law Review* 767.

Dollbaum, JM, Lallouet, M, and Noble, B, *Navalny: Putin's Nemesis, Russia's Future?* (London, Oxford University Press, 2021).

Dworkin, R, *Justice for Hedgehogs* (Cambridge, Belknap Press, 2011).

—— *Taking Rights Seriously* (London, Bloomsbury Academic, 2013).

Dzmitryieva, A, 'Case Selection in the Russian Constitutional Court: The Role of Legal Assistants' (2017) 6(3) *Laws* 12.

Eklof, B, Bushnell, J, and Zakharova, L (eds), *Russia's Great Reforms, 1855–1881* (Bloomington, Indiana University Press, 1994).

Ekins, R, 'The Balance of the Constitution' (2022) 67 *The American Journal of Jurisprudence* 199.

Ellison, HJ, *Boris Yeltsin and Russia's Democratic Transformation* (Seattle, University of Washington Press, 2006).

Felkay, A, *Yeltsin's Russia and the West* (Westport, Praeger, 2002).

Fishkin, J, and Forbath, WE, *The Anti-Oligarchy Constitution: Reconstructing the Economic Foundations of American Democracy* (Cambridge MA, Harvard University Press, 2022).

Fortescue, S, 'The Policymaking Process in Putin's Prime Ministership' in L Jonson and S White (eds), *Waiting for Reform under Putin and Medvedev* (New York, Palgrave Macmillan, 2012) 119–39.

Frankenberg, G, *Authoritarianism: Constitutional Perspectives* (Cheltenham, Edward Elgar, 2020).

Friedman, B, *The Will of the People: How Public Opinion Has Shaped the Meaning of the Constitution* (New York, Farrar, Strauss, and Giroux, 2010).

Frye, T, *Weak Strongman: The Limits of Power in Putin's Russia* (Princeton, Princeton University Press, 2021).

Fukuda, A, *Sovereignty and the Sword: Harrington, Hobbes, and Mixed Government in the English Civil Wars* (Oxford, Clarendon Press, 1997).

Fukuyama, F, *The End of History and the Last Man* (New York, The Free Press, 1992).

—— 'The End of History?' (1989) 16 *The National Interest* 3.

Frantz, E, *Authoritarianism: What Everyone Needs to Know* (New York, Oxford University Press, 2018).

Ganghof, S, *Beyond Presidentialism and Parliamentarism: Democratic Design and the Separation of Powers* (Oxford, Oxford University Press, 2021).

—— 'A New Political System Model: Semi-Parliamentary Government' (2018) 57 *European Journal of Political Research* 261.

Gardbaum, S, 'The Myth and the Reality of American Constitutional Exceptionalism' (2008) 107 *Michigan Law Review* 391.

Gargarella, R, *Latin American Constitutionalism, 1810–2010: The Engine Room of the Constitution* (Oxford, Oxford University Press, 2013).

Geddes, B, Wright, J, and Frantz, E, *How Dictatorships Work: Power, Personalization, and Collapse* (Cambridge, Cambridge University Press, 2018).

Gee, G, and Webber, GCN, 'What is a Political Constitution?' (2010) 30 *Oxford Journal of Legal Studies* 273.

Gel'man, V, *Authoritarian Russia: Analyzing Post-Soviet Regime Changes* (Pittsburgh, University of Pittsburgh Press, 2015).

—— 'Constitution, Authoritarianism, and Bad Governance: The Case of Russia' (2021) 6 *Russian Politics* 71.

—— *The Politics of Bad Governance in Contemporary Russia* (Ann Arbor, University of Michigan Press, 2022).

Gessen, M, *The Man Without a Face: The Unlikely Rise of Vladimir Putin* (New York, Riverhead Books, 2012).

Ginsburg, T, *Judicial Review in New Democracies: Constitutional Courts in Asian Cases* (Cambridge, Cambridge University Press, 2003).

Ginsburg, T and Simpser, A, 'Introduction' in T Ginsburg and A Simpser (eds), *Constitutions in Authoritarian Regimes* (New York, Cambridge University Press, 2014) 1–18.

Glazunova, S, '"Four Populisms" of Alexey Navalny: An Analysis of Russian Non-Systemic Opposition Discourse on YouTube' (2020) 8 *Media and Communication* 121.

Goldman, M, 'Putin and the Oligarchs' (2004) 83 *Foreign Affairs* 33.

Goldsmith, J and Levinson, D, 'Law for States: International Law, Constitutional Law, Public Law' (2009) 122 *Harvard Law Review* 1791.

Gooding, J, 'The Liberalism of Michael Speransky' (1986) 64 *Slavonic and East European Review* 401.

Hahn, GM, 'Medvedev, Putin, and Perestroika 2.0' (2010) 18 *Demokratizatsiya: The Journal of Post-Soviet Democratization* 228.

Hale, HE, 'The Informal Politics of Formal Constitutions: Rethinking the Effects of "Presidentialism" and "Parliamentarism" in the Cases of Kyrgyzstan, Moldova, and Ukraine in Constitutions' in T Ginsburg and A Simpser (eds), *Constitutions in Authoritarian Regimes* (New York, Cambridge University Press, 2014) 218–44.

Hamburg, GM, *Boris Chicherin and Early Russian Liberalism, 1828–1866* (Stanford, Stanford University Press, 1992).

—— 'Peasant Emancipation and Russian Social Thought: The Case of Boris N Chicherin' (1991) 50 *Slavic Review* 890.

—— *Russia's Path toward Enlightenment: Faith, Politics, and Reason, 1500–1801* (New Haven, Yale University Press, 2016).

Harrison, J, 'Sovereignty: Dual, Plural, and One' in N Aroney and I Leigh (eds), *Christianity and Constitutionalism* (New York, Oxford University Press, 2022) 173–92.

Hausminger, H, 'From the Soviet Committee of Constitutional Supervision to the Russian Constitutional Court' (1992) 25(2) *Cornell International Law Journal* 305.

Hayek, F, *Law, Legislation, and Liberty: Rules and Order*, vol 1 (Chicago, Chicago University Press, 1973).

Heiman, G (ed), *Otto Gierke: Associations and the Law: The Classical and Early Christian Stages* (Toronto, University of Toronto Press, 1977).

Henderson, J, *The Constitution of the Russian Federation: A Contextual Analysis*, 2nd edn (Oxford, Hart Publishing, 2022).

Hill, F and Gaddy, CG, *Mr Putin: Operative in the Kremlin* (Washington DC, Brookings Institution Press, 2013).

Hirschl, R, *Towards Juristocracy: The Origins and Consequences of the New Constitutionalism* (Cambridge MA, Harvard University Press, 2007).

Hobbes, T, *Leviathan*, vol 2, N Malcolm (ed) (Oxford, Oxford University Press, 2012).
Hoffman, D, *The Oligarchs: Wealth and Power in the New Russia* (New York, Public Affairs, 2011).
Holmes, L, 'Corruption and Organised Crime in Putin's Russia' (2008) 60 *Europe-Asia Studies* 1011.
Holmes, S, 'What Russia Teaches Us Now: How Weak States Threaten Freedom' (1997) 33 *The American Prospect* 30.
Horvath, R, *The Legacy of Soviet Dissent: Dissidents, Democratisation and Radical Nationalism in Russia* (New York, Routledge Curzon, 2005).
Huntington, SP, 'Democracy's Third Wave' (1991) 2(2) *Journal of Democracy* 12.
Hutcheson, DS and Petersson, B, 'Shortcut to Legitimacy: Popularity in Putin's Russia' (2016) 68 *Europe-Asia Studies* 1107.
Judt, T, *Ill Fares the Land: A Treatise on Our Present Discontents* (New York, Penguin, 2010).
Kahn, J, *Federalism, Democratization, and the Rule of Law in Russia* (Oxford, Oxford University Press, 2002).
——— 'Vladimir Putin and the Rule of the Law in Russia' (2008) 36 *Georgia Journal of International Law* 511.
——— 'What is the New Russian Federalism?' in A Brown (ed), *Contemporary Russian Politics: A Reader* (Oxford, Oxford University Press, 2001) 374–83.
Khaitan, T, 'Killing a Constitution with a Thousand Cuts: Executive Aggrandizement and Party-State Fusion in India' (2020) 14 *Law and Ethics of Human Rights* 49.
Khosla, M and Tushnet, M, 'Courts, Constitutionalism, and State Capacity: A Preliminary Inquiry' (2022) 70 *The American Journal of Comparative Law* 9.
Khramova, T, 'Russia: Legal Response to Covid-19' in J King and OLM Ferraz et al (eds), *The Oxford Compendium of National Legal Responses to Covid-19* (online, Oxford University Press, 2021).
King, J, 'The Rule of Law' in R Bellamy and J King (eds), *The Cambridge Handbook of Constitutional Theory* (Cambridge, Cambridge University Press, forthcoming).
King, WR and Cleland, DI, *Strategic Planning and Policy* (New York, Van Nostrand Reinhold, 1978).
Kovalev, S, 'Andrei Dmitrievich Sakharov: Meeting the Demands of Reason' in *Andrei Sakharov and Human Rights* (Strasbourg, Council of Europe Publishing, 2010) 131–38.
Kramer, LD, *The People Themselves: Popular Constitutionalism and Judicial Review* (Oxford, Oxford University Press, 2004).
Krasnov, M, *A Personalist Regime in Russia: The Experience of Constitutional Analysis* (in Russian) (Moscow, Moscow Liberal Mission, 2006).
Krastev, I and Holmes, S, 'Putinism under Siege: An Autopsy of Managed Democracy' (2012) 23(3) *Journal of Democracy* 33.
Kryshtanovskaya, O, 'The Tandem and the Crisis' (2011) 27 *The Journal of Communist Studies and Transition Politics* 407.
Kryshtanovskaya, O and White, S, 'The Sovietization of Russian Politics' (2009) 25 *Post-Soviet Affairs* 283.
Landau, D, 'Abusive Constitutionalism' (2013) 47 *University of California Davis Law Review* 189.
Larionov, A, *Fundamentals of Russian Statehood: A Textbook for Students of Natural Sciences and Engineering Specialties* (Moscow, Delo Publishing House, 2023).
Laski, H, 'The Pluralistic State' (1919) 28 *The Philosophical Review* 562.
Law, DS and Versteeg, M, 'Sham Constitutions' (2013) 101 *California Law Review* 863.

Lenin, VI, *The State and Revolution*, R Service trans (London, Penguin, 1992).

Levinger, M, 'Kant and the Origins of Prussian Constitutionalism' (1998) 19 *History of Political Thought* 241.

Levinson, S, 'Do Constitutions Have a Point? Reflections on "Parchment Barriers" and Preambles' (2011) 28(1) *Social Philosophy and Policy* 150.

—— *Framed: America's 51 Constitutions and the Crisis of Governance* (New York, Oxford University Press, 2012).

Levitsky, S and Way, LA, *Competitive Authoritarianism: Hybrid Regimes after the Cold War* (Cambridge, Cambridge University Press, 2010).

Levitsky, S and Ziblatt, D, *Tyranny of the Minority: How to Reverse an Authoritarian Turn and Forge a Democracy for All* (New York, Penguin, 2023).

Li-Ann, T, 'Varieties of Constitutionalism in Asia' (2021) 16 *Asian Journal of Comparative Law* 285.

Linz, J, 'The Perils of Presidentialism' (1990) 1 *Journal of Democracy* 51.

—— 'Presidential or Parliamentary Democracy: Does it Make a Difference?' in JJ Linz and A Valenzuela (eds), *The Failure of Presidential Democracy* (Baltimore, Johns Hopkins University Press, 1994) 3–90.

Loughlin, M, *Against Constitutionalism* (Cambridge MA, Harvard University Press, 2022).

Ludwikowski, R, 'Judicial Review in the Socialist Legal System: Current Developments' (1988) 37 *ICLQ* 89.

—— '"Mixed" Constitutions: Product of an East-Central European Constitutional Melting Pot' (1998) 16 *Boston University International Law Journal* 41.

Lukashuk, A, 'Constitutionalism in Belarus: A False Start' in J Zielonka (ed), *Democratic Consolidation in Eastern Europe: Institutional Engineering*, vol 1 (Oxford, Oxford University Press, 2001) 293–318.

Lynn, NJ and Novikov, AV, 'Refederalizing Russia: Debates on the Idea of Federalism in Russia' (1997) 27 *Publius* 187.

Mair, P, *Ruling The Void: The Hollowing of Western Democracy* (London, Verso, 2013).

Maitland, FW (trans), 'Introduction' in O Gierke, *Political Theories of the Middle Ages* (Boston, Beacon Press, 1958) vii–xiv.

—— *Township and Borough: Being the Ford Lectures Delivered in the University of Oxford in the October Term of 1897* (Cambridge, Cambridge University Press, 1898).

March, L, 'Populism in the Post-Soviet States' in CR Kaltwasser et al (eds), *The Oxford Handbook of Populism* (Oxford, Oxford University Press, 2017) 214–31.

Martin, B, 'The Sakharov-Medvedev Debate on Détente and Human Rights: From the Jackson-Vanik Amendment to the Helsinki Accords' (2021) 23 *Journal of Cold War Studies* 138.

Matheson, C, 'Weber and the Classification of Forms of Legitimacy' (1987) 38 *The British Journal of Sociology* 199.

Matthews-Ferraro, D, 'Book Review: *Technopopulism: The New Logic of Democratic Politics*' (2022) 25 *European Journal of Social Theory* 189.

Mazmanyan, A, 'The Judicialization of Politics: The Post-Soviet Way' (2015) 13 *International Journal of Constitutional Law* 200.

McCarthy, LA, Rice, D, and Lokhmutov, A, 'Four Months of "Discrediting the Military": Repressive Law in Wartime Russia' (2023) 31 *Demokratizatsiya: The Journal of Post-Soviet Democratization* 125.

McClure, ML, 'An Analysis of the New Russian Constitution' (1995) 4 *Journal of International Law and Practice* 601.

McFaul, M, *Russia's Unfinished Revolution: Political Change from Gorbachev to Putin* (Ithaca, NY, Cornell University Press, 2001).

Miliukov, PN, *Russia and its Crisis* (Chicago, University of Chicago Press, 1905).

Miller, LL, 'Checks and Balances, Veto Exceptionalism, and Constitutional Folk Wisdom: Class and Race Power in American Politics' (2023) 76 *Political Research Quarterly* 1604.

Monaghan, A, 'The *Vertikal*: Power and Authority in Russia' (2012) 88 *International Affairs* 1.

Moore, R, 'The Path to the New Russian Constitution: A Comparison of Executive-Legislative Relations in the Major Drafts' (1995) 3(1) *Demokratizatsiya: The Journal of Post-Soviet Democratization* 44.

Moyn, S, *Not Enough: Human Rights in an Unequal World* (Cambridge MA, Harvard University Press, 2018).

—— *The Last Utopia: Human Rights in History* (Cambridge MA, Harvard University Press, 2012).

Muraviev, N, 'Project for a Constitution' in WJ Leatherbarrow and DC Offord (eds), *A Documentary History of Russian Thought: From the Enlightenment to Marxism* (Ann Arbor, Ardis, 1987) 42–50.

Myers, SL, *The New Tsar: The Rise and Reign of Vladimir Putin* (New York, Alfred A Knopf, 2015).

Noble, B, 'Authoritarian Amendments: Legislative Institutions as Intraexecutive Constraints in Post-Soviet Russia' (2020) 53 *Comparative Political Studies* 1417.

Oversloot, H, 'Reordering the State (Without Changing the Constitution): Russia under Putin's Rule, 2000–2008' (2007) 32 *Review of Central and East European Law* 41.

Oxford English Dictionary, 3rd edn (Oxford University Press, 2021).

Pacer, VA, *Russian Foreign Policy under Dmitry Medvedev, 2008–2012* (London, Routledge, 2016).

Pallin, C, 'Russia's Presidential Domestic Policy Directorate: HQ for Defeat-Proofing Russian Politics' (2017) 25 *Demokratizatsiya: The Journal of Post-Soviet Democratization* 255.

Partlett, W, 'Crown-Presidentialism' (2022) 20 *International Journal of Constitutional Law* 204.

—— 'Historiography and Comparative Constitutional Scholarship' (2023) 1 *Comparative Constitutional Studies* 267.

—— 'Russia's 2020 Constitutional Amendments: A Comparative Analysis' (2021) 23 *Cambridge Yearbook of European Legal Studies* 311.

—— 'Putin's Artful Jurisprudence' (2013) 123 *National Interest* 35.

—— 'Separation of Powers without Checks and Balances: The Failure of Semi-Presidentialism and the Making of the Russian Constitutional System, 1991–1993' in T Borisova and WB Simons (eds), *The Legal Dimension in Cold War Interactions: Some Notes from the Field* (Leiden, Martinus Nijhoff Publishers, 2012) 105–40.

—— 'The Dangers of Popular Constitution-Making' (2012) 38 *Brooklyn Journal of International Law* 193.

—— 'The Historical Roots of Socialist Law' in F Hualing et al (eds), *Socialist Law in Socialist East Asia* (Cambridge, Cambridge University Press, 2018) 37–71.

Partlett, W and Ip, EC, 'Is Socialist Law Really Dead?' (2016) 48 *New York University Journal of International Law and Politics* 463.

Partlett, W and Krasnov, M, 'Russia's Non-Transformative Constitutional Founding' (2019) 15 *European Constitutional Law Review* 644.

Partlett, W, and Kupper, H, *The Post-Soviet as Post-Colonial: A New Paradigm for Understanding Constitutional Dynamics in the Former Soviet Empire* (Cheltenham, Edward Elgar, 2022).

Partlett, W and Samararatne, D, 'Redeeming the National in Constitutional Argument' (2021) 54 *World Constitutional Law* 461.

Pettit, P, *The State* (Princeton, Princeton University Press, 2003).

Pipes, R (ed), *Karamzin's Memoir on Ancient and Modern Russia* (New York, Atheneum, 1969).

Pistor, K, *The Code of Capital: How the Law Creates Wealth and Inequality* (Princeton, Princeton University Press, 2019).

Pocock, JGA, *The Machiavellian Moment: Florentine Political Thought and the Atlantic Republican Tradition* (Princeton, Princeton University Press, 2016).

Pomeranz, WE, 'Judicial Review and the Russian Constitutional Court: The Chechen Case' (1997) 23 *Review of Central and East European Law* 9.

—— *Law and the Russian State: Russia's Legal Evolution from Peter the Great to Vladimir Putin* (London, Bloomsbury, 2018).

—— 'President Medvedev and the Contested Constitutional Underpinnings of Russia's Power Vertical' (2009) 17 *Demokratizatsiya: The Journal of Post-Soviet Democratization* 179.

—— 'Uneasy Partners: Russia and the European Court of Human Rights' (2012) 19(3) *Human Rights Brief* 17.

Posner, EA and Vermeule, A, *The Executive Unbound: After the Madisonian Republic* (New York, Oxford University Press, 2010).

Price, M, *The Perilous Crown: France between Revolutions, 1814–1848* (London, Macmillan, 2007).

Prutsch, MJ, '"Monarchical Constitutionalism" in Post-Napoleonic Europe: Concept and Practice' in KL Grotke and MJ Prutsch (eds), *Constitutionalism, Legitimacy, and Power: Nineteenth-Century Experiences* (Oxford, Oxford University Press, 2014) 69–83.

Rabow-Edling, S, 'The Decembrists and the Concept of a Civic Nation' (2007) 35 *Nationalities Papers* 369.

Rawls, J, *Political Liberalism* (New York, Columbia University Press, 1993).

Reddaway, P and Glinsky, D, *The Tragedy of Russia's Reforms: Market Bolshevism Against Democracy* (Washington DC, United States Institute for Peace, 2001).

Remington, TF, *Presidential Decrees in Russia: A Comparative Perspective* (New York, Cambridge University Press, 2014).

Robinson, JH (trans), *Constitution of the Kingdom of Prussia* (Philadelphia, American Academy of Political and Social Science, 1894).

Robinson, N, 'Russia's Response to Crisis: The Paradox of Success' (2013) 65 *Europe-Asia Studies* 450.

Rosenblum, NL, *On the Side of Angels: An Appreciation of Politics and Partisanship* (Princeton, Princeton University Press, 2008).

Ross, C, 'Putin's Federal Reforms and the Consolidation of Federalism in Russia: One Step Forward, Two Steps Back!' (2003) 36 *Communist and Post-Communist Studies* 29.

—— 'Regional Elections in Russia: Instruments of Authoritarian Legitimacy or Instability?' (2018) 4 *Palgrave Communications* 1.

Rumiantsev, OG, 'From Confrontation to Social Contract' (1991) 5 *East European Politics and Societies* 113.

—— 'Russia's New Constitution' (1991) 2 *Journal of Democracy* 35.

Sakwa, R, *The Crisis of Russian Democracy: The Dual State, Factionalism and the Medvedev Succession* (Cambridge, Cambridge University Press, 2012).
—— 'The Struggle for the Constitution in Russia and the Triumph of Ethical Individualism' (1996) 48 *Studies in East European Thought* 115.
Sautman, B, 'The Devil to Pay: The 1989 Debate and the Intellectual Origins of Yeltsin's "Soft Authoritarianism"' (1995) 28 *Communist and Post-Communist Studies* 131.
Schapiro, L, 'The Political Thought of the First Provisional Government' in R Pipes (ed), *Revolutionary Russia* (Cambridge MA, Harvard University Press, 1968) 97–113.
Scheppele, KL, 'Autocratic Legalism' (2018) 85 *University of Chicago Law Review* 545.
—— 'The Rule of Law and the Frankenstate: Why Governance Checklists Do Not Work' (2013) 26 *Governance: An International Journal of Policy, Administration, and Institutions* 559.
Schneider, E, 'The Russian Federal Security Service under President Putin' in S White (ed), *Politics and the Ruling Group in Putin's Russia* (New York, Palgrave Macmillan, 2008) 42–62.
Schwartz, V, 'The Influences of the West on the 1993 Russian Constitution' (2009) 32 *Hastings International and Comparative Law Review* 101.
Scott, JC, *Seeing Like a State: How Certain Schemes to Improve the Human Condition Have Failed* (New Haven, Yale University Press, 1998).
Shah, SAA, 'Genesis of the Chechen Resistance Movement' (2004) 24(4) *Strategic Studies* 84.
Sharlet, R, 'Legal Transplants and Political Mutations: The Reception of Constitutional Law in Russia and the Newly Independent States' (1998) 7 *East European Constitutional Review* 59.
—— 'Putin and the Politics of Law in Russia' (2001) 17 *Post-Soviet Affairs* 195.
—— 'Transitional Constitutionalism: Politics and Law in the Second Russian Republic' (1996) 14 *Wisconsin International Law Journal* 495.
Smyth, R and Turovsky, R, 'Legitimising Victories: Electoral Authoritarian Control in Russia's Gubernatorial Elections' (2018) 70(2) *Europe-Asia Studies* 182.
Snyder, T, *The Road to Unfreedom: Russia, Europe, America* (New York, Tim Duggan Books, 2018).
Solvang, O, 'Russia and the European Court of Human Rights: The Price of Non-Cooperation' (2008) 15(2) *Human Rights Brief* 14.
Son, BN, *Constitutional Change in the Contemporary Socialist World* (Oxford, Oxford University Press, 2020).
Southall, R, 'Democracy in Southern Africa: Moving beyond a Difficult Legacy' (2003) 30 *Review of African Political Economy* 255.
St Augustine, *Concerning the City of God against the Pagans*, Henry Bettenson trans (New York, Penguin, 2003).
Stockdale, MK, *Paul Miliukov and the Quest for a Liberal Russia, 1880–1918* (Ithaca NY, Cornell University Press, 1997).
Stoner-Weiss, K, 'Russia and the Global Financial Crisis: The End of "Putinism"?' (2009) 15 *The Brown Journal of World Affairs* 103.
Sunstein, CR, 'Against Positive Rights' (1993) 2 *East European Constitutional Review* 35.
Taylor, B, *State Building in Putin's Russia: Policing and Coercion After Communism* (Cambridge, UK, Cambridge University Press, 2011).
Teague, E, 'Russia's Return to the Direct Elections of Governors: Re-Shaping the Power Vertical?' (2014) 3 *Region: Regional Studies of Russia, Eastern Europe, and Central Asia* 37.
Tushnet, M, *Why the Constitution Matters* (New Haven, Yale University Press, 2010).

Treadgold, DW, 'The Constitutional Democrats and the Russian Liberal Tradition' (1951) 10 *The American Slavic and East European Review* 85.

Tribe, LH, *The Invisible Constitution* (Oxford, Oxford University Press, 2008).

Trochev, A, *Judging Russia: The Role of the Constitutional Court in Russian Politics, 1990–2006* (Cambridge, Cambridge University Press, 2008).

Trochev, A and Solomon Jr, PH, 'Authoritarian Constitutionalism in Putin's Russia: A Pragmatic Constitutional Court in a Dual State' (2018) 51 *Communist and Post-Communist Studies* 201.

Tsygankov, AP, *The Strong State in Russia: Development and Crisis* (New York, Oxford University Press, 2012).

Tucker, R, 'The Theory of Charismatic Leadership' (1968) 97(3) *Daedalus* 731.

Tushnet, MV, 'Popular Constitutionalism as Political Law' (2006) 81 *Chicago Kent Law Review* 991.

Twomey, A, 'The Prerogative and the Courts in Australia' (2021) 3 *Journal of Commonwealth Law* 55.

Urban, ME, 'Boris El'tsin, Democratic Russia and the Campaign for the Russian Presidency' (1992) 44 *Soviet Studies* 187.

Vile, MJC, *Constitutionalism and the Separation of Powers*, 2nd edn (Indianapolis, Liberty Fund, 1998).

von Fritz, K, *The Theory of the Mixed Constitution in Antiquity* (New York, Columbia University Press, 1954).

von Humboldt, W, 'Denkschrift über ständische Verfassung (October 1819)' in B Gebhardt (ed), *Wilhelm von Humboldts Gesammelte Schriften*, vol 12 (Berlin, De Gruyter, 1904).

von Mohl, R, *Die Geschichte und Literatur der Staatswissenschaften*, vol 1 (Erlangen, 1855).

Walker, MC, *The Strategic Use of Referendums: Power, Legitimacy, and Democracy* (New York, Palgrave McMillan, 2003).

Way, L, *Pluralism by Default: Weak Autocrats and the Rise of Competitive Politics* (Baltimore, John Hopkins University Press, 2015).

Weber, M, *Theory of Social and Economic Organization* (T Parsons (ed), AM Henderson and T Parsons (trans)) (New York, Free Press, 1947).

Wendt, A, *Social Theory of International Politics* (Cambridge, Cambridge University Press, 1999).

White, S and McAllister, I, 'The Putin Phenomenon' (2008) 24 *Journal of Communist Studies and Transition Politics* 604.

de Wilde, M, 'The Dictator's Trust: Regulating and Constraining Emergency Powers in the Roman Republic (2012) 33(4) *History of Political Thought* 555.

Wilson, A, *Political Technology: The Globalisation of Political Manipulation* (Cambridge, Cambridge University Press, 2023).

——— *Virtual Politics: Faking Democracy in the Post-Soviet World* (New Haven, Yale University Press, 2005).

Wood, GS, *Power and Liberty: Constitutionalism in the American Revolution* (New York, Oxford University Press, 2021).

Wortman, R, *Russian Monarchy: Representation and Rule* (Boston, Academic Studies Press, 2013).

Yavuz, MH, 'A Torn Country: Erdogan's Turkey and the Elections of 2023' (2023) 30(3) *Middle East Policy* 81.

Yudin, G, 'Governing Through Polls: Politics of Representation and Presidential Support in Putin's Russia' (2020) 27 *Javnost – The Public* 2.

Index

A
Accountability
  constitutional dark arts 3
  creation of 'crown-presidential'
    constitutional system by
    Yeltsin 5–6
  intellectual roots of Russian democratic
    constitutionalism 38
  justification for Russian
    Constitution 71–2
  lessons from Russian experience 12
  Medvedev's presidency 2008–2012
    domestic legal
      accountability 129–34
    international legal
      accountability 134–6
    popular accountability 128–9
  misleading basis of centralised
    democracy 23
  Putin as a managerial president
    2000–2008
    domestic legal
      accountability 110–4
    international legal
      accountability 114–5
    popular accountability 109–10
  Putin as an imperial president 2012
    to present
    domestic legal
      accountability 153–7
    international legal
      accountability 157
    popular accountability 152
  reform in a post-Putin Russia 174–8
  Russia's post-Soviet constitutional
    experience 4
  struggle for power between Yeltsin and
    Russian legislature 4–5
  Yeltsin's personalised rule 1994–1999
    domestic legal
      accountability 86–92
    international legal
      accountability 92–4

  popular accountability 84–6
Authoritarianism
  see also **Centralised authority and**
    power
  challenges to conventional approach
    role of structural constitutional rules
      in Constitution 3
    effect of centralised presidential
      authority 3
  failure to understand the Russian
    Constitution
    dangers of legal
      constitutionalism 202–10
    key deficiency in understanding
      of democratic
      constitutionalism 221–2
    need for better understanding
      of benefits of a balanced
      Constitution 215–21
    need for better understanding
      of normative goals 213–5
    need to study constitutional
      rules 211–3
    overview of key points 13
    persistent failure to *see*
      structural constitutional
      provisions 202
    US misgivings in 1993 201
  lessons from Russian experience
    importance of structural legal
      rules 11
    relationship between written
      Constitutions and populist
      authoritarianism 11
    structural-normative approach
      to Russia's post- Soviet
      constitutional experience 9–11
  personalised rule of Yeltsin 1994–1999
    'bulldozer' approach to
      governance 76
    concluding remarks 94
    strong strain of liberal
      authoritarianism in team 84

in a post-Putin Russia
  continuation of dark arts 162–3
  endless cycle of imperial
    authoritarianism 171
  false attribution to Putin 161
  lessons from history 168
  new constitutional discourse 174
  Russia's ongoing resilience 164
Putin as a managerial president
    2000–2008
  concluding remarks 115–6
  controlling the oligarchs 104–6
  'dictatorship of the law' 100–2
  domestic legal accountability 110–4
  effectiveness 106–9
  importance of Kursk tragedy 95
  institution-building 97–100
  international legal
    accountability 114–5
  overview of key points 12
  popular accountability 109–10
  project of presidential
    dominance 96
  recentralising of power in
    Moscow 102–4
  reliance on centralising power 96
Putin as an imperial president 2012
    to present
  closing of Russian
    politics 139–41
  concluding remarks 157–9
  confrontation with the West 141–2
  constitutional reform 2020 138–9,
    142–8
  domestic legal
    accountability 153–7
  effectiveness 150–2
  full-scale invasion of Ukraine 148–9
  international legal
    accountability 157
  overview of key points 13
  popular accountability 152
Putin's dominance over the Russian
    political system
  product of his personal, non-legal
    authority 1
  relevance of Russia's
    Constitution 2
  reliance on official state
    messaging 2

reform in a post-Putin Russia
  balanced state tradition as the new
    constitutional discourse 174
  change from centralised state
    tradition 164
  concluding remarks 178–9
  continuation of dark arts 162
  need for new democratic
    Constitution 171
relevance of Constitutions globally
  concluding remarks 200
  globally deceptive claims of the
    constitutional dark arts 180–1
  overview of key points 13
  populist attacks on established
    democracy 187–90
  rise of populist
    authoritarianism 181–6
  strengths of the constitutional dark
    arts 190–4
  weaknesses of constitutional dark
    arts 194–9
shaping of Russian politics since 1993
  under President Medvedev
    2008–2012 7
  under Putin 2000–2008 7
  under Putin since 2012 7–8
strengths of constitutional dark arts
  legal tools of
    authoritarianism 191–2
  normative justifications for
    centralised power 192–4
  overview 190
Surkov's critique of Western
    democracy 160–1
understand Russia beyond a focus on
    Putin 224
weaknesses of centralised regimes
  direct democracy rationale 197–8
  overview 194–5
  poor legality and rights
    protection 198–9
  weak and poorly governed
    states 195–7

B
Balanced state tradition see also
    Centralised state tradition
  competing traditions of proper state
    ordering 16 t1

competing visions of good political
   ordering   15–6
concentrated sovereign authority to
   monarchs   15
Constitutional Court   130
constitutional rules   24
failure to understand the Russian
   Constitution   215–21
Germany   16
globally deceptive claims of the
   constitutional dark arts   181
lessons from Russian
   experience   225–7
reform in a post-Putin Russia
   balanced state tradition as
      the new constitutional
      discourse   174–8
   change from centralised state
      tradition   164–5
Rumiantsev's Constitutional
   Commission   43
shaping of written democratic
   Constitutions   14–5
Tsarist liberal statist movement   178
underlying principles   9

C
Centralised authority and power
see also **Authoritarianism**
building of a personalised
   'vertical of power' by
   Yeltsin   45–6
changes to constitutional draft
   1993   58
constitutional dark arts   3
constitutional reform 2020   144,
   145–6
creation of 'crown-presidential'
   constitutional system by
   Yeltsin   5–6
crown-presidentialism   184
deceptive claims about its democratic
   benefits   225
important temporary mechanism   27
justifications for Russian Constitution
   accountability of President   71–2
   centralising provisions to ensure
      stability and unity   70–1
   foundational rights and democratic
      provisions   72–3

key foundation for Putin's
   authoritarianism   3
Medvedev's Presidency
   2008–2012   118
in a post-Putin Russia
   balanced state tradition as
      the new constitutional
      discourse   174–8
   democratic opening for
      reform   163–4
   need for new democratic
      Constitution   170–3
Putin as a managerial president
   2000–2008
   importance   96
   institution-building   99
   recentralising of power in
      Moscow   102–4
relevance of Constitutions
   globally   181–6
role of balanced state tradition   15
roll of democratic written
   Constitutions
   communist states such as China,
      Vietnam, and Cuba   18–9
   France's Constitutional Charter of
      1814   17–8
   mid-nineteenth-century Japan   18
   Prussia's 1850 Constitution   18
   tools for centralising authority   17
   'vanguardism' and 'democratic
      centralism'   19
Russian Constitution   70
Russia's deep tradition   3
Russia's post-Soviet constitutional
   experience   4
shaping of Russian politics since 1993
   under President Medvedev
      2008–2012   7
   under Putin 2000–2008   6–7
   under Putin since 2012   7–8
   under Yeltsin 1993–2000   6
Surkov's critique of Western
   democracy   160–1
Centralised state tradition *see also*
   Balanced state tradition
better way to achieve democracy and
   individual rights   16
competing traditions of proper state
   ordering   16 *t*1

242 *Index*

competing visions of good political
 ordering 15–6
constitutional rules 24
Germany 16
influence on Constitutional Court
 accountability of Putin as an
  imperial president 2012 to
  present 156–7
 accountability of Yeltsin's personalised
  rule 1994–1999 90–1
 advancement during Medvedev's
  presidency 131–3
 continuing influence of the
  centralised state tradition 92
justifications
 Hobbes 20
 influence on absolutist monarchical
  systems 20–1
 link with national identity 21–2
 stability and advance of the common
  good 19
 weakness and instability over
  time 21
misleading bases 23
normative consequences 32
reform in a post-Putin Russia 164–5
rejection of dispersed institutional
 authority 15
Russia's centralised state history 35–7
ultimate source of authority 22
underlying principles 9
Chief executive officer
authority over executive representatives
 in the upper house 65
foundation of constitutional dark arts
 in Russia 67–70
Constitutional Court
accountability of Medvedev's
 presidency 2008–2012
 advancement of centralised state
  tradition 131–3
 changes to the Law 130
 deferral to to presidential
  interests 130–1
 guardian authority 133–4
 importance of unity 134
 management powers 134
 marginalisation of balanced state
  tradition 130

 weakening position and forced
  relocation 129–30
accountability of Putin as a managerial
 president 2000–2008
 balanced constitutional
  tradition 111
 decree power of the President 113
 individual rights 114
 popular sovereignty 111–3
accountability of Putin as an imperial
 president 2012 to present
 centralised state tradition 156–7
 constitutionality of the 2020
  amendments 155–6
 controversial policy
  decisions 153–4
 impact of Ukraine invasion 156
 reductions in the independence of
  the Court 153
accountability of Yeltsin's personalised
 rule 1994–1999
 continuing influence of the centralised
  state tradition 90–1, 92
 power to dissolve the lower
  house 89–90
 power to wage war 86–8
 territorial integrity 88–9
 violations of individual rights 86,
  91–2
deferral to presidential authority 76
draft constitution 51, 59
early conflict with Yeltsin 46–7
foundation of constitutional dark arts
 in Russia 55
power of President as monarch 65
ruling on 'trust' referendum 49
under-enforcement of rights
 provisions 32
Constitutional dark arts
in action
 key question 26–7
 normative consequences 31–2
 weakness of rights and democratic
  guarantees 27–31
causes and consequences 32–3
centralised state tradition
 foundation of a new form of
  populist authoritarianism 22
 misleading bases 23

ultimate source of authority 22
version of democratic rights
    constitutionalism 22
centralised state tradition as the better
    way 16–7
enabling of authoritarianism
    legal tools of
        authoritarianism 191–2
    normative justifications for
        centralised power 192–4
    overview 190
foundation of constitutional dark arts
    in Russia
    changes to constitutional draft
        1993 57–9
    concluding remarks 73–4
    dissolution of elected Russian
        legislature 54–5
    overview of key points 12
    President as chief executive
        officer 67–70
    president as monarch 63–7
    replacement of Yeltsin by Rutskoi 55
    restoration of Yeltsin and governance
        by decree 55–6
    Russian
        crown-presidentialism 60–2
    subsequent significance 59–60
guarantees within a highly centralised
    constitutional structure 3
identification
    avoidance of checklist approach 25
    need for structural-normative
        approach 25–6
    lesson from Russia 223
    misleading claims 3
    overview of key points 12
in a post-Putin Russia 161–4
relevance of Constitutions globally
    globally deceptive claims of the
        constitutional dark arts 180–1
    populist attacks on established
        democracy 187–90
    rise of populist
        authoritarianism 181–6
Russia's post-Soviet constitutional
    experience 4
search for reason-based form of
    constitutional democracy 4

struggle for power between Yeltsin and
    Russian legislature 4–5
two different types of constitutional
    rules
    balanced state tradition 24
    centralised state tradition 24
Ukrainian invasion 148–9
weaknesses of centralised regimes
    direct democracy rationale 197–8
    overview 194–5
    poor legality and rights
        protection 198–9
    weak and poorly governed
        states 195–7
Constitutional law
see also **Constitutional dark arts**
authoritarian populist projects 225
dialogue between courts and non-legal
    political actors 203
failure to understand Russian
    constitutional law as key
    deficiency 221
ideological potential 32
judicially centred understanding of
    Constitutions 23
methodology 8
in a post-Putin Russia
    balanced state tradition as the new
        constitutional discourse 174–8
    concluding remarks 178–9
    continuation of dark arts 161–4
    democratic opening for
        reform 164–9
    grounding of democratic principles
        and values in Russian
        history 165–7
    need for new democratic
        Constitution 170–3
    overview of key points 13
    rejection of anti-political form of
        democracy 167–9
    Surkov's critique of Western
        democracy 160–1
Russia's centralised state
    tradition 133
self-enforcing nature 27
use of the rational-legal, constitutional
    authority of Russia's crown-
    presidential Constitution 107

Constitutional rules
  constitutional dark arts
    balanced state tradition   24
    centralised state tradition   24
  constitutional dark arts in action
    key question   26–7
    normative consequences   31–2
    weakness of rights and democratic guarantees   27–31
  failure to understand the Russian Constitution
    need for better understanding of normative goals   213–5
    need to study constitutional rules   211–3
    persistent failure to *see* structural constitutional provisions   202
  lessons from Russian experience   11, 226–7
  methodology   8
  need for structural-normative approach   25–6
  populist attacks on established democracy   187–8
  shaping of Russian politics since 1993
    under President Medvedev 2008–2012   7
    under Putin 2000–2008   6–7
    under Putin since 2012   7–8
    tools and justifications for Putin to dominate Russian politics   8
    under Yeltsin 1993–2000   6
Constitutionalism
  democratic constitutionalism
    concluding remarks   50–2
    constitutional dark arts   22
    failure to understand the Russian Constitution   13, 201–22
    intellectual roots of Russian democratic constitutionalism   37–9
    lessons from Russian experience   9–11, 226–7
    rise of Yeltsin 1992–1993   43–50
    Rumiantsev's Constitutional Commission   43
    Sakharov's constitutional draft   39–40
    Yeltsin's constitutional draft   50–2

  legal constitutionalism
    anti-political understanding of democracy   205–7
    blindness to centralising structural provisions in the Russian Constitution   202–5
    false association of democracy with libertarian economics and a weak state   209–10
    undermining of international efforts to promoting democracy and rights protection   208–9
Crown-presidentialism
  African continent   183
  Belarus   182
  centralised authority and power   184
  creation of 'crown-presidential' constitutional system by Yeltsin   5–6
  dictatorial style of anti-politics   75
  foundation of constitutional dark arts in Russia   60–2, 63–7
  president as monarch   63–7
  Russian crown-presidentialism   60–2
  hybrid Russian Constitution   5
  Kazakhstan   182
  legal tools of authoritarianism   191
  post-Putin Russia   161
  presidential domination   118
  Putin's systematic use of authority   107
  reliance on popular legitimacy and winning elections   84
  Turkey   187–8
  types of presidential power   61 *t*2

D
Dark arts *see* Constitutional dark arts
Democracy
  approach of key Soviet-era dissidents and reformers   34
  centralised state tradition as the better way   16
  constitutional dark arts   3
  constitutional dark arts in action
    key question   27
    normative consequences   31–2
    weakness of rights and democratic guarantees   27–31

constitutional law in a post-Putin
Russia
overview of key points   13
creation of 'crown-presidential'
constitutional system by
Yeltsin   5
deceptive claims for centralised
power   225
effect of centralised presidential
authority   3
foundation of constitutional dark arts
in Russia
abstract constitutional
guarantees   58
decisive moment in undermining of
Russian democracy   57
justification for Russian
Constitution   72–3
legal constitutionalism
anti-political understanding of
democracy   205–7
blindness to centralising structural
provisions in the Russian
Constitution   202–5
false association of democracy with
libertarian economics and a
weak state   209–10
undermining of international efforts
to promoting democracy and
rights protection   208–9
misleading bases of centralised
democracy   23
reform in a post-Putin Russia
balanced state tradition as the new
constitutional discourse   174–8
change from centralised state
tradition   164–5
grounding of democratic principles
and values in Russian
history   165–7
need for new democratic
Constitution   170–3
rejection of anti-political form of
democracy   167–9
relevance of Constitutions globally
globally deceptive claims of the
constitutional dark arts   181
populist attacks on established
democracy   187–90
struggle for power between Yeltsin and
Russian legislature   4–5
Surkov's critique of Western
democracy   160–1
use of constitutional dark arts in
Russia   4
weaknesses of centralised
regimes   197–8
'Democratic centralism'   19, 37
Democratic constitutionalism
constitutional dark arts   22
failure to understand the Russian
Constitution
dangers of legal
constitutionalism   202–10
key deficiency in understanding
of democratic
constitutionalism   221–2
need for better understanding
of benefits of a balanced
Constitution   215–21
need for better understanding of
normative goals   213–5
need to study constitutional
rules   211–3
overview of key points   13
persistent failure to *see* structural
constitutional provisions   202
US misgivings in 1993   201
intellectual roots of Russian democratic
constitutionalism   37–9
lessons from Russian experience   226–7
importance of structural legal
rules   11
structural-normative approach
to Russia's post- Soviet
constitutional experience   9–11
reform in a post-Putin Russia   165,
167

E
'End of history' debate
Fukuyama's 1989 article   223
Russia's post-Soviet constitutional
experience   224–5

F
Federalism *see* **Unity and Russian**
federalism

G

Guardian authority
  authority of a hereditary
      monarch 133
  constitutional reform 2020 144
  constitutionalisation 66
  draft Constitution 43
  general purposes 63–4
  key amendments 144
  Medvedev's presidency 2008–2012 7, 123
  Putin as a managerial president 2000–2008 100
  Putin's imperial presidency 2012 to present 144
  Russian crown-presidentialism 60, 63–5
  'sole powers' 134
  South Sudan 185
  threat to democratic governance 62
  Yeltsin's personalised rule 1994–1999 75, 76–7, 79, 94

H

Human rights
  see also **Individual rights**
  accountability of Medvedev's presidency 2008–2012 134–6
  accountability of Putin as a managerial president 2000–2008 114–5
  accountability of Putin as an imperial president 2012 to present 157
  foundation of constitutional dark arts in Russia 59
  imperial presidency in action 7
  intellectual roots of Russian democratic constitutionalism 38–9
  justification for Russian Constitution 73
  reform in a post-Putin Russia 165
  Sakharov's constitutional draft 39–40
  Sakharov's Nobel Peace Prize 34
  shaping of Russian politics under Putin 2000–2008 7
  Yeltsin's constitutional draft 51
  Yeltsin's personalised rule 1994–1999
    domestic legal accountability 87
    international legal accountability 93

I

Imperial president of Putin 2012 to present
  closing of Russian politics 139–41
  concluding remarks 157–9
  confrontation with the West 141–2
  constitutional reform 2020 138–9, 142–8
  domestic legal accountability 153–7
  effectiveness 150–2
  full-scale invasion of Ukraine 148–9
  international legal accountability 157
  overview of key points 13
  popular accountability 152
  topdown constitutional reform of 2020 7

Individual rights
  see also **Human rights**
  accountability of Putin as a managerial president 2000–2008 114
  centralised state tradition as the better way 16
  constitutional dark arts in action
    key question 26–7
    misleading claims 3
    normative consequences 31–2
    weakness of rights and democratic guarantees 27–31
  creation of 'crown-presidential' constitutional system by Yeltsin 6
  effect of centralised presidential authority 3
  foundation of constitutional dark arts in Russia 58–9
  impact of balanced state tradition 14–5
  justification for Russian Constitution 72–3
  legal constitutionalism
    blindness of legal constitutionalism to centralising structural provisions in the Russian Constitution 202–5
    undermining of international efforts to promoting democracy and rights protection 208–9
  misleading basis of centralised democracy 23–4
  populist attacks on established democracy 189

struggle for power between Yeltsin and Russian legislature 4–5
version of democratic rights constitutionalism 22
weaknesses of centralised regimes 198–9
Institution-building 97–100

L
Legal constitutionalism
anti-political understanding of democracy 205–7
blindness to centralising structural provisions in the Russian Constitution 202–5
false association of democracy with libertarian economics and a weak state 209–10
undermining of international efforts to promoting democracy and rights protection 208–9

M
Management powers
constitutional reform 2020 144–5
control over the executive-branch government 134
foundation of constitutional dark arts in Russia 68–9
key amendments 144–5
Putin as a managerial president 2000–2008 6–7
Putin as an imperial president 2012 to present 139–40
Putin during presidency of Medvedev, D. 2008–2012 123
threat to democratic governance 62
Turkey 187
Market reform
creation of 'crown-presidential' constitutional system by Yeltsin 5–6
personalised rule of Yeltsin 'bulldozer' approach to governance 76
concluding remarks 94
effectiveness of decree-based form of governance 83–4
'end of history' belief 75
overview of key points 12

rapid privatisation of state-owned assets 81–2
rise of Yeltsin 1992–1993 46
shaping of Russian politics under Putin 2000–2008 6–7
Medvedev, D.
as constrained President 2008–2012
overview of key points 12
as President 2008–2012
concluding remarks 136–7
domestic legal accountability 129–34
foreign policy 125–8
importance of rational-legal authority of the President 117–8
international legal accountability 134–6
normative pull of the term limit rule 118–9
obstacles to Medvedev's authority 119–22
popular accountability 128–9
Putin's role in domestic policy 122–5
two power centres 118
UN resolution on Libya 117
use of guardian powers 7
Methodology 8, 8–9

O
Oligarchs
control over television and print media 85
creation of powerful class under Yeltsin 6
effect of poor governance 196
effect of Yeltin's economic reforms 81
Putin as a managerial president 2000–2008 104–6
Putin's constrained presidency 2008–2012 123
Yeltsin's bulldozer approach 76

P
Populism
anti-politics of legal constitutionalism 206–7
centralised state tradition as foundation of a new form of populist authoritarianism 22

248 *Index*

deceptive claims for centralised
 power 225
lessons from Russian experience 11
misleading basis of centralised
 democracy 23
popular accountability of all-powerful
 sovereign 3
relevance of Constitutions globally
populist attacks on established
 democracy 187–90
rise of populist
 authoritarianism 181–6
Surkov's critique of Western
 democracy 161
weaknesses of centralised
 regimes 197–8
Yeltsin's understanding of democratic
 politics 44
Presidency *see* **Russian presidency**
Prime Minister
changes to constitutional draft 1993 57
constitutional dark arts in India 190
identification of constitutional dark
 arts 25–6
ignorance of Ukrainian invasion 1
President as chief executive
 officer 67–8
Putin during presidency of Medvedev, D.
 2008–2012
 concluding remarks 136–7
 domestic legal
  accountability 129–34
 foreign policy 125–8
 importance of rational-legal authority
  of the President 117–8
 international legal
  accountability 134–6
 normative pull of the term limit
  rule 118–9
 obstacles to Medvedev's
  authority 119–22
 overview of key points 12
 popular accountability 128–9
 role in domestic policy 122–5
 two power centres 118
 UN resolution on Libya 117
Putin, V.
appointment of a status quo
 successor 162–3

decision to invade Ukraine 1
dominance over the Russian political
 system
product of his personal, non-legal
 authority 1
relevance of Russia's
 Constitution 2
reliance on official state
 messaging 2
as an imperial president 2012 to present
 closing of Russian politics 139–41
 concluding remarks 157–9
 confrontation with the West 141–2
 constitutional reform 2020 138–9,
  142–8
 domestic legal
  accountability 153–7
 effectiveness 150–2
 full-scale invasion of Ukraine
  148–9
 international legal
  accountability 157
 overview of key points 13
 popular accountability 152
importance of centralised presidential
 authority 3
importance of Russian Constitution 8
as a managerial president 2000–2008
 concluding remarks 115–6
 controlling the oligarchs 104–6
 'dictatorship of the law' 100–2
 domestic legal accountability 110–4
 effectiveness 106–9
 importance of Kursk tragedy 95
 institution-building 97–100
 international legal
  accountability 114–5
 overview of key points 12
 popular accountability 109–10
 project of presidential
  dominance 96
 recentralising of power in
  Moscow 102–4
 reliance on centralising power 96
as Prime Minister during presidency of
 Medvedev, D. 2008–2012
 concluding remarks 136–7
 domestic legal accountability
  129–34

foreign policy   125–8
importance of rational-legal authority of the President   117–8
international legal accountability   134–6
normative pull of the term limit rule   118–9
obstacles to Medvedev's authority   119–22
overview of key points   12
popular accountability   128–9
role in domestic policy   122–5
two power centres   118
UN resolution on Libya   117
shaping of Russian politics 2000–2008   6–7
since 2012   7–8
understand Russia beyond a focus on Putin   224

R
Rights *see* Human rights; Individual rights
Rules *see* Constitutional rules
Rumiantsev, P.   42–3, 56, 58
Russian Constitution
  centralised presidential authority   3
  changes to constitutional draft 1993   57
  constitutional reform 2020
    absence of serious functional changes   143
    centralised authority and power   144, 145–6
    justification for Russia's increasingly centralised system   146
    management powers   144–5
    national plebiscite   146–8
    neo-imperial version of Russian identity   143
    presidential power over the legislature   144
    Putin as an imperial president 2012 to present   138–9
    Russians to be the 'state-forming' people   144
    stage-managed constitutional reform   142–3
  creation of 'crown-presidential' constitutional system by Yeltsin   5–6, 60–2
  example of hybrid constitutional text   59
  failure to understand the Russian Constitution
    dangers of legal constitutionalism   202–10
    key deficiency in understanding of democratic constitutionalism   221–2
    need for better understanding of benefits of a balanced Constitution   215–21
    need for better understanding of normative goals   213–5
    need to study constitutional rules   211–3
    overview of key points   13
    persistent failure to *see* structural constitutional provisions   202
    US misgivings in 1993   201
  identification of constitutional dark arts   25–6
  justifications
    accountability of President   71–2
    centralising provisions to ensure stability and unity   70–1
    concluding remarks   73–4
    foundational rights and democratic provisions   72–3
    normative blueprint for a centralised state   70
  need for new democratic Constitution in a post-Putin Russia   170–3
  President as chief executive officer   67–70
  president as monarch   63–7
  relevance in Putin's Russia   2
  role of structural constitutional rules   3
  Rumiantsev's Constitutional Commission   42–3
  shaping of Russian politics since 1993
    under President Medvedev 2008–2012   7
    under Putin 2000–2008   6–7
    under Putin since 2012   7–8
    tools and justifications for Putin to dominate Russian politics   8
    under Yeltsin 1993–2000   6

struggle for power between Yeltsin and
    Russian legislature 4–5
  system of 'pluralism by default' 76
  understand Russia beyond a focus on
    Putin 224
  Yeltsin's constitutional draft 50–2
Russian presidency
  crown-presidentialism 5–6, 60–2
  early Russian democratic development
    1988–1991 40–2
  identification of constitutional dark
    arts 25–6
  Medvedev, D. 2008–2012
    commitment to centralised
      management 118
    concluding remarks 136–7
    domestic legal
      accountability 129–34
    foreign policy 125–8
    importance of rational-legal authority
      of the President 117–8
    international legal
      accountability 134–6
    normative pull of the term limit
      rule 118–9
    obstacles to Medvedev's
      authority 119–22
    overview of key points 12
    popular accountability 128–9
    Putin's role in domestic
      policy 122–5
    two power centres 118
    UN resolution on Libya 117
  need for new democratic Constitution
    in a post-Putin Russia 170–3
  President as chief executive
    officer 67–70
  president as monarch 63–7
  Putin as a managerial president
    2000–2008
    concluding remarks 115–6
    controlling the oligarchs 104–6
    'dictatorship of the law' 100–2
    domestic legal
      accountability 110–4
    effectiveness 106–9
    importance of Kursk tragedy 95
    institution-building 97–100
    international legal
      accountability 114–5
  overview of key points 12
  popular accountability 109–10
  project of presidential
    dominance 96
  recentralising of power in
    Moscow 102–4
  reliance on centralising power 96
  Putin as an imperial president 2012 to
    present
    closing of Russian politics 139–41
    concluding remarks 157–9
    confrontation with the West 141–2
    constitutional reform 2020 138–9,
      142–8
    domestic legal
      accountability 153–7
    effectiveness 150–2
    full-scale invasion of Ukraine
      148–9
    international legal
      accountability 157
    overview of key points 13
    popular accountability 152
  shaping of Russian politics since
    1993
    under President Medvedev
      2008–2012 7
    under Putin 2000–2008 6–7
    under Putin since 2012 7–8
    under Yeltsin 1993–2000 6
  types of presidential power 61 t2
  Yeltsin's personalised rule 1994–1999
    ad hoc federalism 79–80
    'bulldozer' approach to
      governance 76
    centre-periphery relations 76–80
    concluding remarks 94
    domestic legal
      accountability 86–92
    effectiveness of decree-based form of
      governance 83–4
    first Chechen War 77–9
    highly personalised and dictatorial
      style of anti-politics 75–6
    international legal
      accountability 92–4
    popular accountability 84–6
    rapid privatisation of state-owned
      assets 81–2
Rutskoi, A. 55

S

State tradition *see* Centralised state tradition *see* Balanced state tradition

U

Ukrainian invasion
 full-scale invasion by Putin   148–9
 impact on Constitutional Court   156
 imperial presidency in action   7
 Putin as sole decision-maker   1

Unity and Russian federalism
 anti-political tradition   21
 centralised state tradition   19
 centralising provisions of the constitutional dark arts   198
 competing visions of good political ordering   16 *t*1
 constitutional dark arts   24, 26
 constitutional requirement   15
 foundation of constitutional dark arts in Russia   55, 57, 68
 foundational rational-legal powers of the managerial President   7
 importance   222
 internal normativity of constitutional dark arts   193–4
 justification for Russian Constitution   70
 Medvedev's presidency 2008–2012   132–4
 post-Putin Russia   170, 181
 Putin as a managerial president 2000–2008   97, 101–2, 112–3
 Putin's imperial presidency 2012 to present   140
 rise of Yeltsin 1992–1993   47
 Russian crown-presidentialism   63
 Russia's centralised state history   35
 Russia's historical role   2
 types of presidential power   61 *t*2
 Yeltsin's constitutional draft   52
 Yeltsin's personalised rule 1994–1999   83

V

'Vanguardism'   19, 74

W

Written Constitutions
 constitutional centralisation communist states such as China, Vietnam, and Cuba   18–9
 France's Constitutional Charter of 1814   17–8
 mid-nineteenth-century Japan   18
 Prussia's 1850 Constitution   18
 tools for centralising authority   17
 'vanguardism' and 'democratic centralism'   19
 impact of balanced state tradition   14–5
 introduction in America   14
 lessons from Russian experience   11
 relevance of Constitutions globally concluding remarks   200
 globally deceptive claims of the constitutional dark arts   180–1
 overview of key points   13
 populist attacks on established democracy   187–90
 rise of populist authoritarianism   181–6
 strengths of the constitutional dark arts   190–4
 weaknesses of constitutional dark arts   194–9

Y

Yeltsin, B.
 alliance with Russian democratic movement 1992–1919   3
 building of a personalised 'vertical of power'   45–6, 46
 conflicts with Constitutional Court   46–7
 confrontation with the Congress of People's Deputies   47–8
 establishment of Russian Federation   49–50
 key moment in Yeltsin's appeal   45
 leader of the Russian liberal democratic reform movement   44
 populist understanding of democratic politics   44
 Yeltsin's constitutional draft   50–2
 chairman of Congress 1990   40
 creation of 'crown-presidential' constitutional system   5–6
 foundation of constitutional dark arts in Russia

changes to constitutional draft
   1993   57–9
concluding remarks   73–4
dissolution of elected Russian
   legislature   54–5
overview of key points   12
President as chief executive
   officer   67–70
president as monarch   63–7
replacement of Yeltsin by
   Rutskoi   55
restoration of Yeltsin and governance
   by decree   55–6
Russian crown-presidentialism
   60–2
subsequent significance   59–60
need for more than non-legal, personal
   authority   8
personalised rule 1994–1999
   ad hoc federalism   79–80

'bulldozer' approach to
   governance   76
centre-periphery relations   76–80
concluding remarks   94
domestic legal accountability   86–92
effectiveness of decree-based form of
   governance   83–4
first Chechen War   77–9
highly personalised and dictatorial
   style of anti-politics   75–6
international legal
   accountability   92–4
overview of key points   12
popular accountability   84–6
rapid privatisation of state-owned
   assets   81–2
shaping of Russian politics since
   1993   6
struggle for power between Yeltsin and
   Russian legislature   4–5